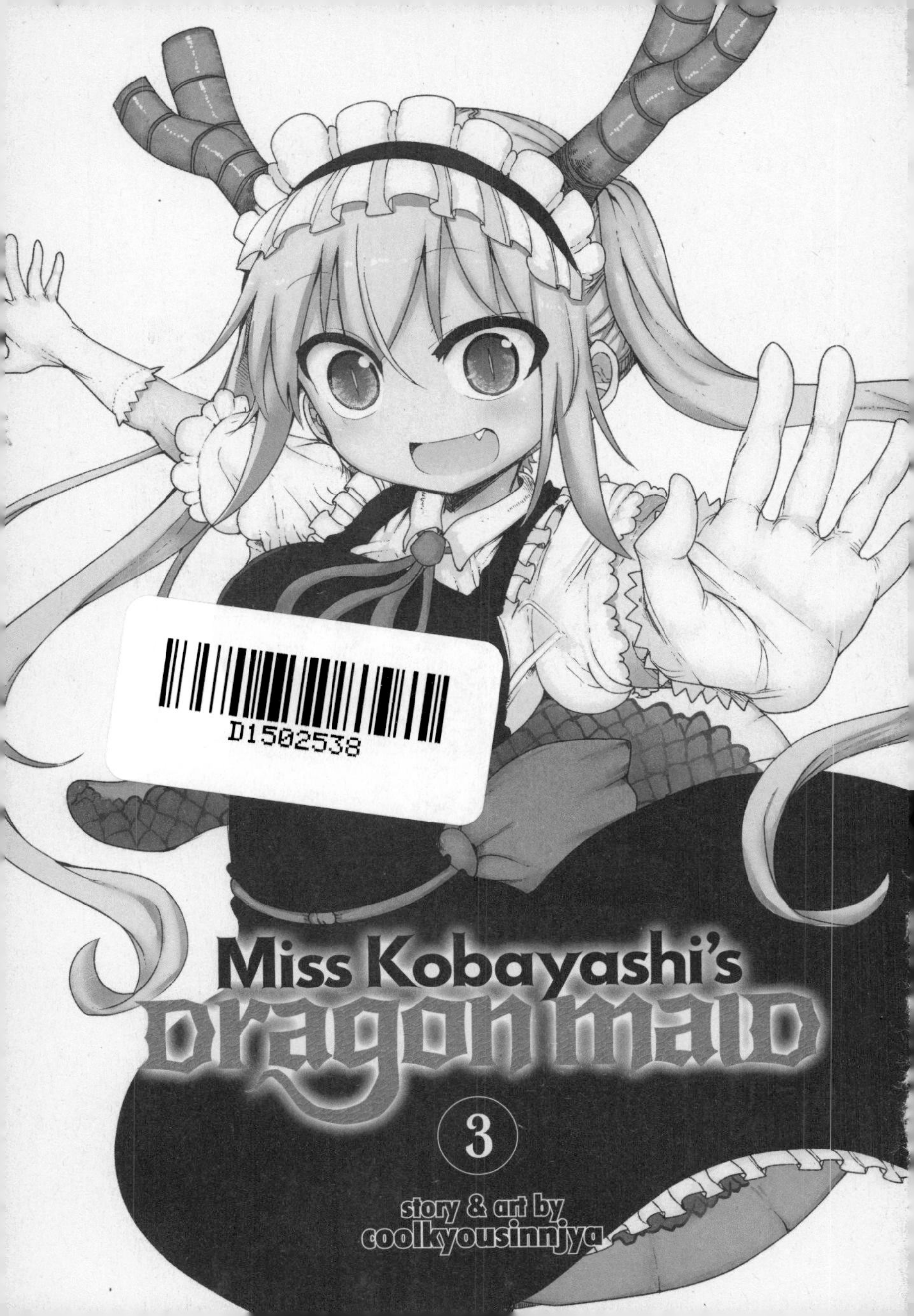

Miss Kobayashi's Dragon Maid

3

story & art by
coolkyousinnjya

Miss Kobayashi's Dragon Maid

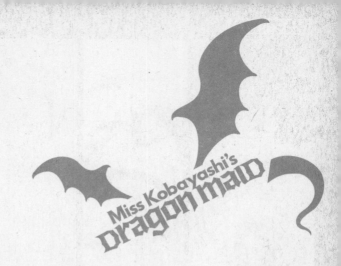

CHAPTER 21

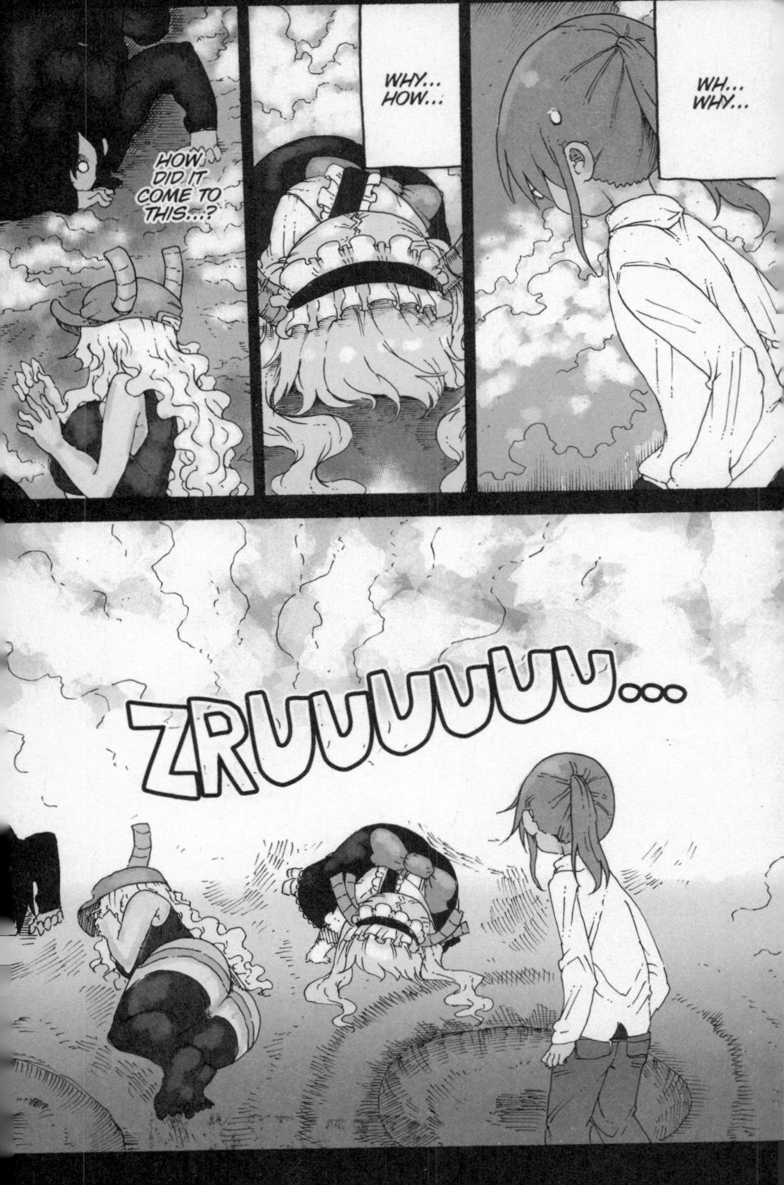
WH... WHY...
WHY... HOW...
HOW DID IT COME TO THIS...?
ZRUUUUUU...

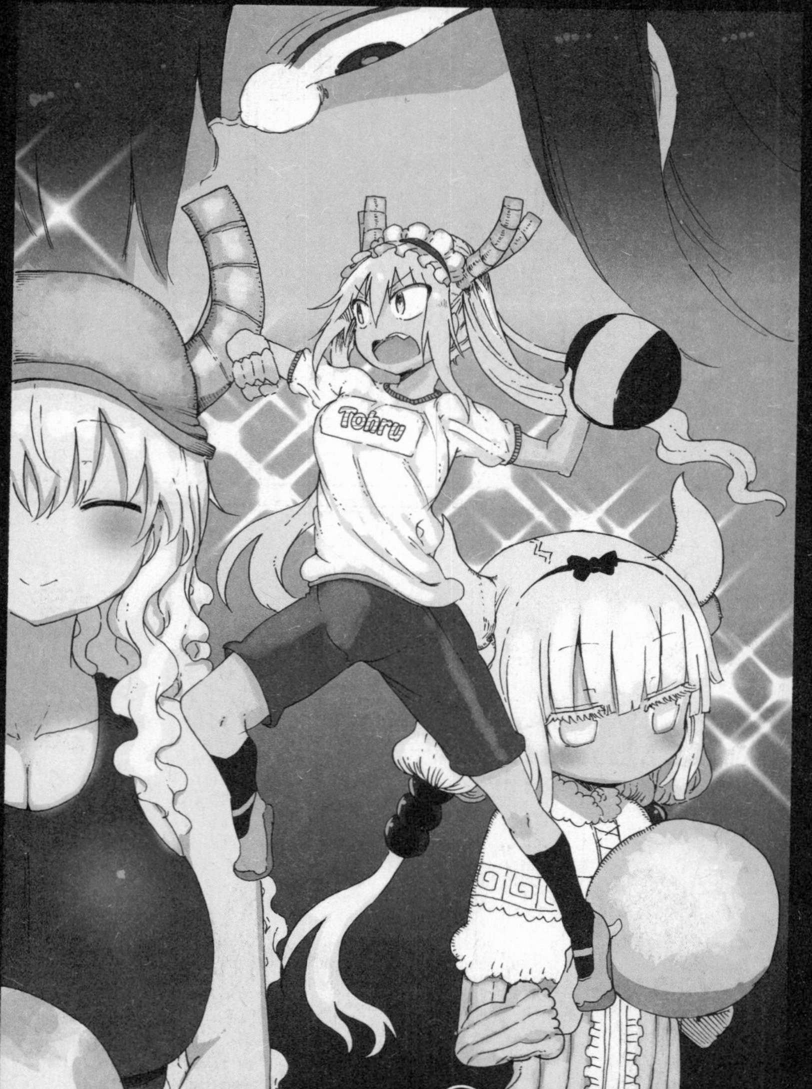
Tohru
CHAPTER 21: TOHRU & DODGEBALL

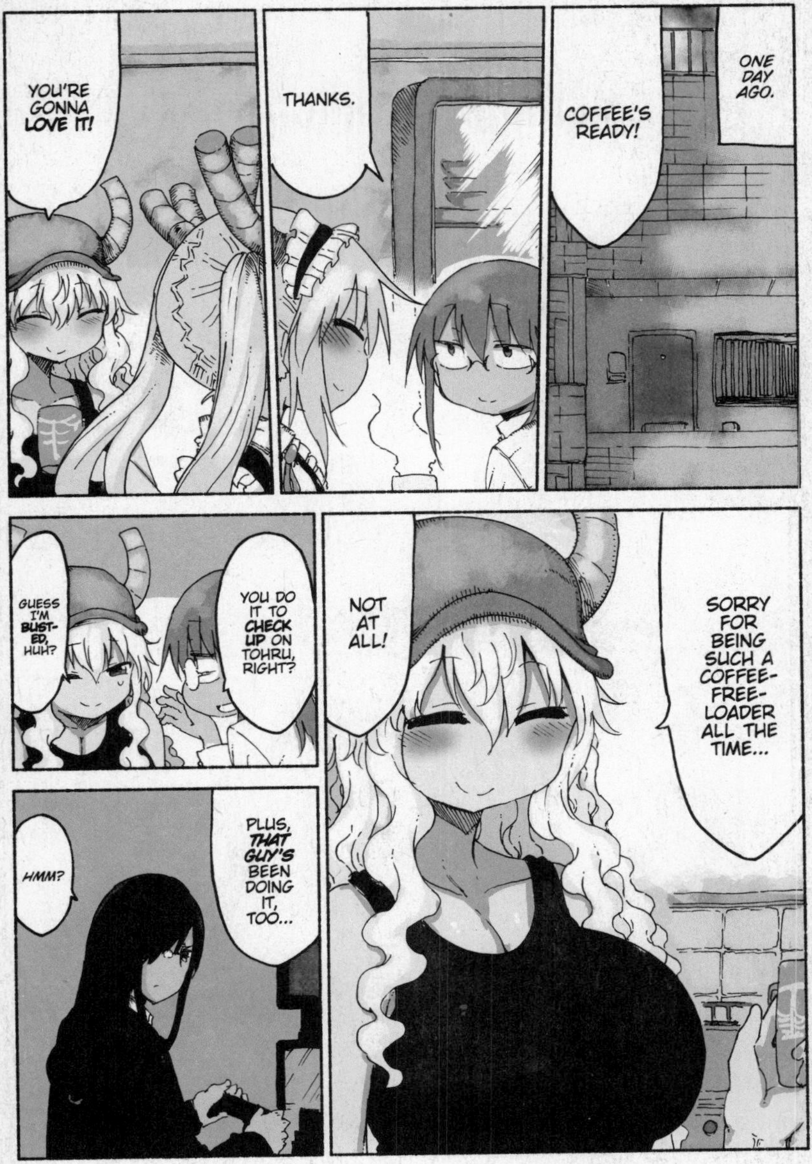
ONE DAY AGO.
COFFEE'S READY!
THANKS.
YOU'RE GONNA LOVE IT!
SORRY FOR BEING SUCH A COFFEE-FREE-LOADER ALL THE TIME...
NOT AT ALL!
YOU DO IT TO CHECK UP ON TOHRU, RIGHT?
GUESS I'M BUST-ED, HUH?
PLUS, THAT GUY'S BEEN DOING IT, TOO...
HMM?

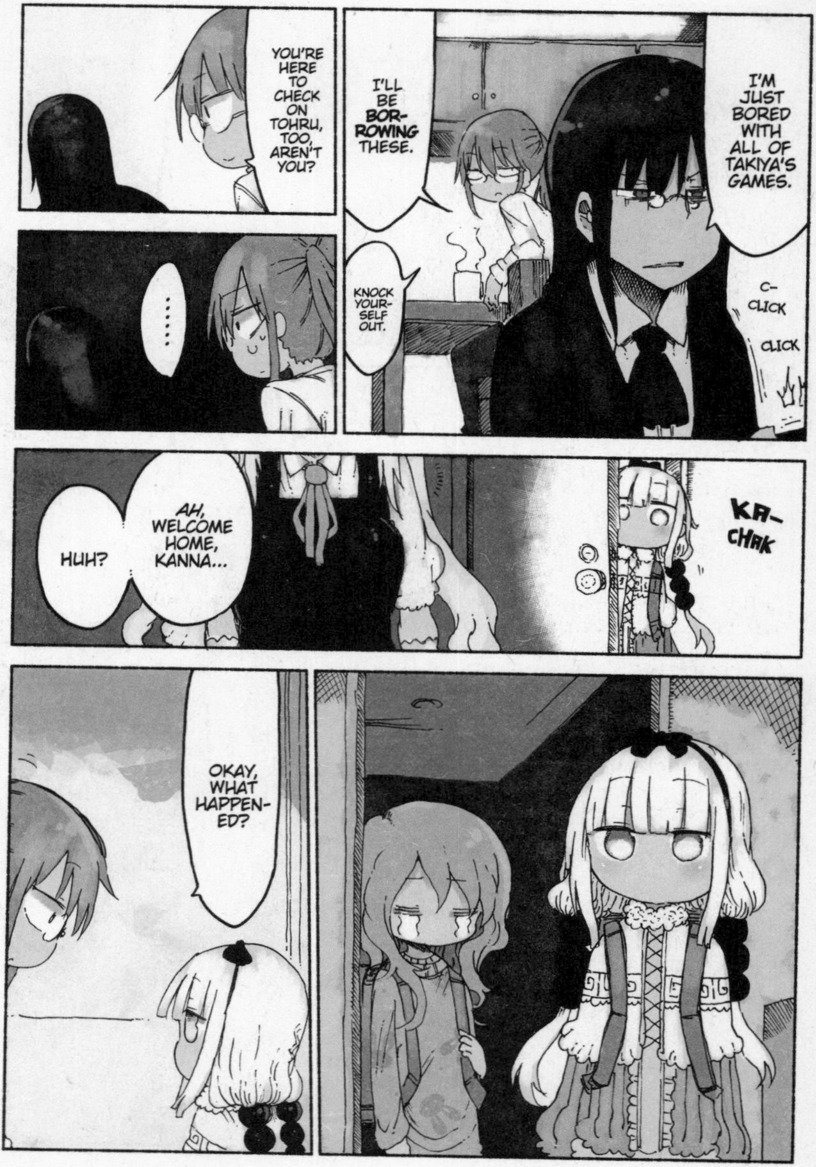
I'M JUST BORED WITH ALL OF TAKIYA'S GAMES.
C-CLICK
CLICK
I'LL BE BOR-ROWING THESE.
KNOCK YOUR-SELF OUT.
YOU'RE HERE TO CHECK ON TOHRU, TOO, AREN'T YOU?
......
KA-CHAK
AH, WELCOME HOME, KANNA...
HUH?
OKAY, WHAT HAPPEN-ED?

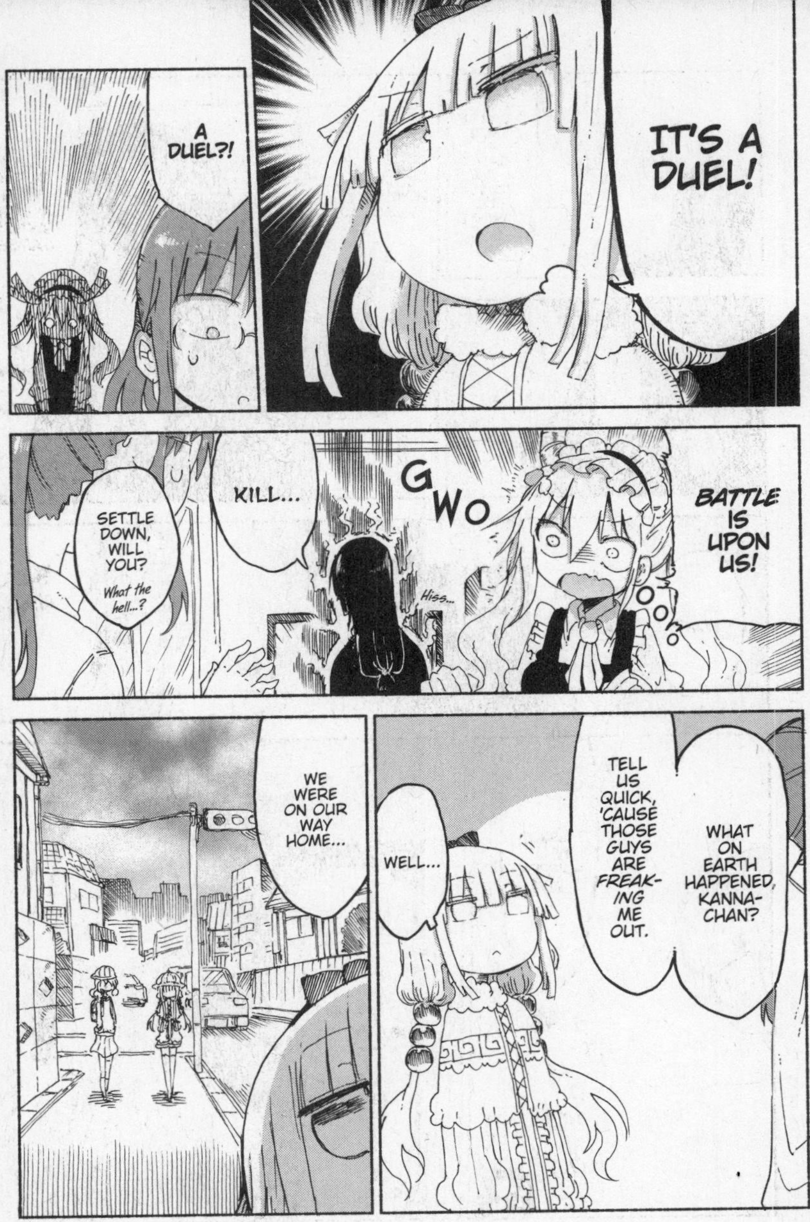
IT'S A DUEL!
A DUEL?!
BATTLE IS UPON US!
GWOOOOO
Hiss...
KILL...
SETTLE DOWN, WILL YOU?
What the hell...?
WHAT ON EARTH HAPPENED, KANNA-CHAN?
TELL US QUICK, 'CAUSE THOSE GUYS ARE FREAKING ME OUT.
WELL...
WE WERE ON OUR WAY HOME...

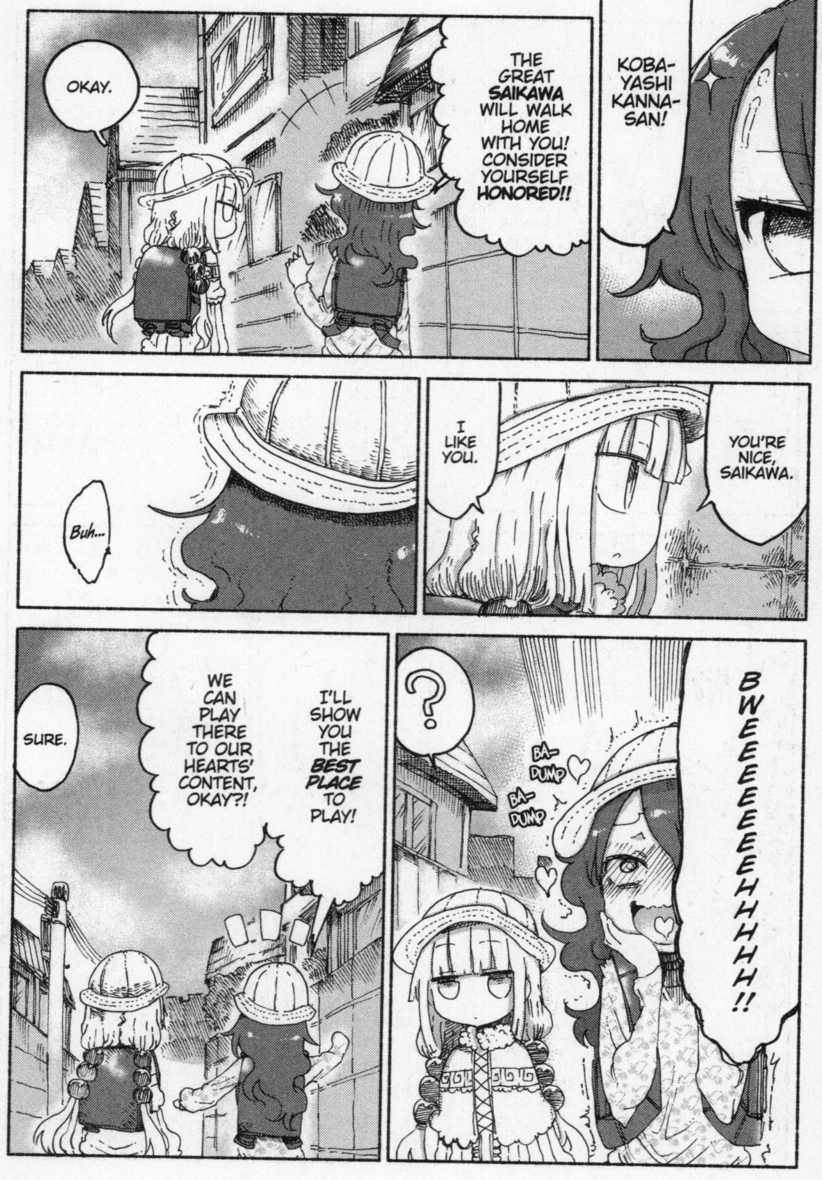
KOBA-YASHI KANNA-SAN!
THE GREAT **SAIKAWA** WILL WALK HOME WITH YOU! CONSIDER YOURSELF **HONORED!!**
OKAY.
YOU'RE NICE, SAIKAWA.
I LIKE YOU.
Buh...
BWEEEEEEEEHHHHH!!
?
BA-DUMP
BA-DUMP
I'LL SHOW YOU THE ***BEST PLACE*** TO PLAY!
WE CAN PLAY THERE TO OUR HEARTS' CONTENT, OKAY?!
SURE.

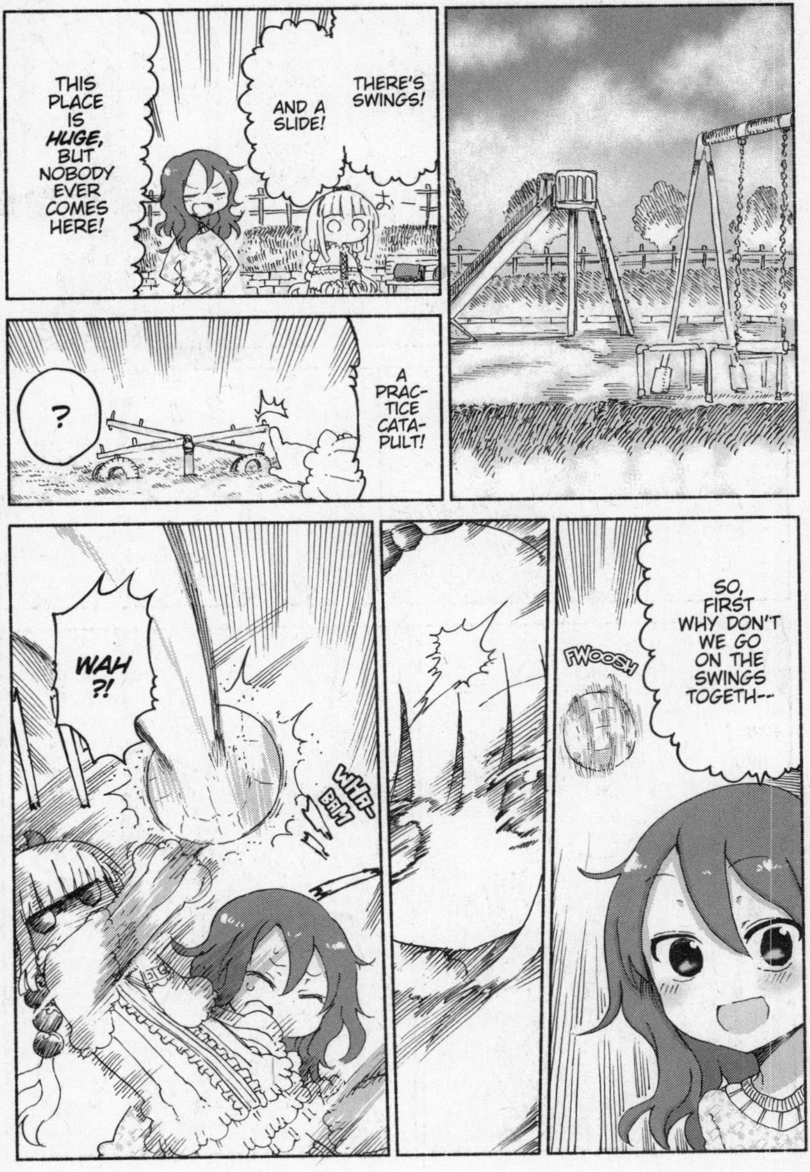
THERE'S SWINGS!
AND A SLIDE!
THIS PLACE IS HUGE, BUT NOBODY EVER COMES HERE!
A PRAC-TICE CATA-PULT!
?
SO, FIRST WHY DON'T WE GO ON THE SWINGS TOGETH--
FWOOSH
WHR-BAM
WAH?!

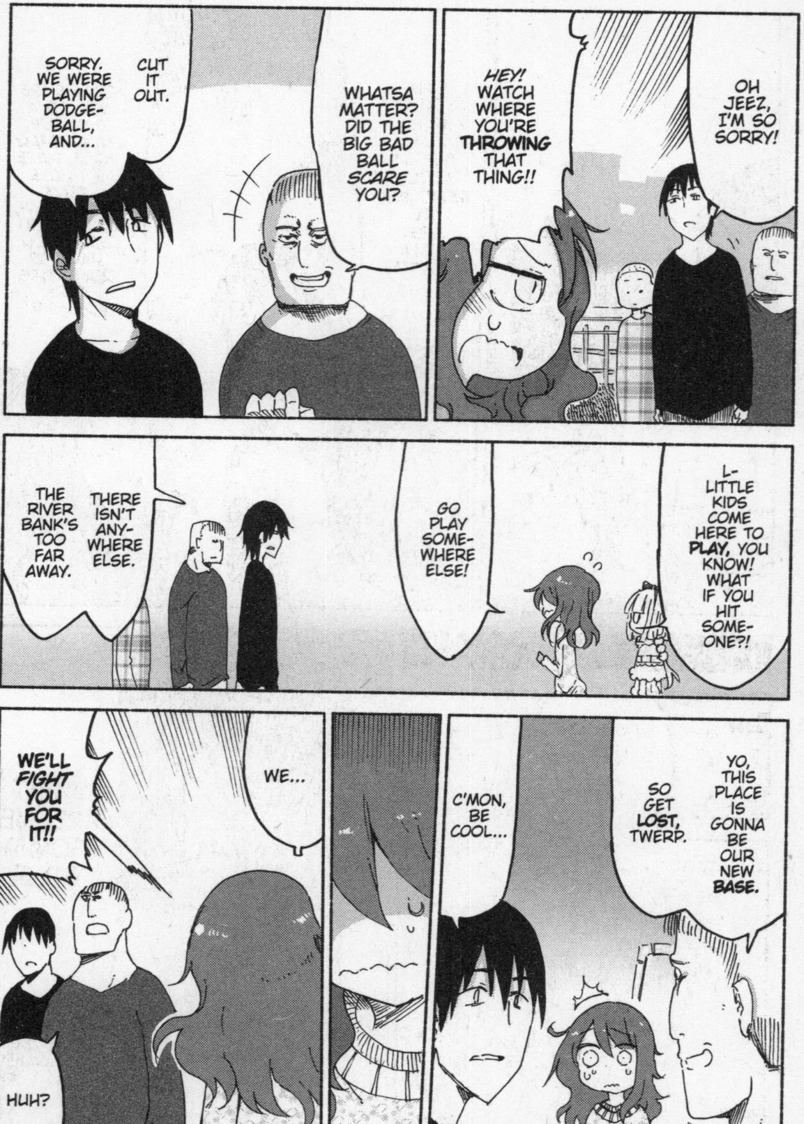
OH JEEZ, I'M SO SORRY!
HEY! WATCH WHERE YOU'RE **THROWING** THAT THING!!
WHATSA MATTER? DID THE BIG BAD BALL *SCARE* YOU?
CUT IT OUT.
SORRY. WE WERE PLAYING DODGEBALL, AND...
L-LITTLE KIDS COME HERE TO **PLAY,** YOU KNOW! WHAT IF YOU HIT SOMEONE?!
GO PLAY SOMEWHERE ELSE!
THERE ISN'T ANYWHERE ELSE.
THE RIVER BANK'S TOO FAR AWAY.
YO, THIS PLACE IS GONNA BE OUR NEW **BASE.**
SO GET **LOST,** TWERP.
C'MON, BE COOL...
WE...
WE'LL *FIGHT* YOU FOR IT!!
HUH?

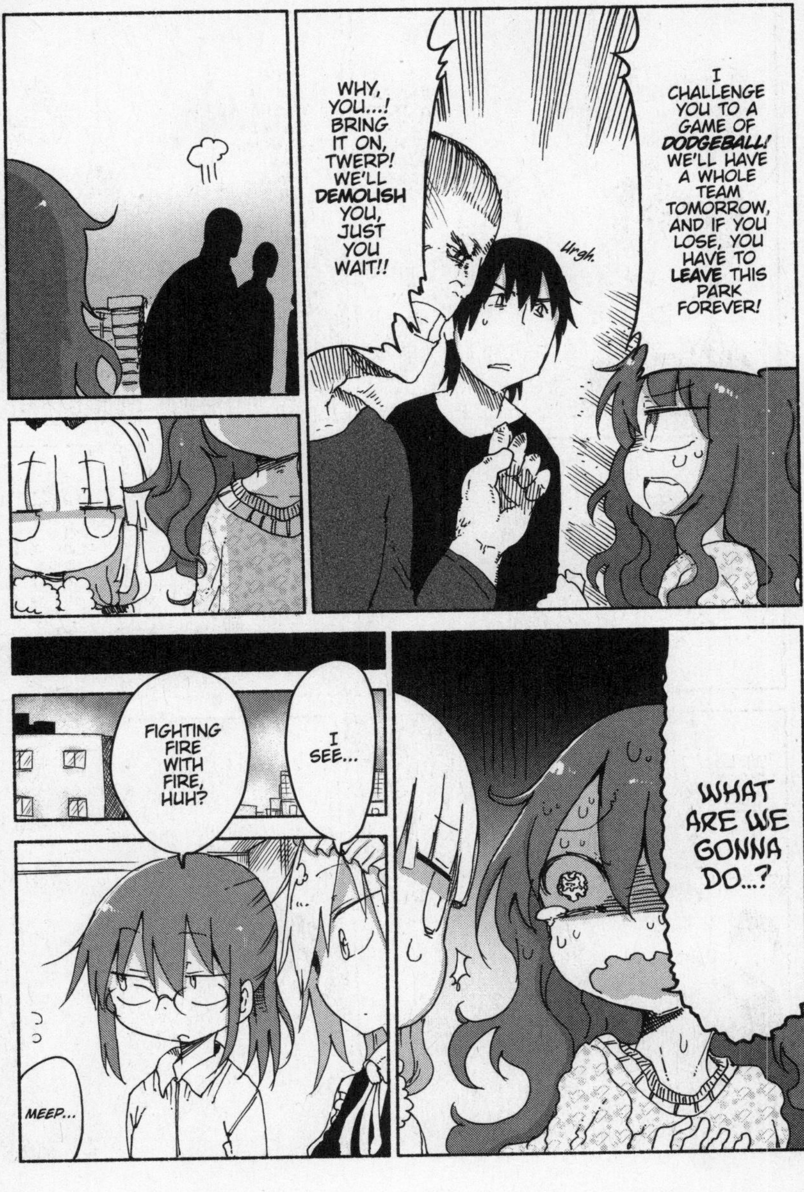
I CHALLENGE YOU TO A GAME OF DODGEBALL! WE'LL HAVE A WHOLE TEAM TOMORROW, AND IF YOU LOSE, YOU HAVE TO LEAVE THIS PARK FOREVER!
Urgh.
WHY, YOU...! BRING IT ON, TWERP! WE'LL DEMOLISH YOU, JUST YOU WAIT!!
WHAT ARE WE GONNA DO...?
I SEE...
FIGHTING FIRE WITH FIRE, HUH?
...
MEEP...

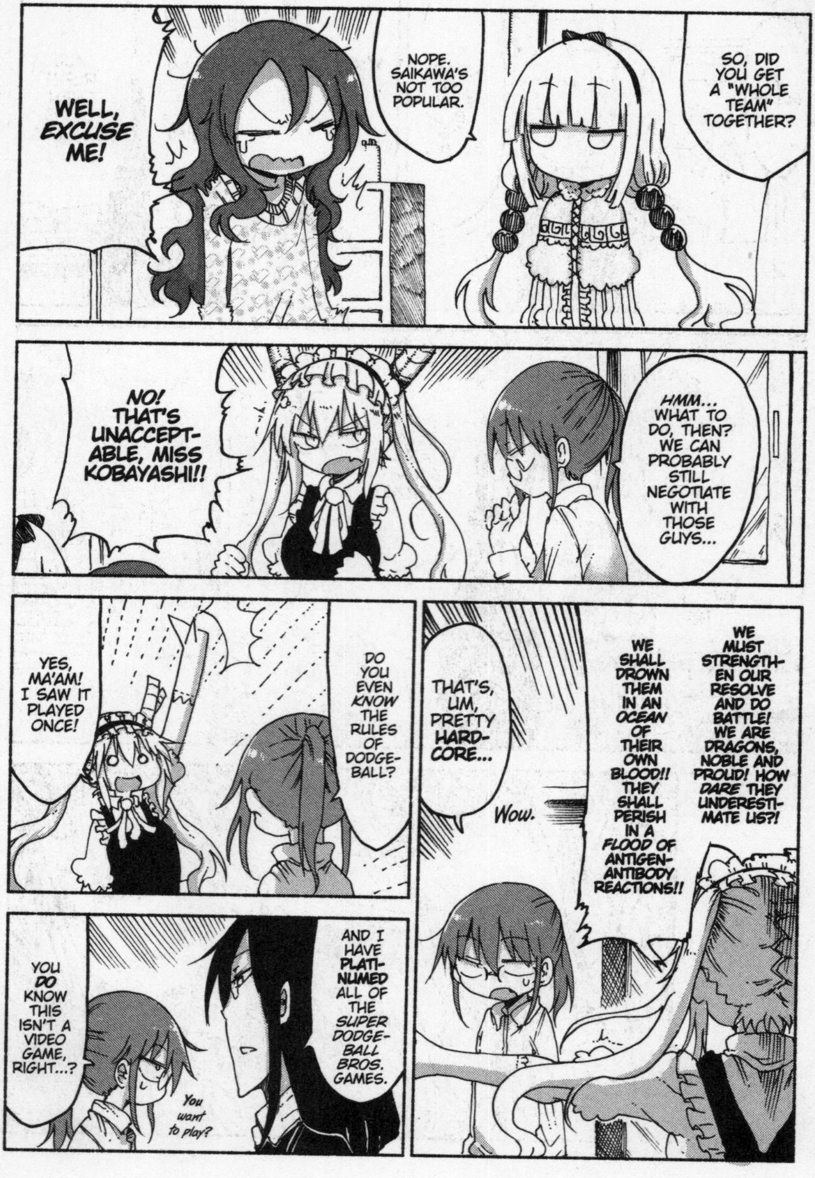
SO, DID YOU GET A "WHOLE TEAM" TOGETHER?
NOPE. SAIKAWA'S NOT TOO POPULAR.
WELL, *EXCUSE* ME!
HMM... WHAT TO DO, THEN? WE CAN PROBABLY STILL NEGOTIATE WITH THOSE GUYS...
NO! THAT'S UNACCEPTABLE, MISS KOBAYASHI!!
WE MUST STRENGTHEN OUR RESOLVE AND DO BATTLE! WE ARE DRAGONS, NOBLE AND PROUD! HOW *DARE* THEY UNDERESTIMATE US?!
WE SHALL DROWN THEM IN AN *OCEAN* OF THEIR OWN BLOOD!! THEY SHALL PERISH IN A *FLOOD* OF ANTIGEN-ANTIBODY REACTIONS!!
THAT'S, UM, PRETTY **HARDCORE...**
Wow.
DO YOU EVEN *KNOW* THE RULES OF DODGEBALL?
YES, MA'AM! I SAW IT PLAYED ONCE!
AND I HAVE **PLATINUMED** ALL OF THE *SUPER DODGEBALL BROS.* GAMES.
YOU *DO* KNOW THIS ISN'T A VIDEO GAME, RIGHT...?
You want to play?

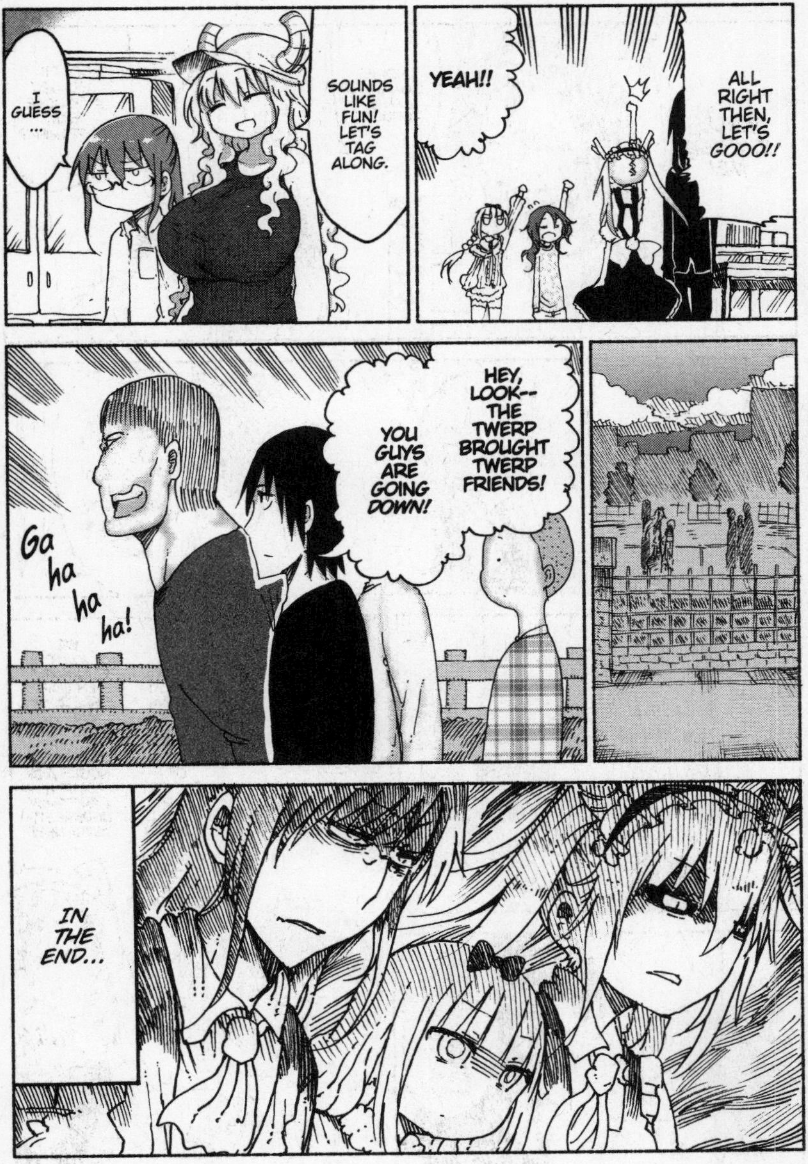
ALL RIGHT THEN, LET'S GOOO!!
YEAH!!
SOUNDS LIKE FUN! LET'S TAG ALONG.
I GUESS ...
HEY, LOOK-- THE TWERP BROUGHT TWERP FRIENDS!
YOU GUYS ARE GOING DOWN!
Ga ha ha ha!
IN THE END...

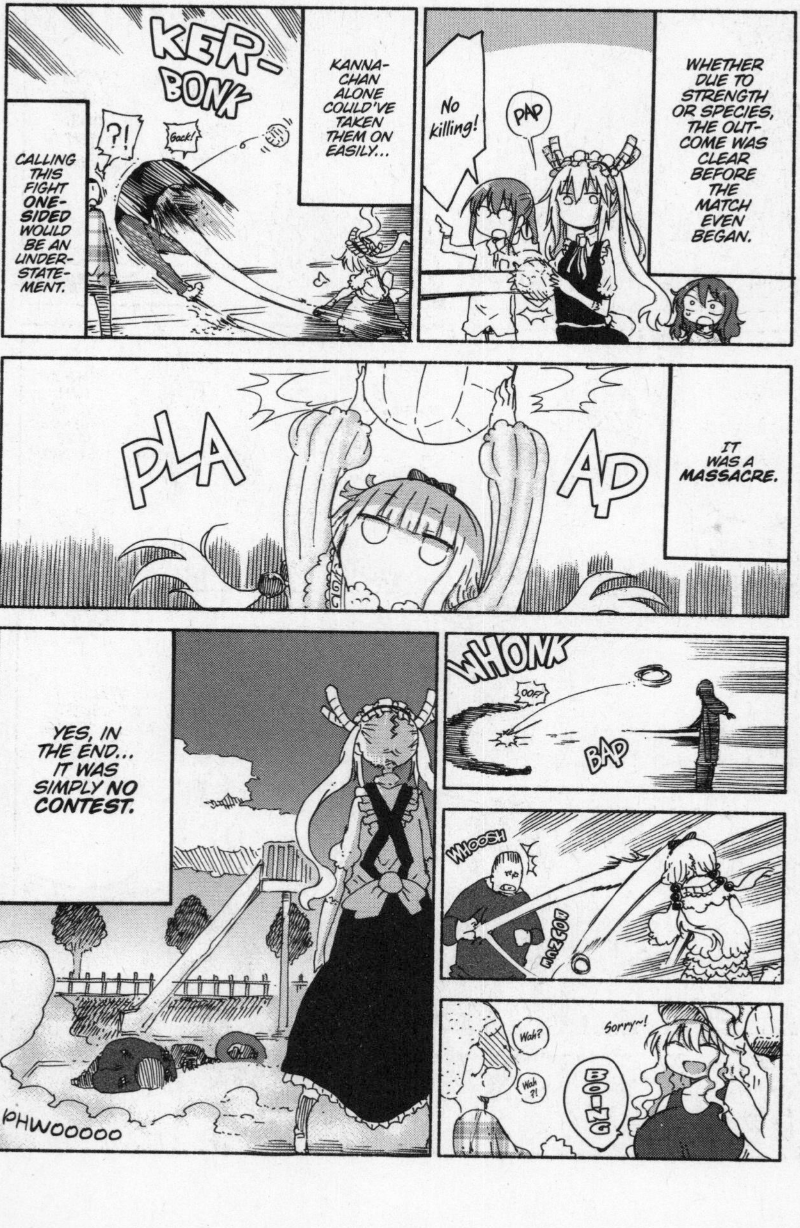
WHETHER DUE TO STRENGTH OR SPECIES, THE OUTCOME WAS CLEAR BEFORE THE MATCH EVEN BEGAN.
No killing!
PAP
KANNA-CHAN ALONE COULD'VE TAKEN THEM ON EASILY...
KER-BONK
?!
Gack!
CALLING THIS FIGHT ONE-SIDED WOULD BE AN UNDERSTATEMENT.
IT WAS A MASSACRE.
PLA AP
WHONK
OOF!?
BAP
WHOOSH
BOUNCE
Sorry~!
Wah?
Wah?!
BOING
YES, IN THE END... IT WAS SIMPLY NO CONTEST.
PHWOOOOO

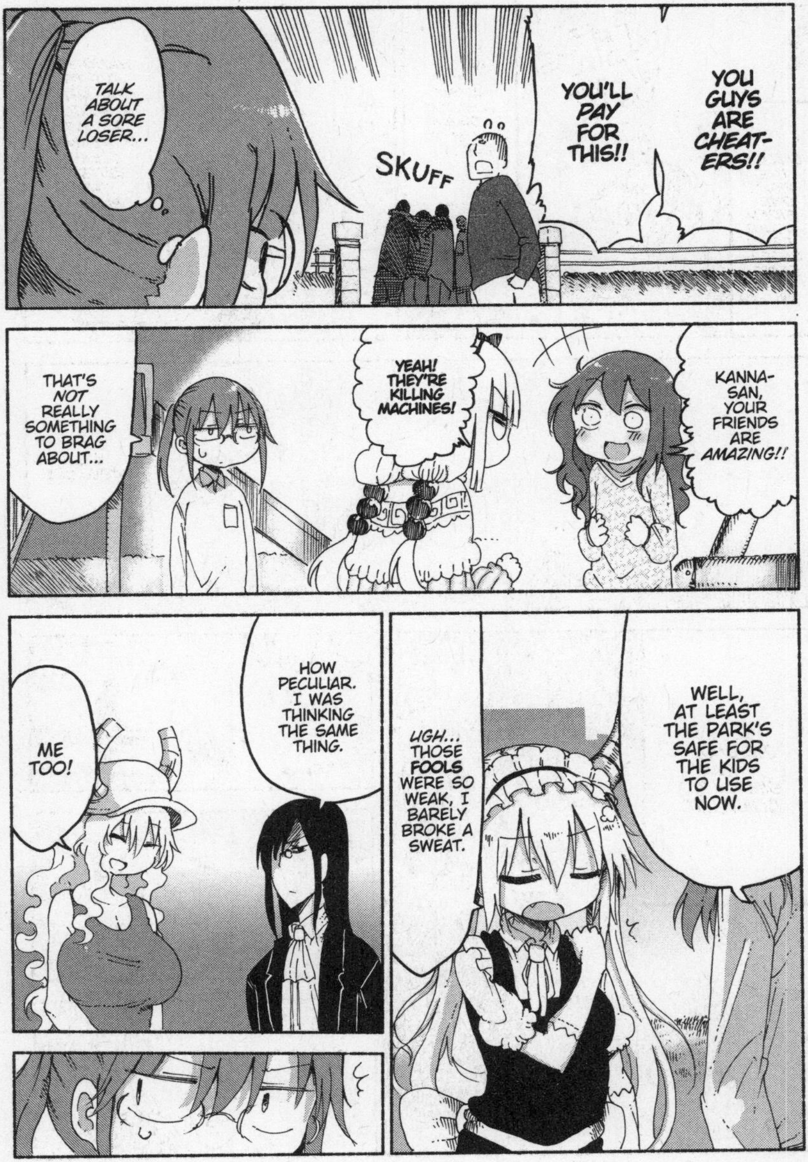
YOU GUYS ARE CHEATERS!!
YOU'LL PAY FOR THIS!!
SKUFF
TALK ABOUT A SORE LOSER...
KANNA-SAN, YOUR FRIENDS ARE AMAZING!!
YEAH! THEY'RE KILLING MACHINES!
THAT'S NOT REALLY SOMETHING TO BRAG ABOUT...
WELL, AT LEAST THE PARK'S SAFE FOR THE KIDS TO USE NOW.
UGH... THOSE FOOLS WERE SO WEAK, I BARELY BROKE A SWEAT.
HOW PECULIAR. I WAS THINKING THE SAME THING.
ME TOO!

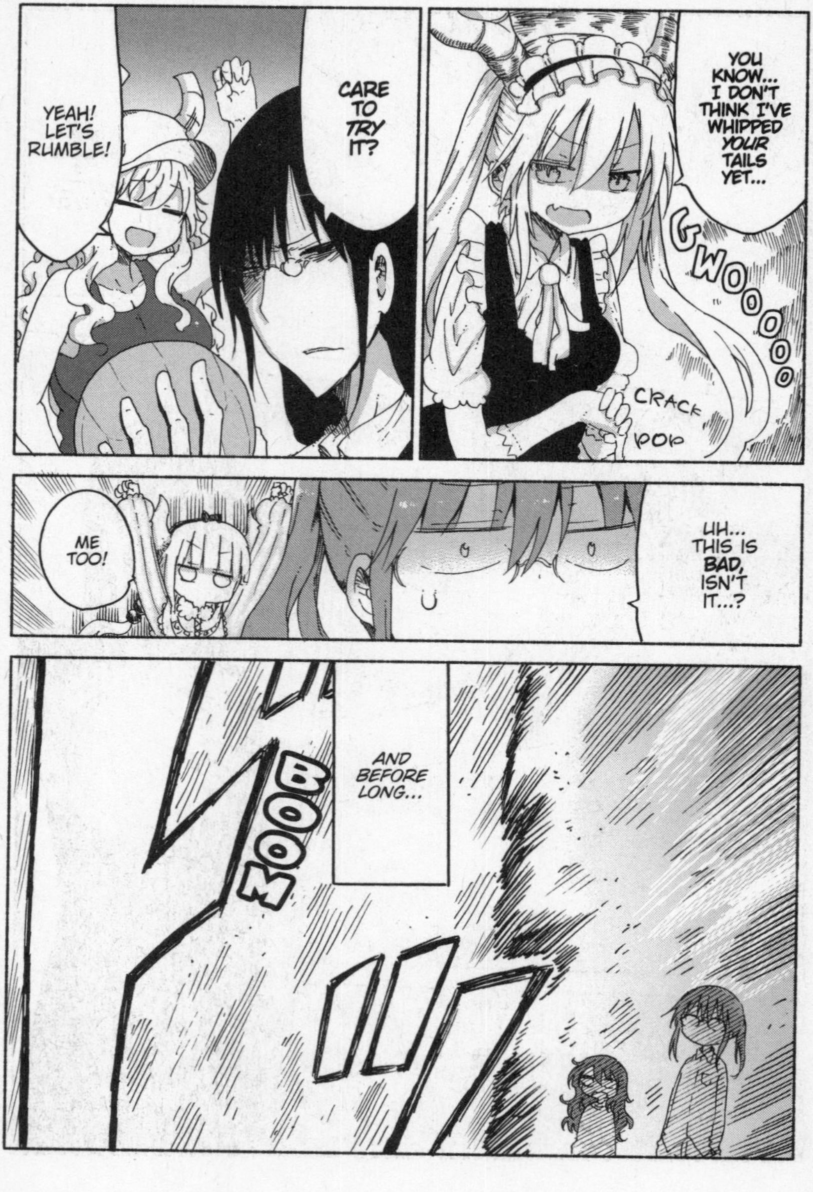
YOU KNOW... I DON'T THINK I'VE WHIPPED YOUR TAILS YET...
GWOOOOOO
CRACK
POP
CARE TO TRY IT?
YEAH! LET'S RUMBLE!
UH... THIS IS BAD, ISN'T IT...?
ME TOO!
AND BEFORE LONG...
BOOM

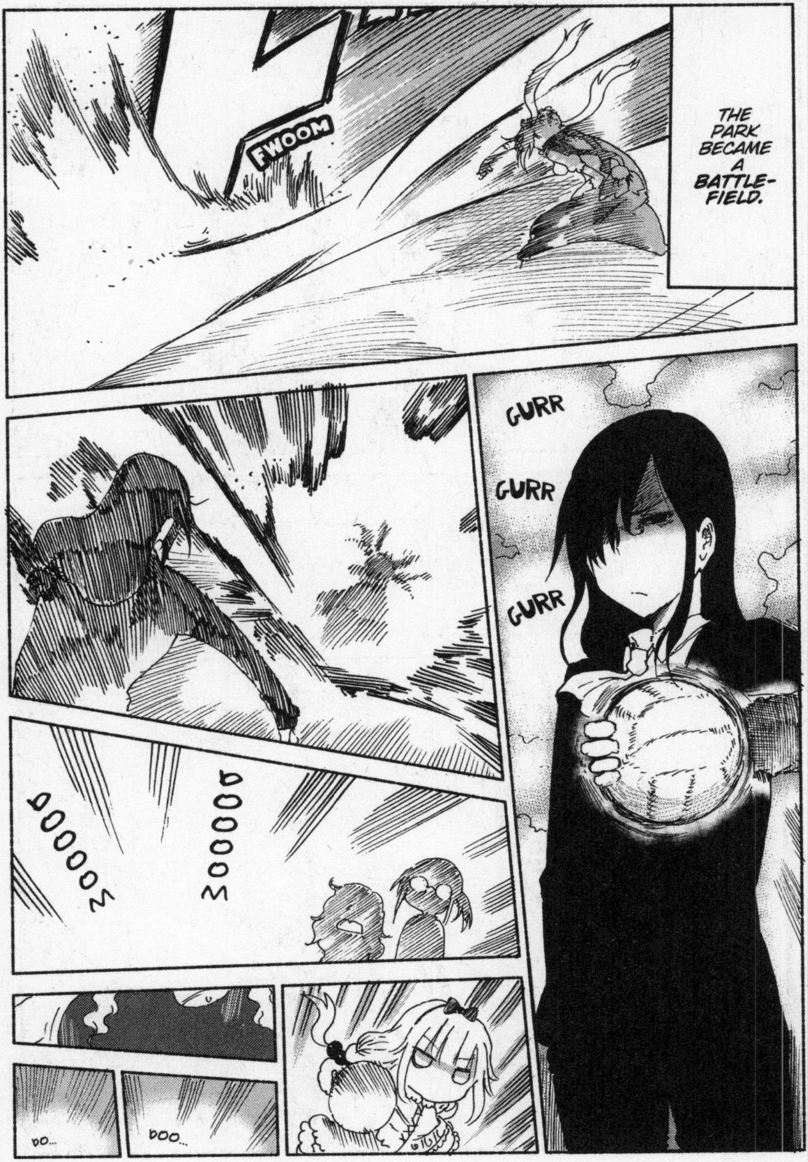
THE PARK BECAME A BATTLE-FIELD.
FWOOM
GURR
GURR
GURR
ZOOOOD
ZOOOOD
DOO...
DO...

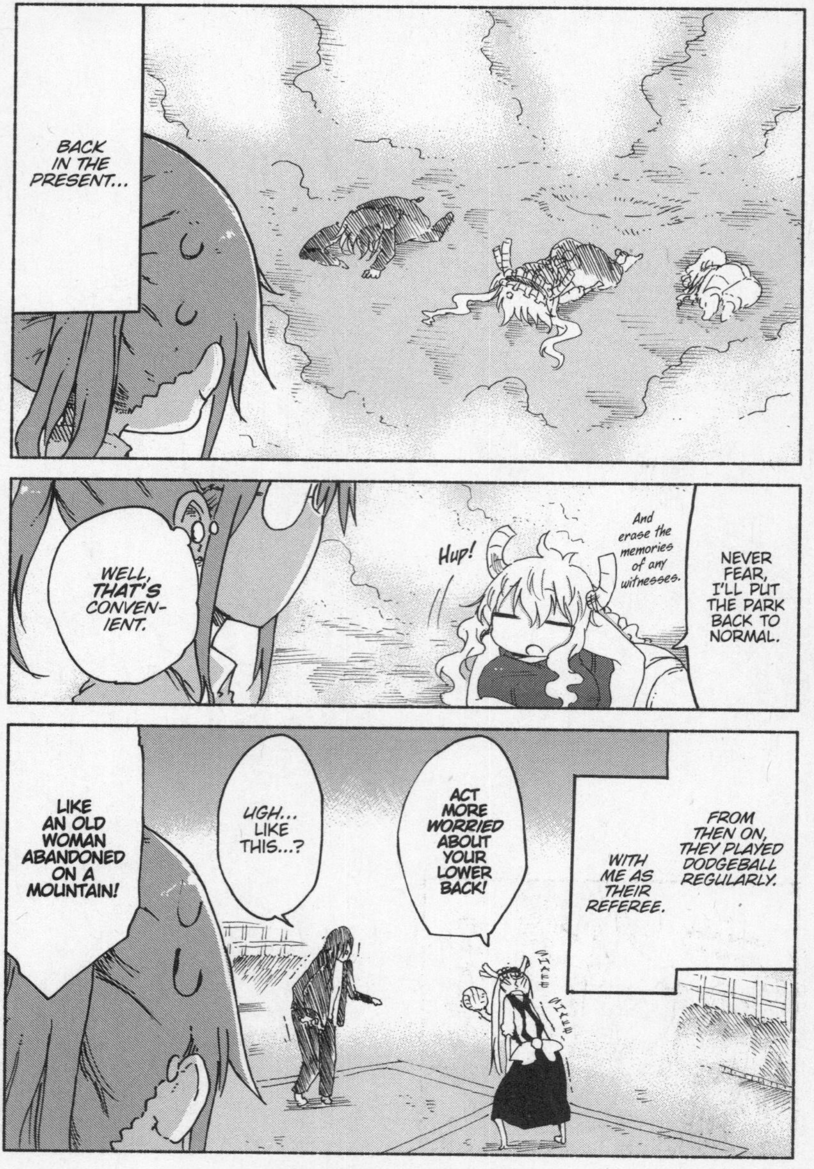
BACK IN THE PRESENT...
NEVER FEAR, I'LL PUT THE PARK BACK TO NORMAL.
And erase the memories of any witnesses.
Hup!
WELL, THAT'S CONVEN-IENT.
FROM THEN ON, THEY PLAYED DODGEBALL REGULARLY.
WITH ME AS THEIR REFEREE.
ACT MORE WORRIED ABOUT YOUR LOWER BACK!
UGH... LIKE THIS...?
LIKE AN OLD WOMAN ABANDONED ON A MOUNTAIN!

CHAPTER 21/END

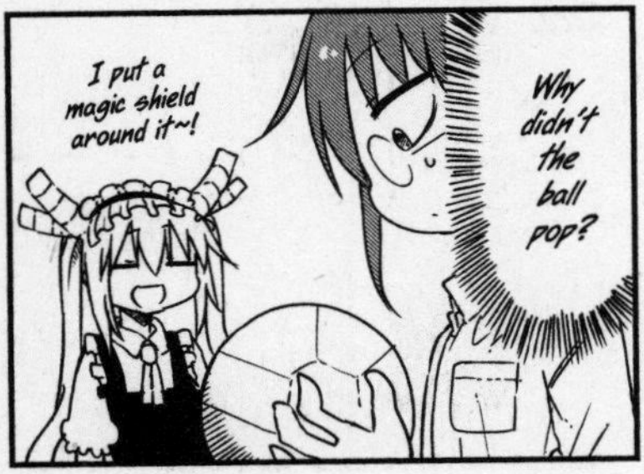
Why didn't the ball pop?
I put a magic shield around it~!

Miss Kobayashi's Dragon Maid

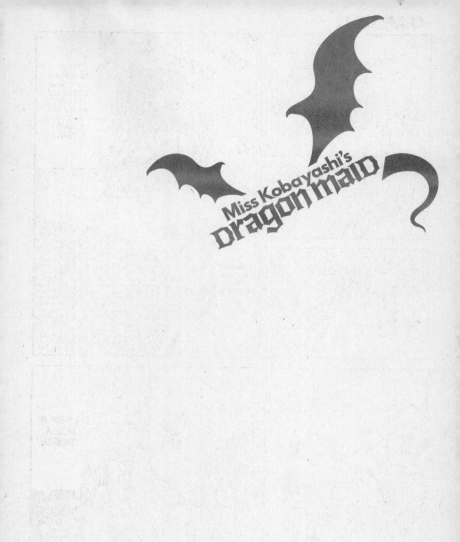

CHAPTER 22

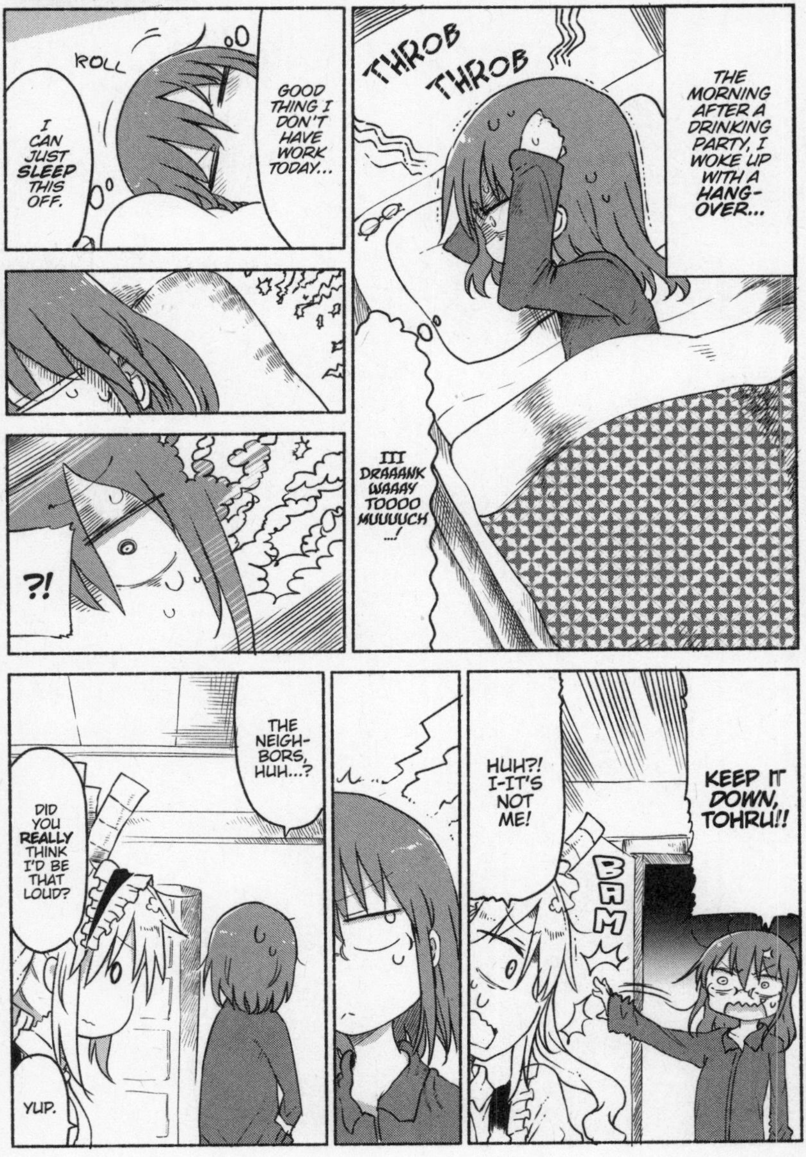
THE MORNING AFTER A DRINKING PARTY, I WOKE UP WITH A HANG-OVER...
THROB THROB
III DRAAANK WAAAY TOOOO MUUUUCH ...!
GOOD THING I DON'T HAVE WORK TODAY...
ROLL
I CAN JUST SLEEP THIS OFF.
?!
KEEP IT DOWN, TOHRU!!
BAM
HUH?! I-IT'S NOT ME!
THE NEIGHBORS, HUH...?
DID YOU REALLY THINK I'D BE THAT LOUD?
YUP.

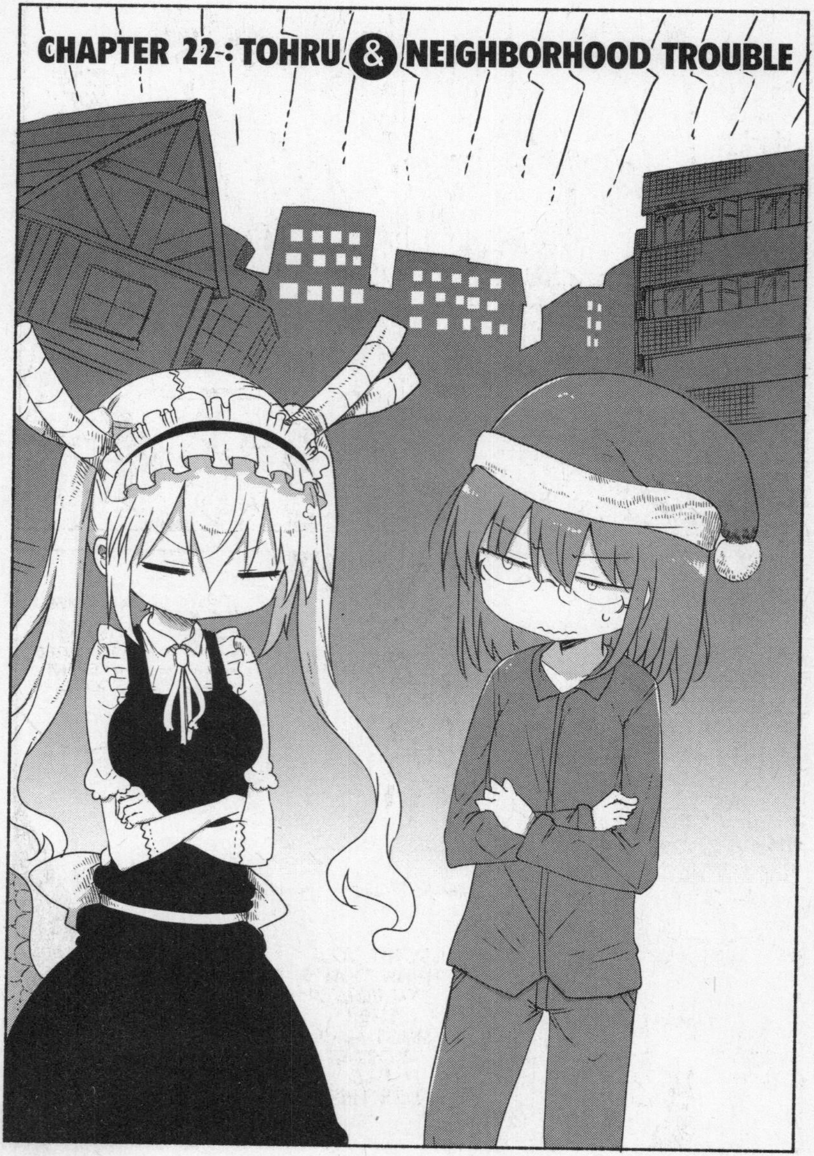
CHAPTER 22 : TOHRU & NEIGHBORHOOD TROUBLE

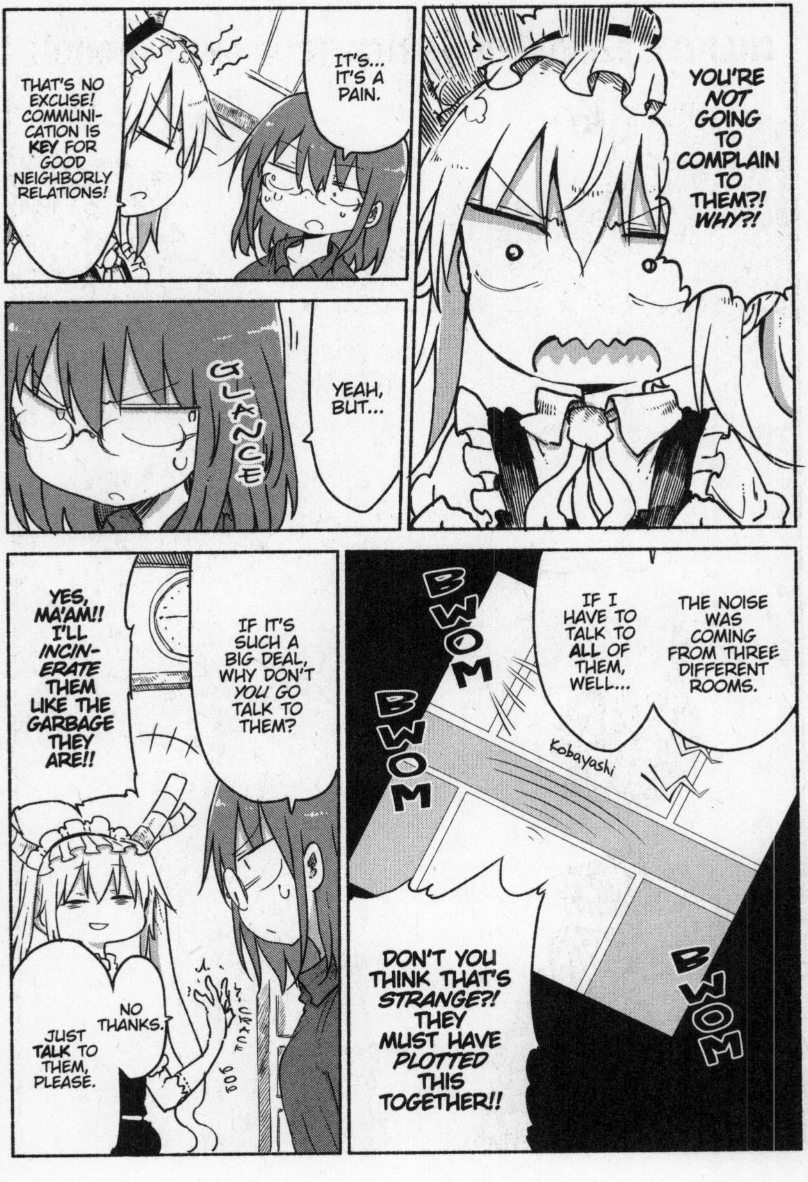
YOU'RE *NOT* GOING TO COMPLAIN TO THEM?! *WHY?!*
IT'S... IT'S A PAIN.
THAT'S NO EXCUSE! COMMUNICATION IS **KEY** FOR GOOD NEIGHBORLY RELATIONS!
YEAH, BUT...
GLANCE
THE NOISE WAS COMING FROM THREE DIFFERENT ROOMS.
IF I HAVE TO TALK TO **ALL** OF THEM, WELL...
BWOM
BWOM
BWOM
Kobayashi
DON'T YOU THINK THAT'S *STRANGE?!* THEY MUST HAVE *PLOTTED* THIS TOGETHER!!
BWOM
IF IT'S SUCH A BIG DEAL, WHY DON'T *YOU* GO TALK TO THEM?
YES, MA'AM!! I'LL *INCINERATE* THEM LIKE THE GARBAGE THEY ARE!!
NO THANKS.
JUST TALK TO THEM, PLEASE.

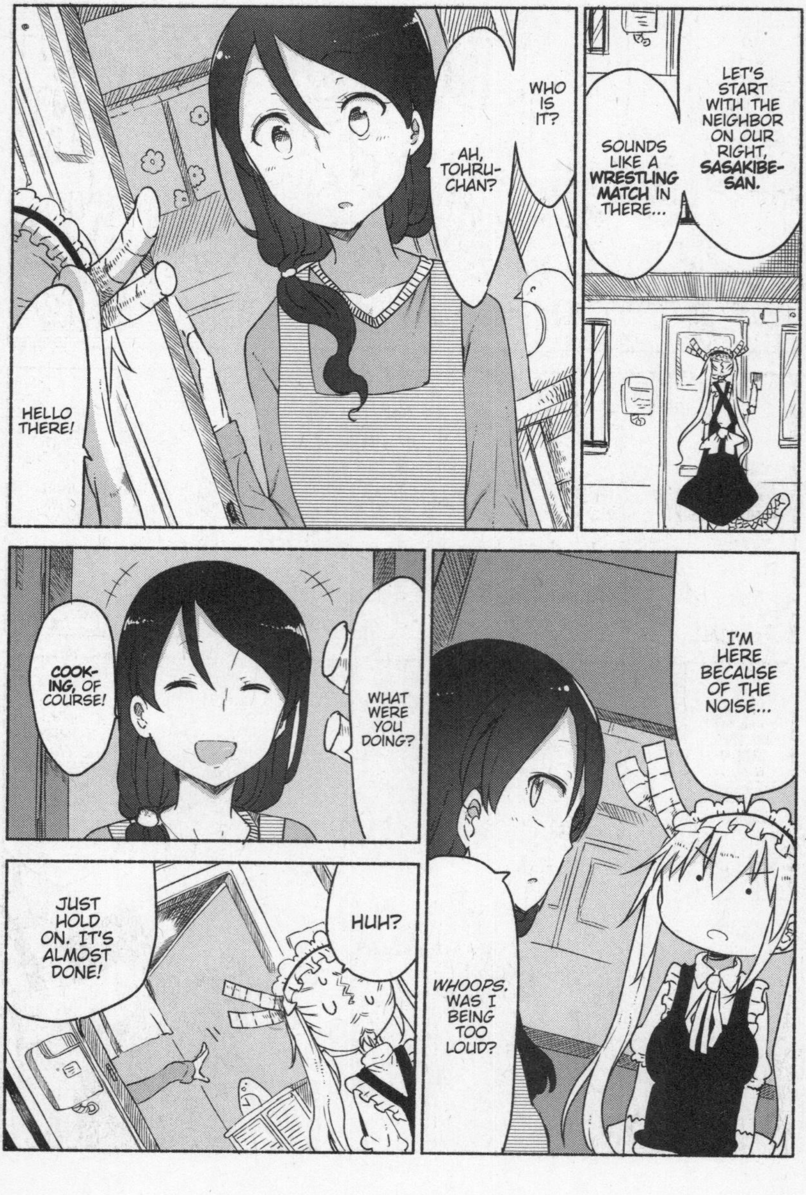
LET'S START WITH THE NEIGHBOR ON OUR RIGHT, SASAKIBE-SAN.
SOUNDS LIKE A WRESTLING MATCH IN THERE...
WHO IS IT?
AH, TOHRU-CHAN?
HELLO THERE!
I'M HERE BECAUSE OF THE NOISE...
WHOOPS. WAS I BEING TOO LOUD?
WHAT WERE YOU DOING?
COOKING, OF COURSE!
HUH?
JUST HOLD ON. IT'S ALMOST DONE!

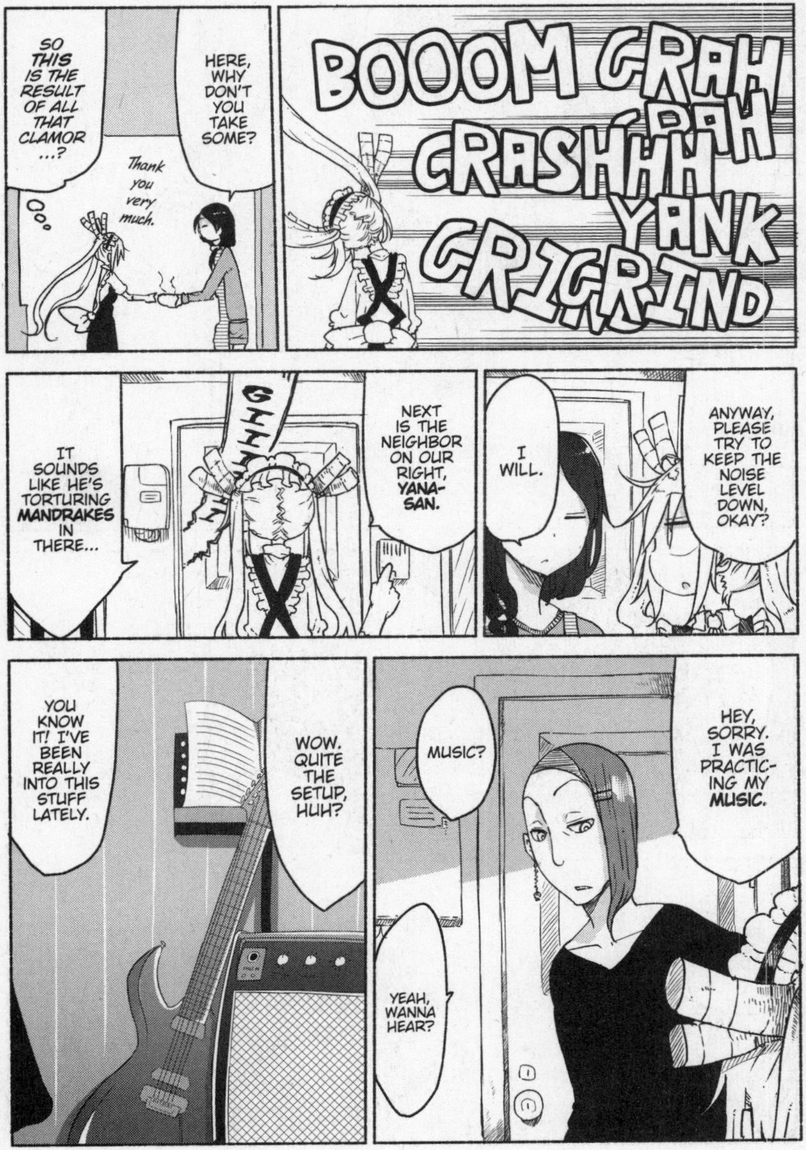
BOOOM GRAH
GRAH
CRASHHH
YANK
GRIGRIND
HERE, WHY DON'T YOU TAKE SOME?
Thank you very much.
SO THIS IS THE RESULT OF ALL THAT CLAMOR ...?
ANYWAY, PLEASE TRY TO KEEP THE NOISE LEVEL DOWN, OKAY?
I WILL.
NEXT IS THE NEIGHBOR ON OUR RIGHT, YANA-SAN.
GIIII
IT SOUNDS LIKE HE'S TORTURING MANDRAKES IN THERE...
HEY, SORRY. I WAS PRACTIC-ING MY MUSIC.
MUSIC?
YEAH, WANNA HEAR?
WOW. QUITE THE SETUP, HUH?
YOU KNOW IT! I'VE BEEN REALLY INTO THIS STUFF LATELY.

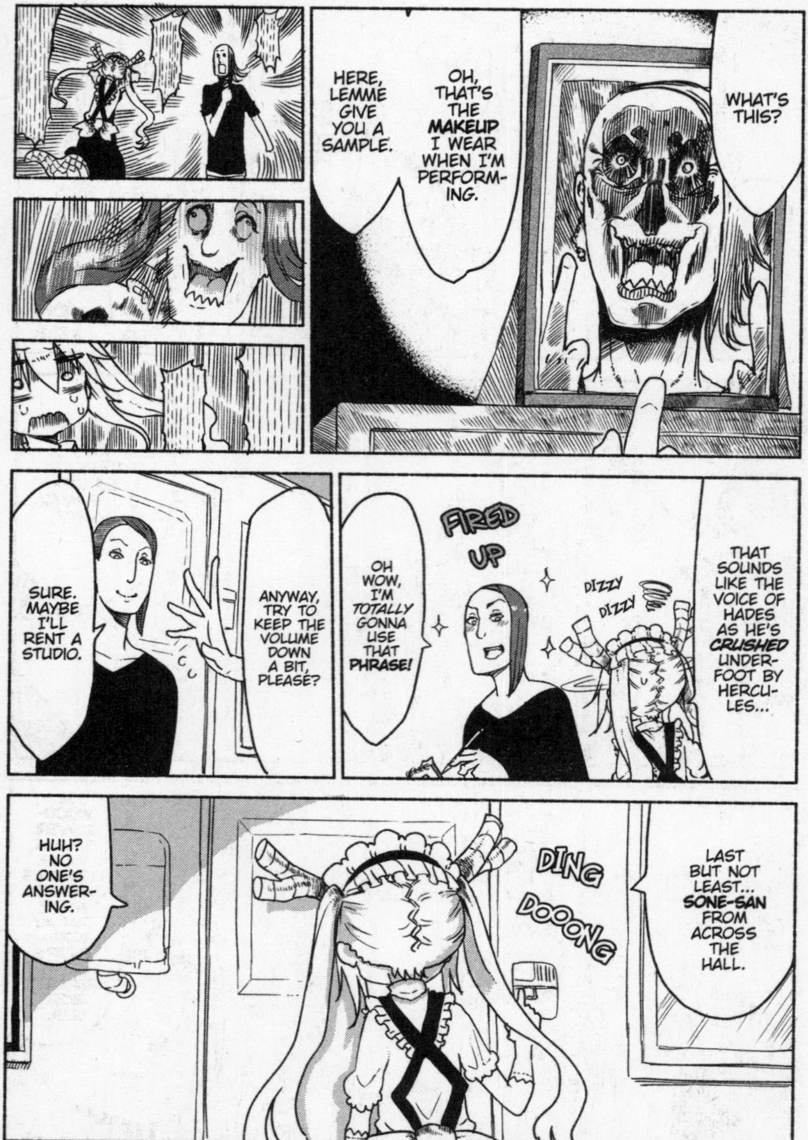
WHAT'S THIS?
OH, THAT'S THE MAKEUP I WEAR WHEN I'M PERFORMING.
HERE, LEMME GIVE YOU A SAMPLE.
THAT SOUNDS LIKE THE VOICE OF HADES AS HE'S CRUSHED UNDERFOOT BY HERCULES...
DIZZY DIZZY
FIRED UP
OH WOW, I'M TOTALLY GONNA USE THAT PHRASE!
ANYWAY, TRY TO KEEP THE VOLUME DOWN A BIT, PLEASE?
SURE. MAYBE I'LL RENT A STUDIO.
LAST BUT NOT LEAST... SONE-SAN FROM ACROSS THE HALL.
DING DOOONG
HUH? NO ONE'S ANSWERING.

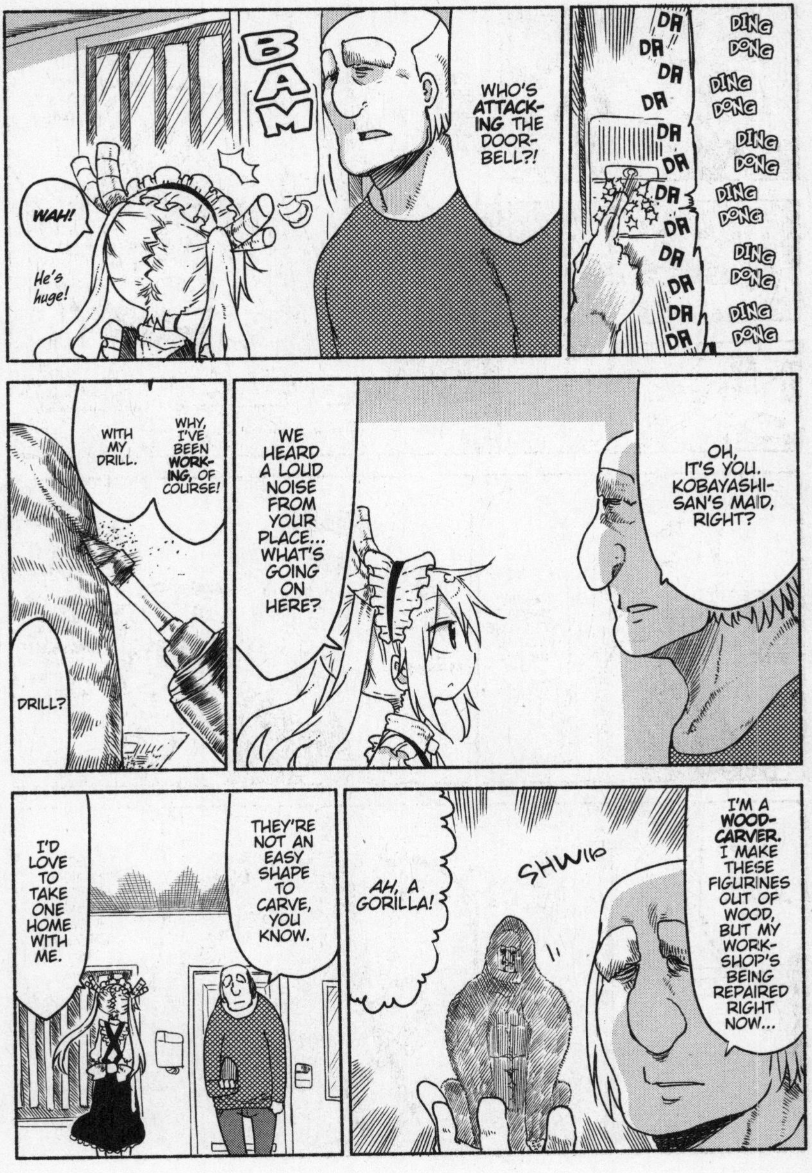
DING DONG DING DONG DING DONG DING DONG DING DONG DING DONG
DA DA DA DA DA DA DA DA DA DA DA DA
WHO'S ATTACKING THE DOORBELL?!
BAM
WAH!
He's huge!
OH, IT'S YOU. KOBAYASHI-SAN'S MAID, RIGHT?
WE HEARD A LOUD NOISE FROM YOUR PLACE... WHAT'S GOING ON HERE?
WHY, I'VE BEEN WORKING, OF COURSE!
WITH MY DRILL.
DRILL?
I'M A WOODCARVER. I MAKE THESE FIGURINES OUT OF WOOD, BUT MY WORKSHOP'S BEING REPAIRED RIGHT NOW...
AH, A GORILLA!
THEY'RE NOT AN EASY SHAPE TO CARVE, YOU KNOW.
I'D LOVE TO TAKE ONE HOME WITH ME.

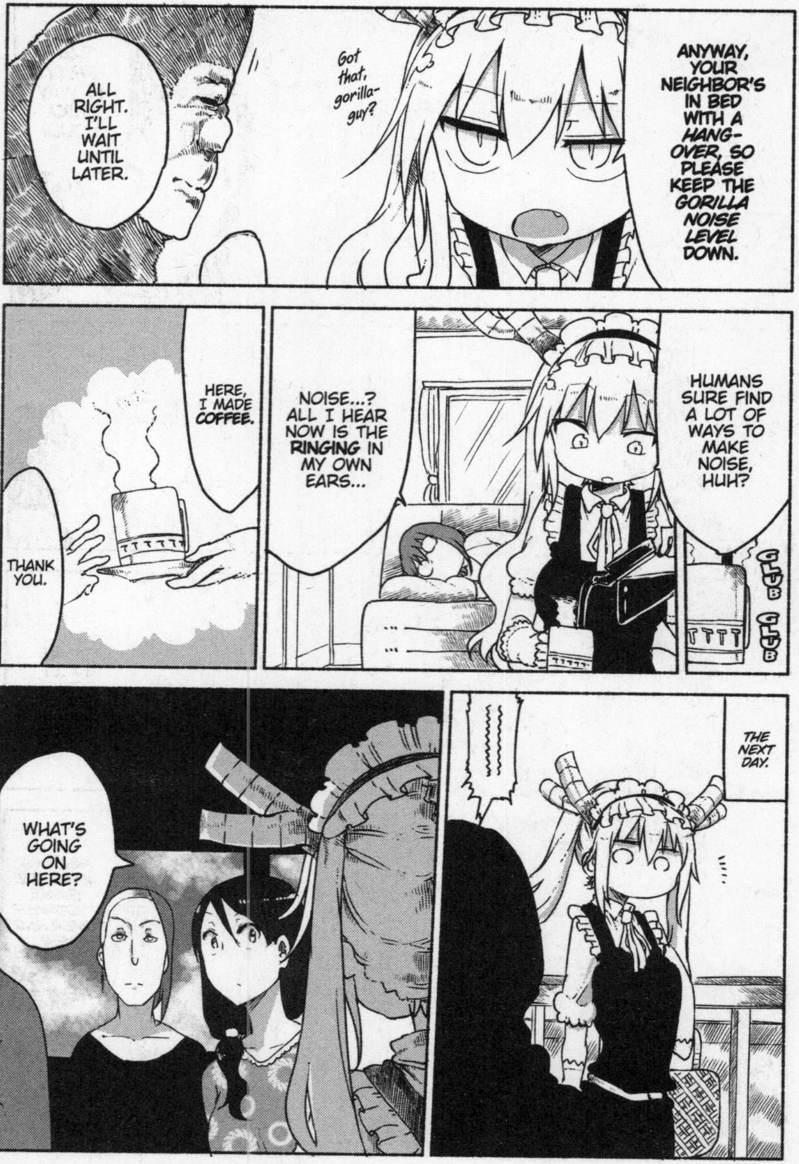
ANYWAY, YOUR NEIGHBOR'S IN BED WITH A HANG-OVER, SO PLEASE KEEP THE GORILLA NOISE LEVEL DOWN.
Got that, gorilla-guy?
ALL RIGHT. I'LL WAIT UNTIL LATER.
HUMANS SURE FIND A LOT OF WAYS TO MAKE NOISE, HUH?
GLUB GLUB
NOISE...? ALL I HEAR NOW IS THE RINGING IN MY OWN EARS...
.....
.....
HERE, I MADE COFFEE.
THANK YOU.
THE NEXT DAY.
WHAT'S GOING ON HERE?

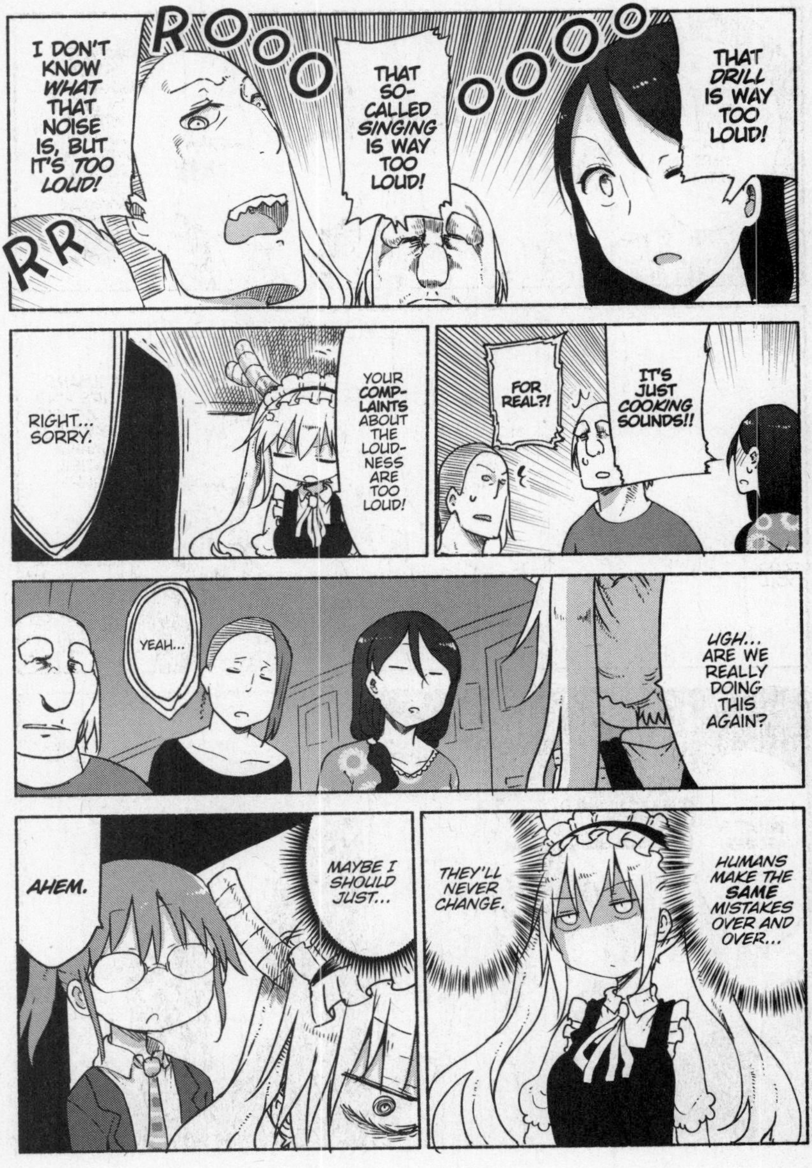
THAT DRILL IS WAY TOO LOUD!
ROOOOOOOOO
THAT SO-CALLED SINGING IS WAY TOO LOUD!
I DON'T KNOW WHAT THAT NOISE IS, BUT IT'S TOO LOUD!
RR
IT'S JUST COOKING SOUNDS!!
FOR REAL?!
YOUR COMPLAINTS ABOUT THE LOUDNESS ARE TOO LOUD!
RIGHT... SORRY.
UGH... ARE WE REALLY DOING THIS AGAIN?
YEAH...
HUMANS MAKE THE SAME MISTAKES OVER AND OVER...
THEY'LL NEVER CHANGE.
MAYBE I SHOULD JUST...
AHEM.

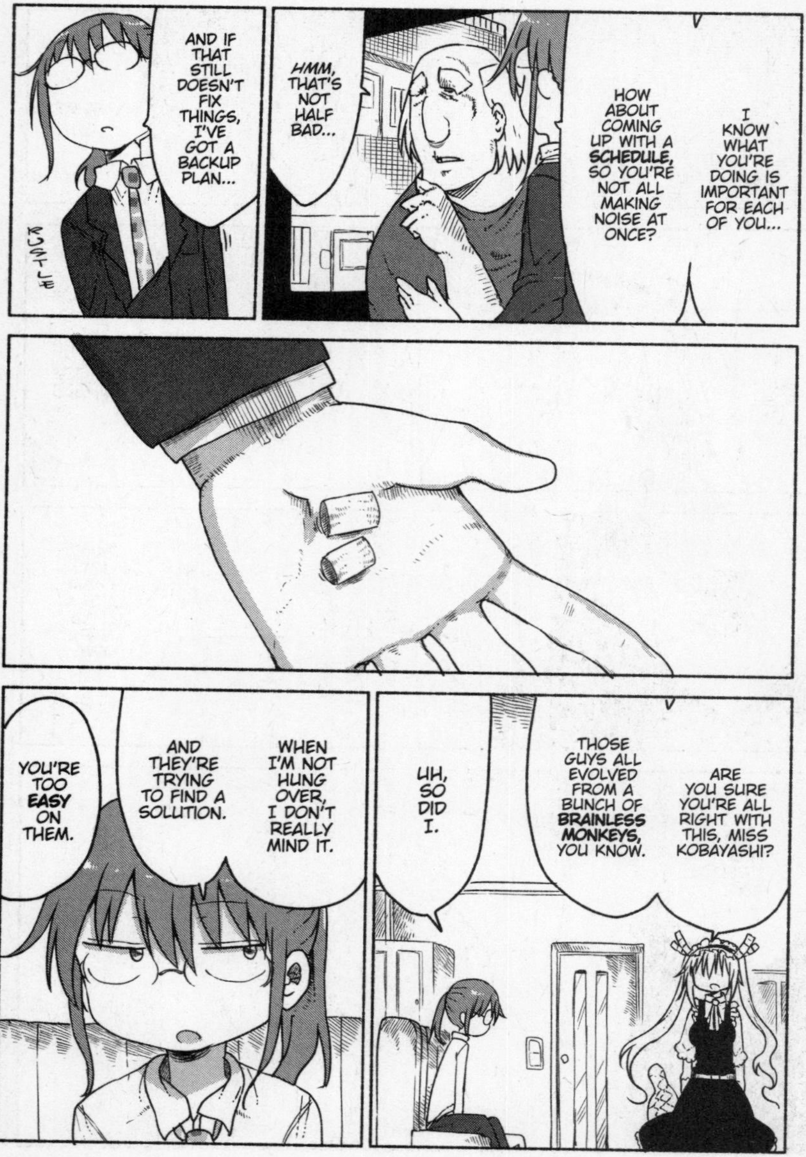
I KNOW WHAT YOU'RE DOING IS IMPORTANT FOR EACH OF YOU...
HOW ABOUT COMING UP WITH A **SCHEDULE,** SO YOU'RE NOT ALL MAKING NOISE AT ONCE?
HMM, THAT'S NOT HALF BAD...
AND IF THAT STILL DOESN'T FIX THINGS, I'VE GOT A BACKUP PLAN...
RUSTLE
ARE YOU SURE YOU'RE ALL RIGHT WITH THIS, MISS KOBAYASHI?
THOSE GUYS ALL EVOLVED FROM A BUNCH OF **BRAINLESS MONKEYS,** YOU KNOW.
UH, SO DID I.
WHEN I'M NOT HUNG OVER, I DON'T REALLY MIND IT.
AND THEY'RE TRYING TO FIND A SOLUTION.
YOU'RE TOO **EASY** ON THEM.

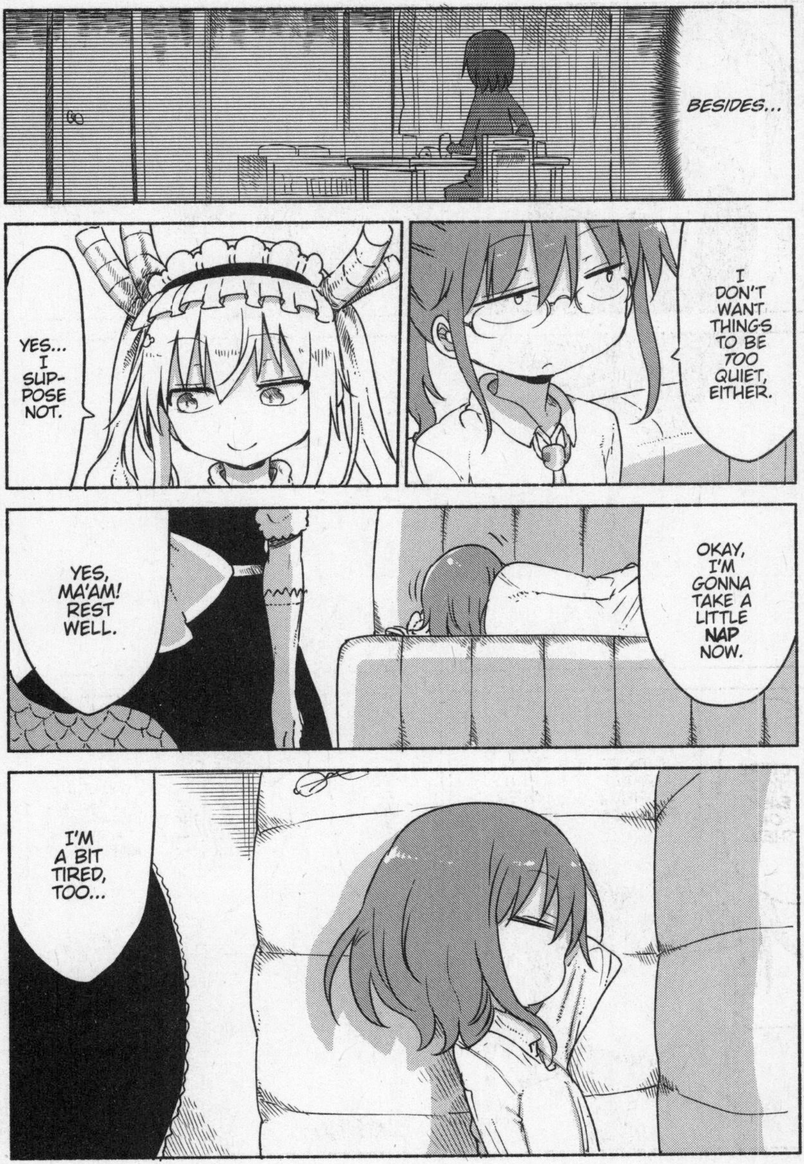
BESIDES...
I DON'T WANT THINGS TO BE TOO QUIET, EITHER.
YES... I SUPPOSE NOT.
OKAY, I'M GONNA TAKE A LITTLE NAP NOW.
YES, MA'AM! REST WELL.
I'M A BIT TIRED, TOO...

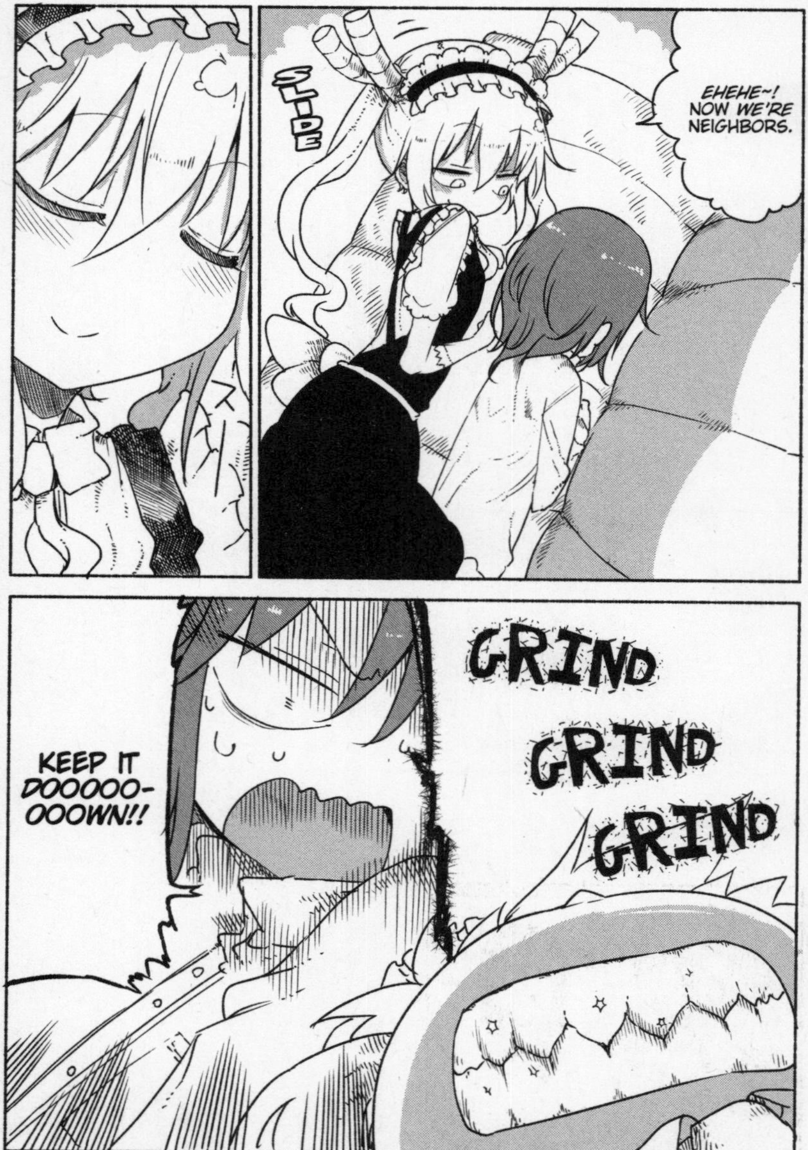
SLIDE
EHEHE~! NOW WE'RE NEIGHBORS.
GRIND GRIND GRIND
KEEP IT DOOOOO-OOOWN!!

CHAPTER 22/END

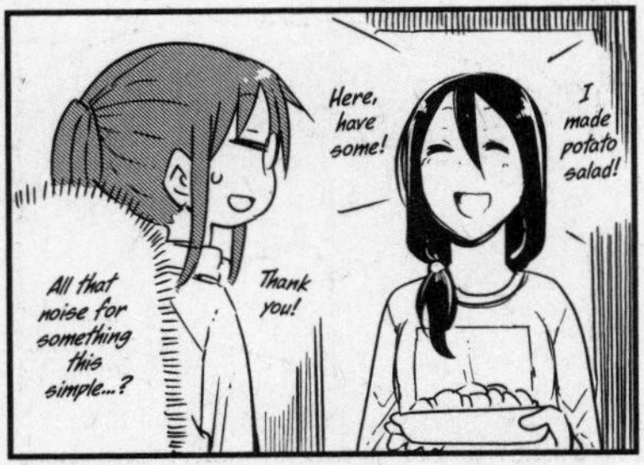
I made potato salad!
Here, have some!
Thank you!
All that noise for something this simple...?

Miss Kobayashi's
Dragon Maid

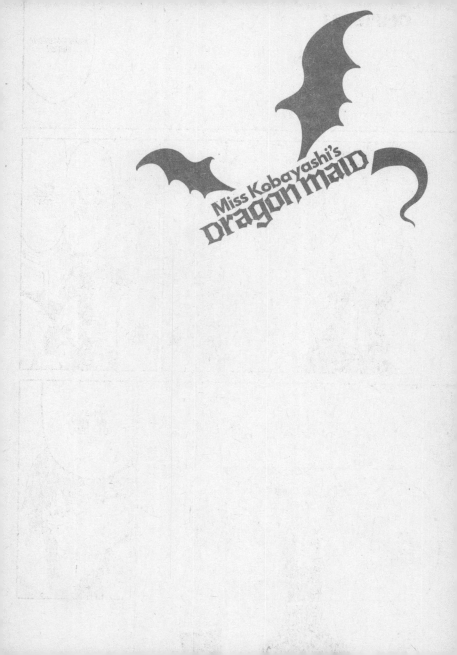

CHAPTER 23

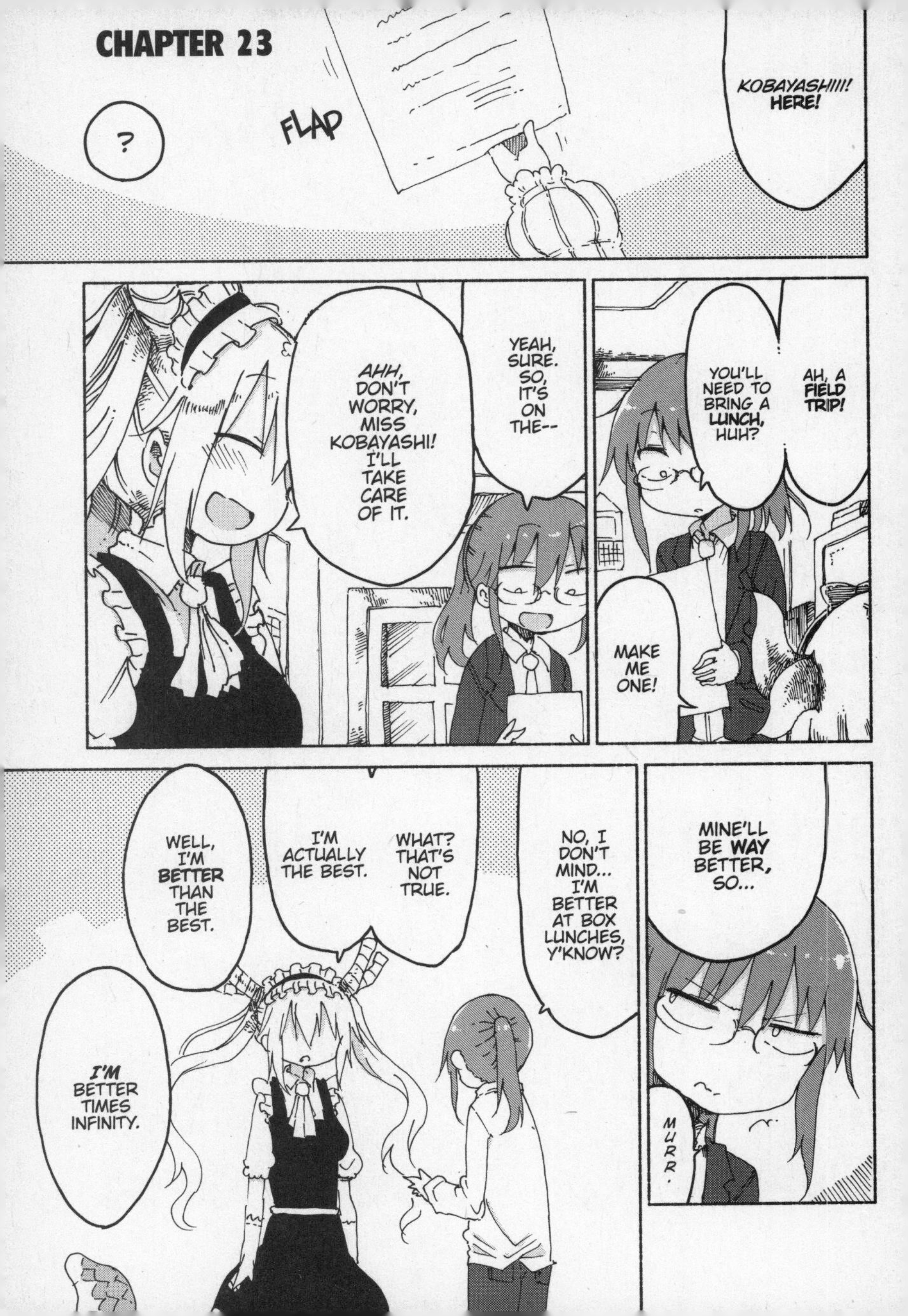
KOBAYASHIIII! HERE!
FLAP
?
AH, A FIELD TRIP!
YOU'LL NEED TO BRING A LUNCH, HUH?
MAKE ME ONE!
YEAH, SURE. SO, IT'S ON THE--
AHH, DON'T WORRY, MISS KOBAYASHI! I'LL TAKE CARE OF IT.
MINE'LL BE WAY BETTER, SO...
MURR.
NO, I DON'T MIND... I'M BETTER AT BOX LUNCHES, Y'KNOW?
WHAT? THAT'S NOT TRUE.
I'M ACTUALLY THE BEST.
WELL, I'M BETTER THAN THE BEST.
I'M BETTER TIMES INFINITY.

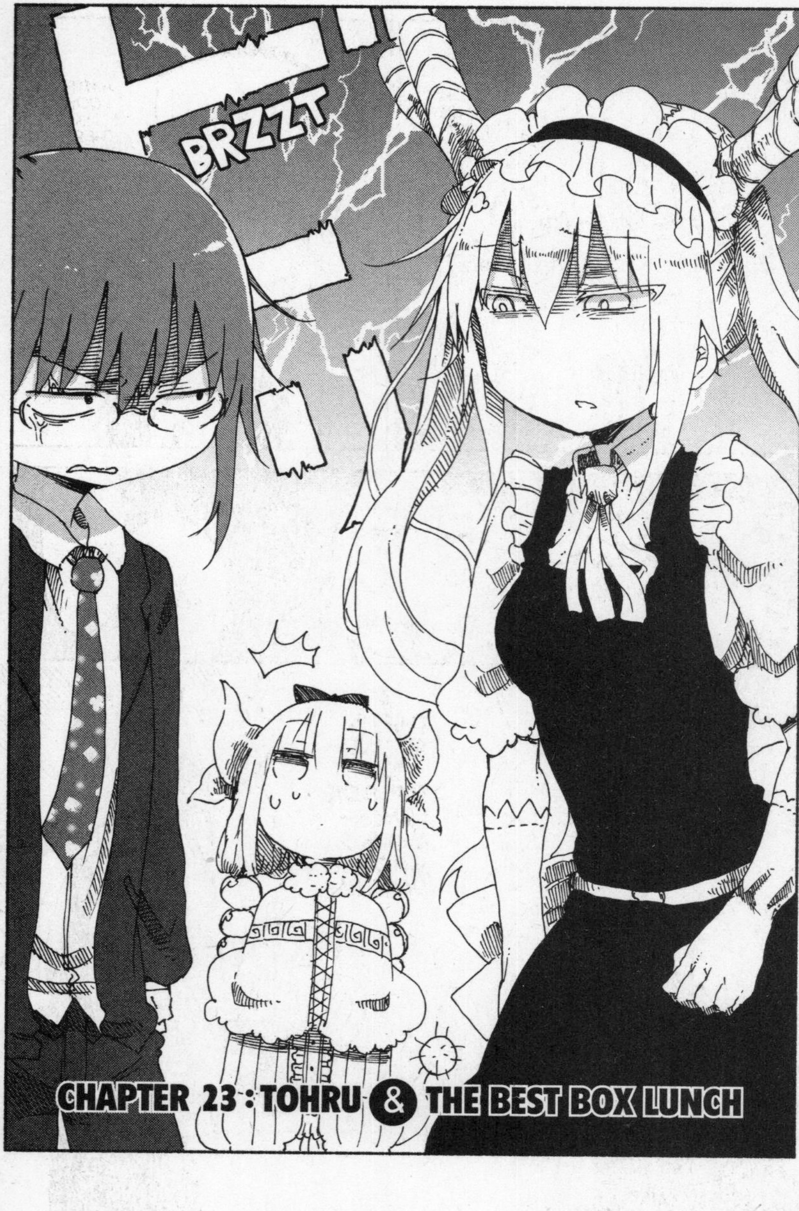
BRZZT
CHAPTER 23: TOHRU & THE BEST BOX LUNCH

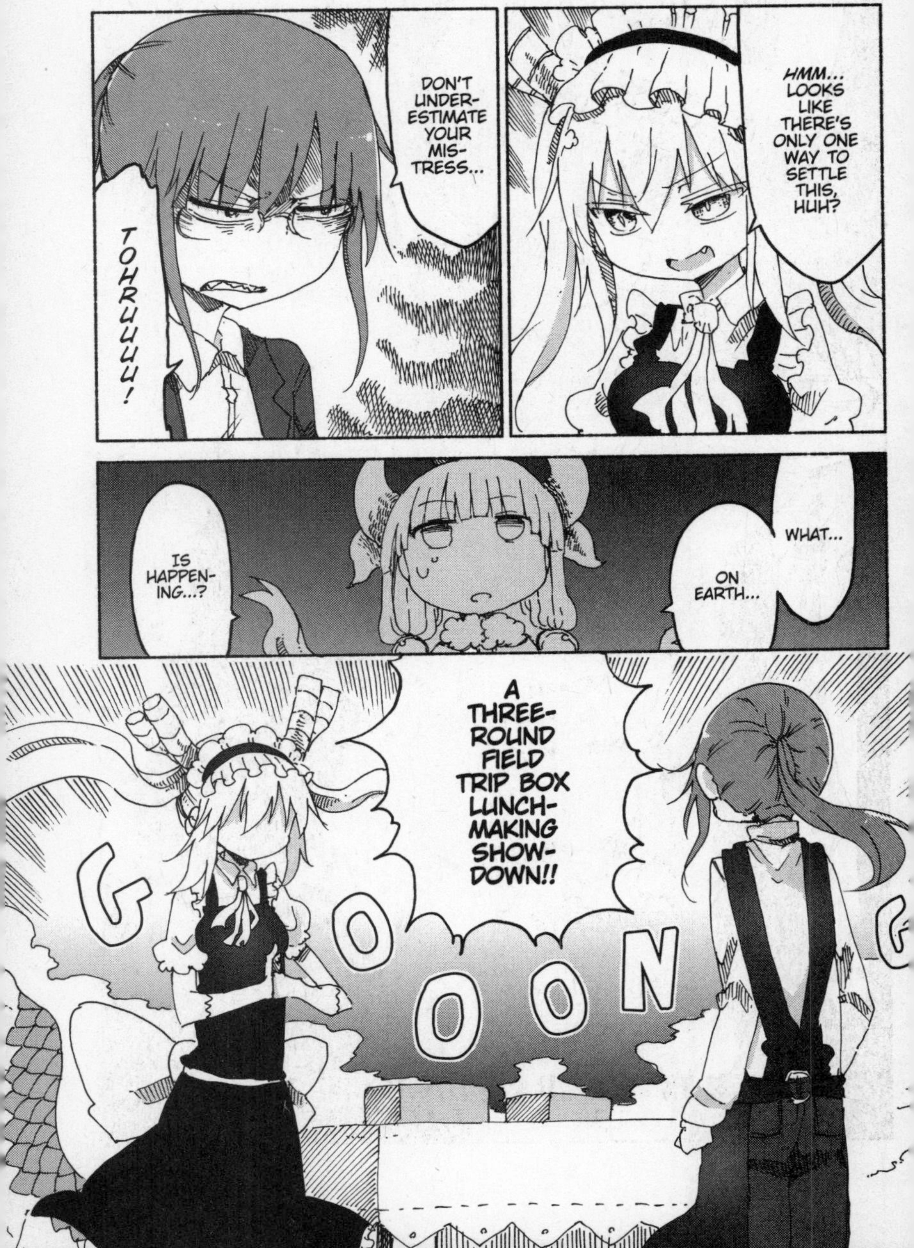
HMM... LOOKS LIKE THERE'S ONLY ONE WAY TO SETTLE THIS, HUH?
DON'T UNDER-ESTIMATE YOUR MIS-TRESS...
TOHRUUUU!
WHAT... ON EARTH...
IS HAPPEN-ING...?
A THREE-ROUND FIELD TRIP BOX LUNCH-MAKING SHOW-DOWN!!
GOOONG

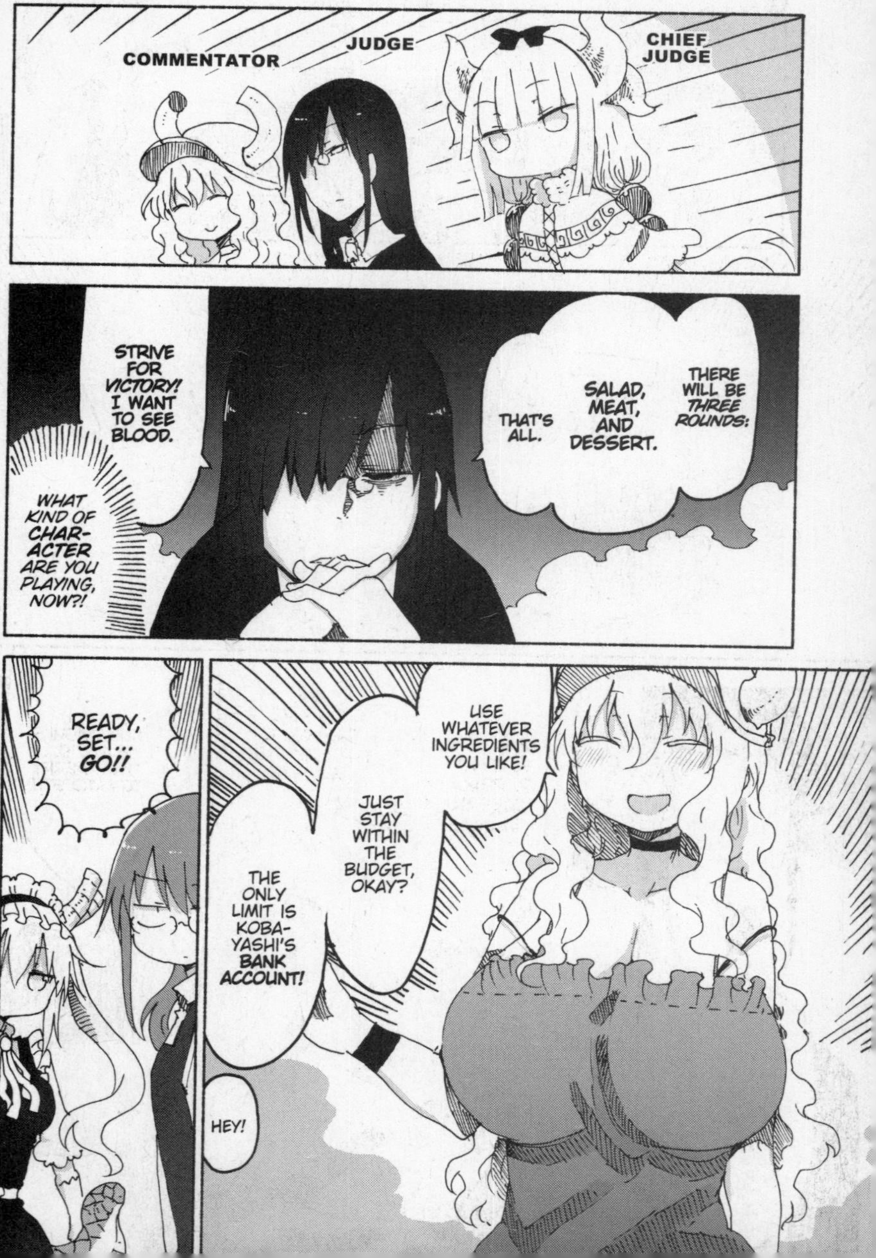
CHIEF JUDGE
JUDGE
COMMENTATOR
THERE WILL BE *THREE ROUNDS:*
SALAD, MEAT, AND DESSERT.
THAT'S ALL.
STRIVE FOR *VICTORY!* I WANT TO SEE BLOOD.
WHAT KIND OF CHAR-ACTER ARE YOU PLAYING, NOW?!
USE WHATEVER INGREDIENTS YOU LIKE!
JUST STAY WITHIN THE BUDGET, OKAY?
THE ONLY LIMIT IS KOBA-YASHI'S BANK ACCOUNT!
HEY!
READY, SET... **GO!!**

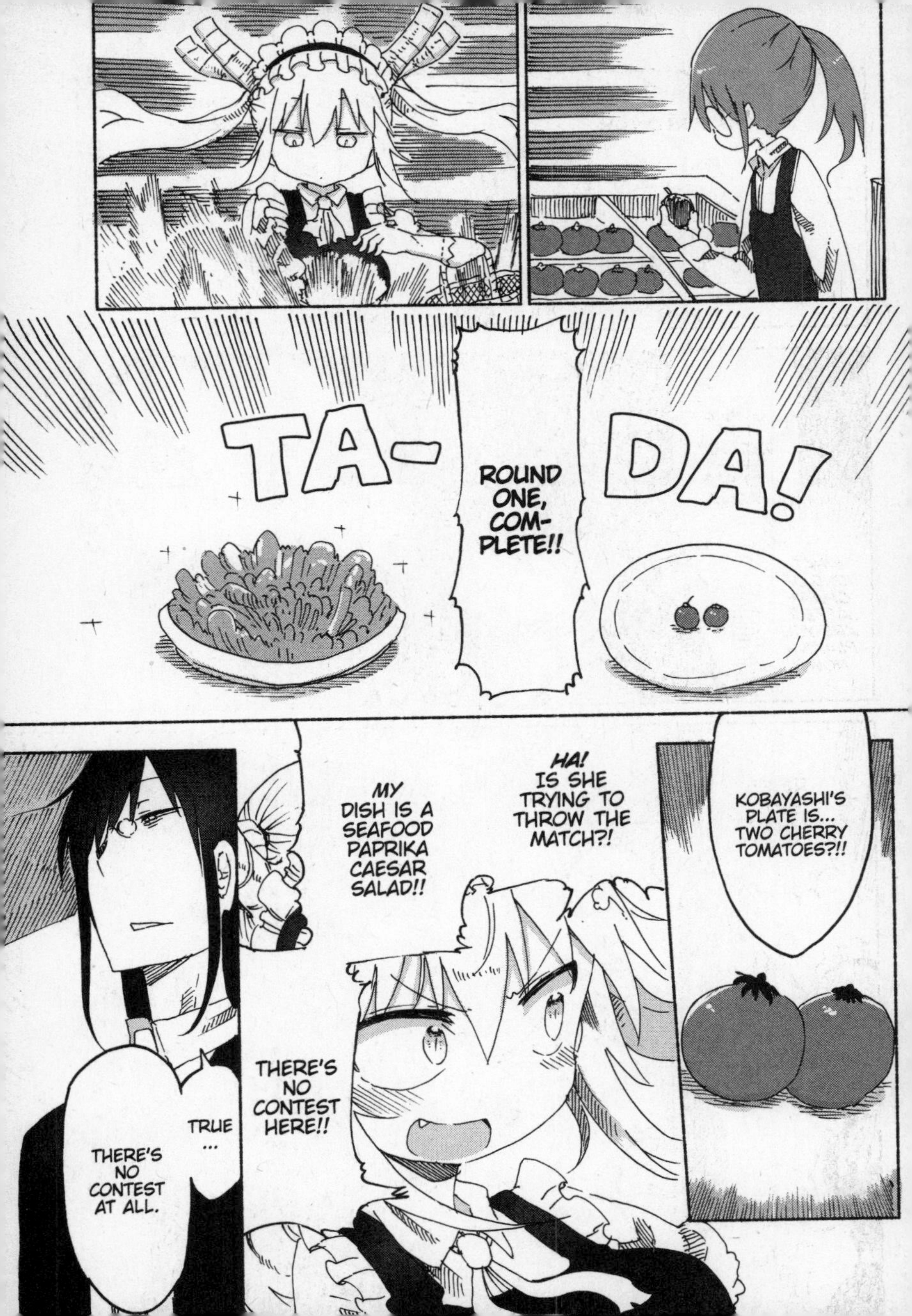
TA-DA!
ROUND ONE, COMPLETE!!
KOBAYASHI'S PLATE IS... TWO CHERRY TOMATOES?!!
HA! IS SHE TRYING TO THROW THE MATCH?!
MY DISH IS A SEAFOOD PAPRIKA CAESAR SALAD!!
THERE'S NO CONTEST HERE!!
TRUE ...
THERE'S NO CONTEST AT ALL.

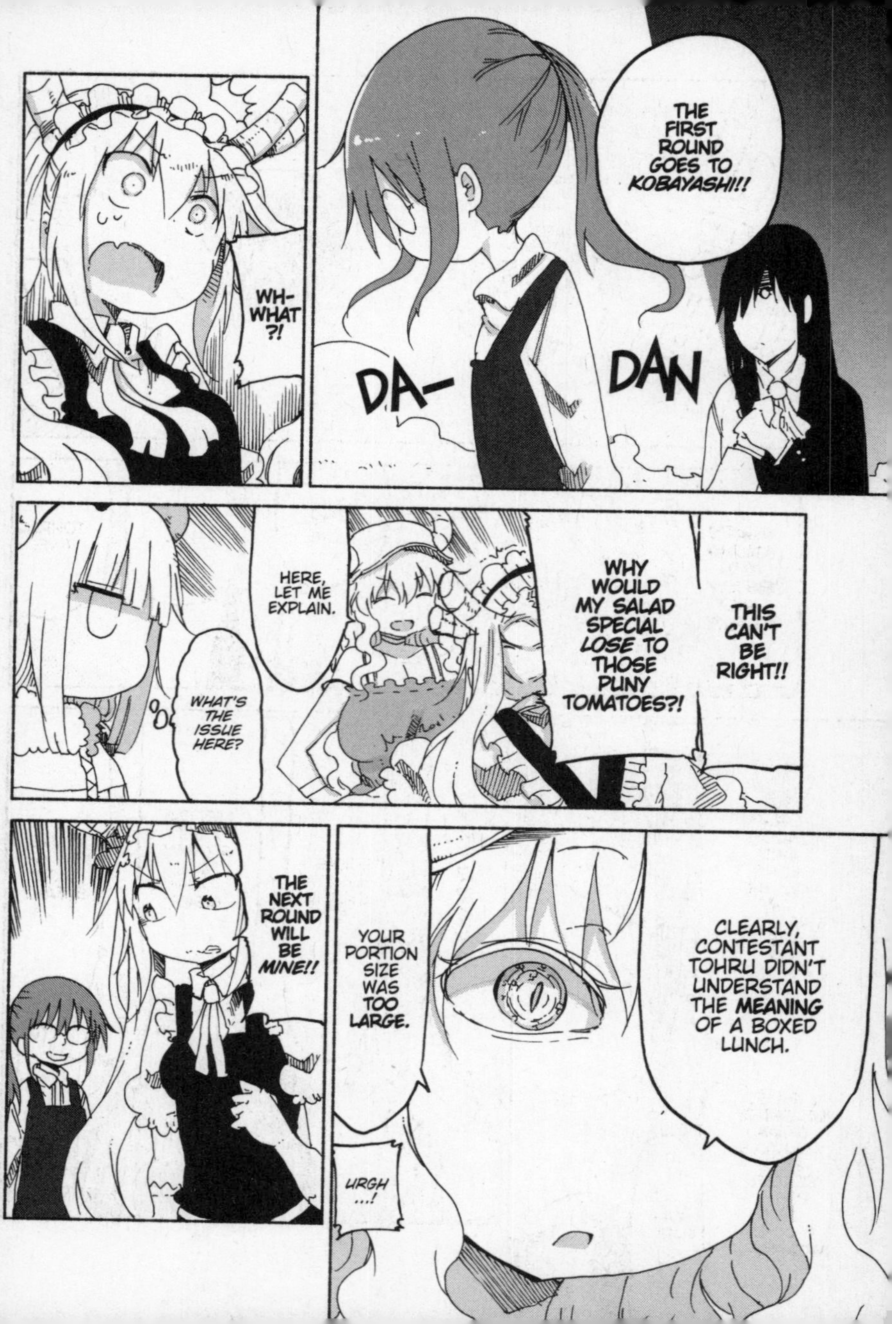
THE FIRST ROUND GOES TO *KOBAYASHI!!*
DA- DAN
WH-WHAT?!
THIS CAN'T BE RIGHT!!
WHY WOULD MY SALAD SPECIAL *LOSE* TO THOSE PUNY TOMATOES?!
WHAT'S THE ISSUE HERE?
HERE, LET ME EXPLAIN.
CLEARLY, CONTESTANT TOHRU DIDN'T UNDERSTAND THE *MEANING* OF A BOXED LUNCH.
YOUR PORTION SIZE WAS TOO LARGE.
URGH ...!
THE NEXT ROUND WILL BE *MINE!!*

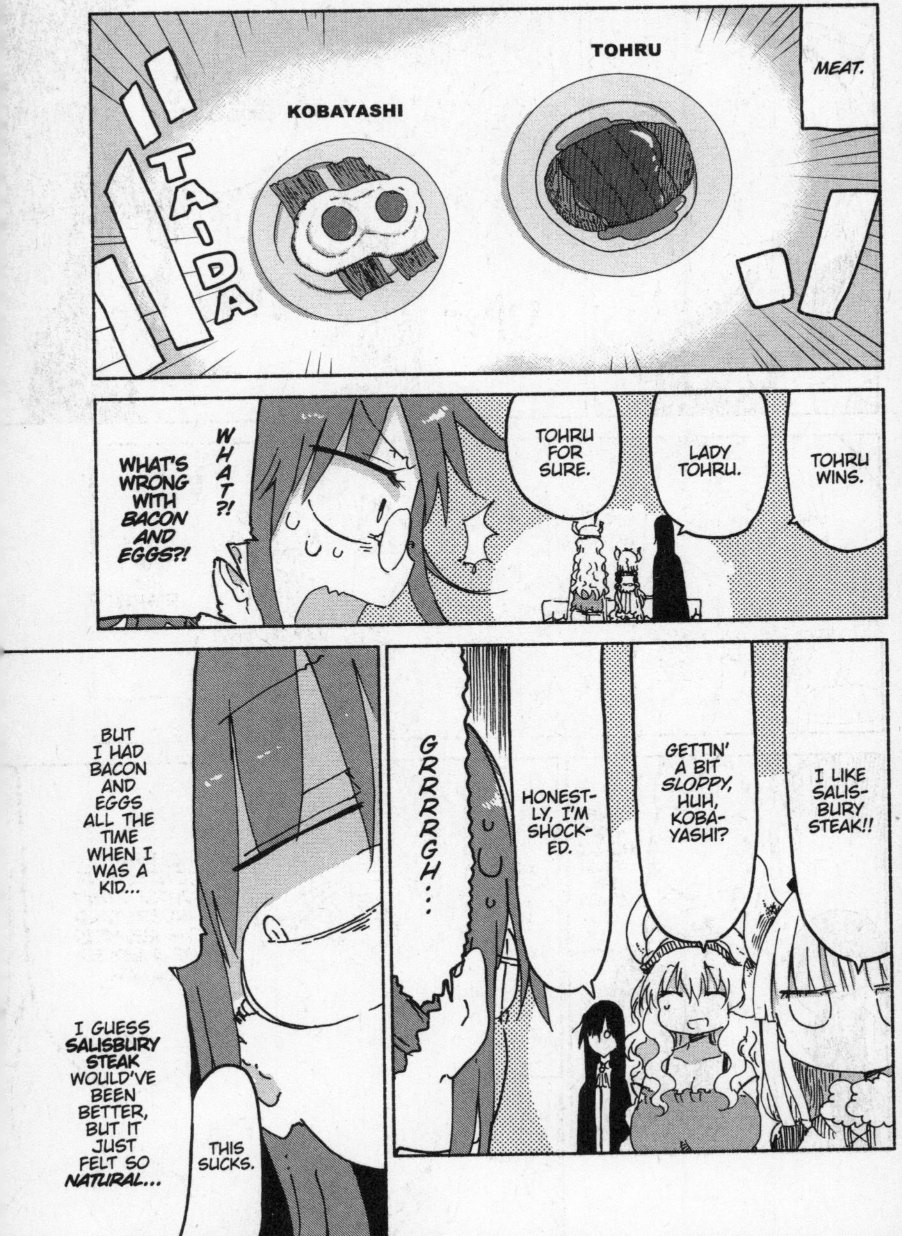
MEAT.
TOHRU
KOBAYASHI
TA-I-DA
TOHRU WINS.
LADY TOHRU.
TOHRU FOR SURE.
WHAT?!
WHAT'S WRONG WITH BACON AND EGGS?!
I LIKE SALISBURY STEAK!!
GETTIN' A BIT SLOPPY, HUH, KOBAYASHI?
HONESTLY, I'M SHOCKED.
GRRRRGH...
BUT I HAD BACON AND EGGS ALL THE TIME WHEN I WAS A KID...
I GUESS SALISBURY STEAK WOULD'VE BEEN BETTER, BUT IT JUST FELT SO NATURAL...
THIS SUCKS.

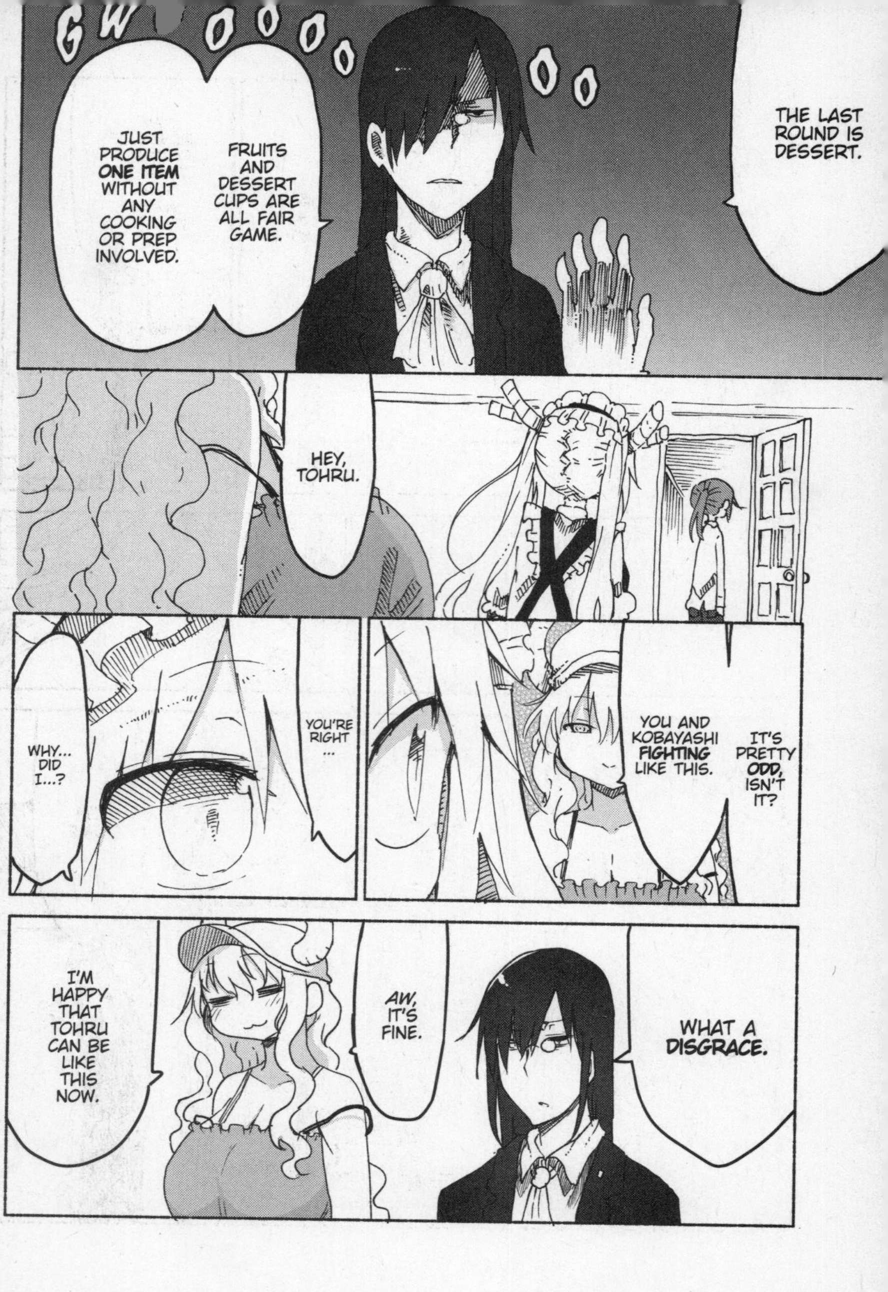
GWOOOOOOO
THE LAST ROUND IS DESSERT.
FRUITS AND DESSERT CUPS ARE ALL FAIR GAME.
JUST PRODUCE ONE ITEM WITHOUT ANY COOKING OR PREP INVOLVED.
HEY, TOHRU.
IT'S PRETTY ODD, ISN'T IT?
YOU AND KOBAYASHI FIGHTING LIKE THIS.
YOU'RE RIGHT...
WHY... DID I...?
WHAT A DISGRACE.
AW, IT'S FINE.
I'M HAPPY THAT TOHRU CAN BE LIKE THIS NOW.

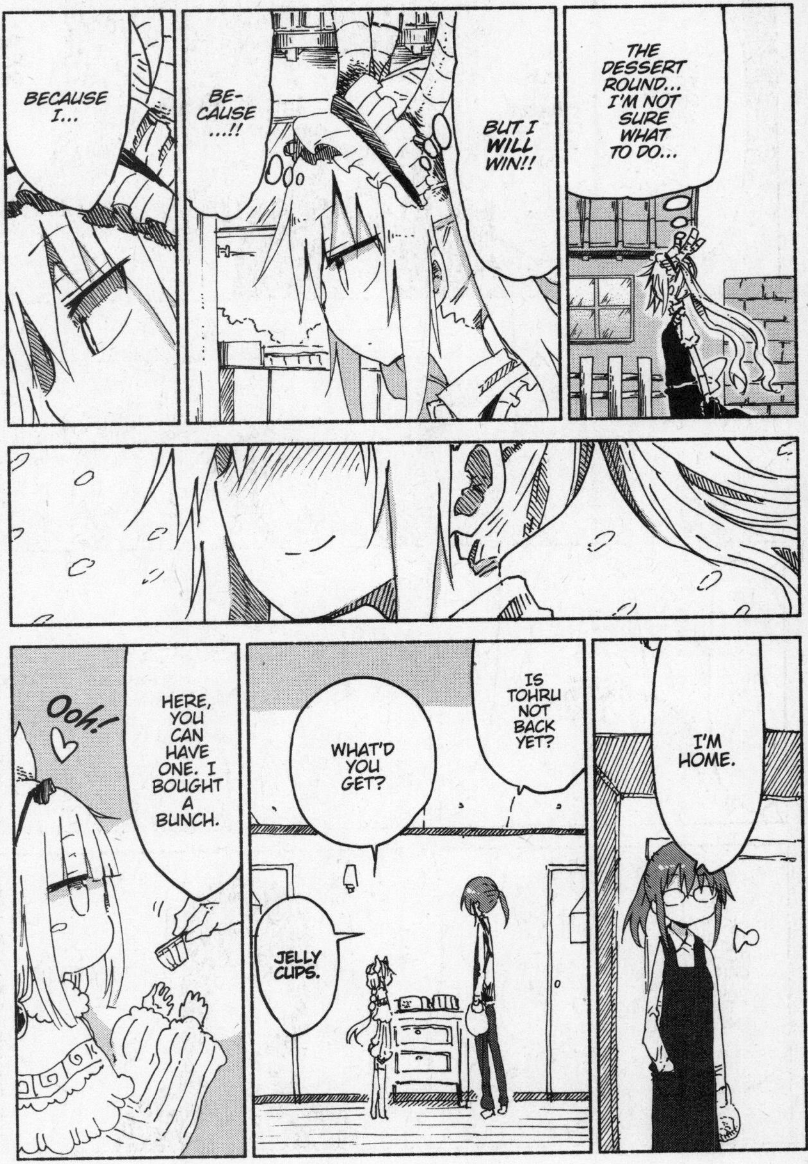
THE DESSERT ROUND... I'M NOT SURE WHAT TO DO...
BUT I WILL WIN!!
BE-CAUSE ...!!
BECAUSE I...
I'M HOME.
IS TOHRU NOT BACK YET?
WHAT'D YOU GET?
JELLY CUPS.
HERE, YOU CAN HAVE ONE. I BOUGHT A BUNCH.
Ooh! ♥

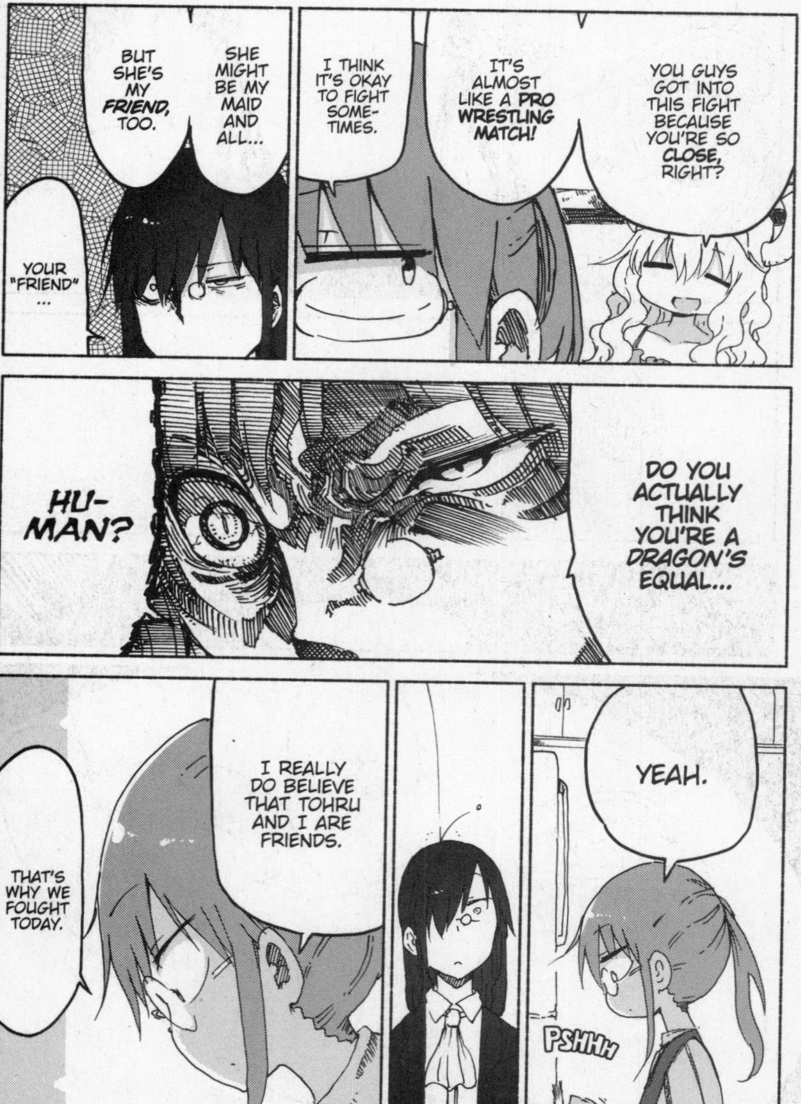
YOU GUYS GOT INTO THIS FIGHT BECAUSE YOU'RE SO CLOSE, RIGHT?
IT'S ALMOST LIKE A PRO WRESTLING MATCH!
I THINK IT'S OKAY TO FIGHT SOME-TIMES.
SHE MIGHT BE MY MAID AND ALL...
BUT SHE'S MY FRIEND, TOO.
YOUR "FRIEND" ...
DO YOU ACTUALLY THINK YOU'RE A DRAGON'S EQUAL...
HU-MAN?
YEAH.
PSHHH
I REALLY DO BELIEVE THAT TOHRU AND I ARE FRIENDS.
THAT'S WHY WE FOUGHT TODAY.

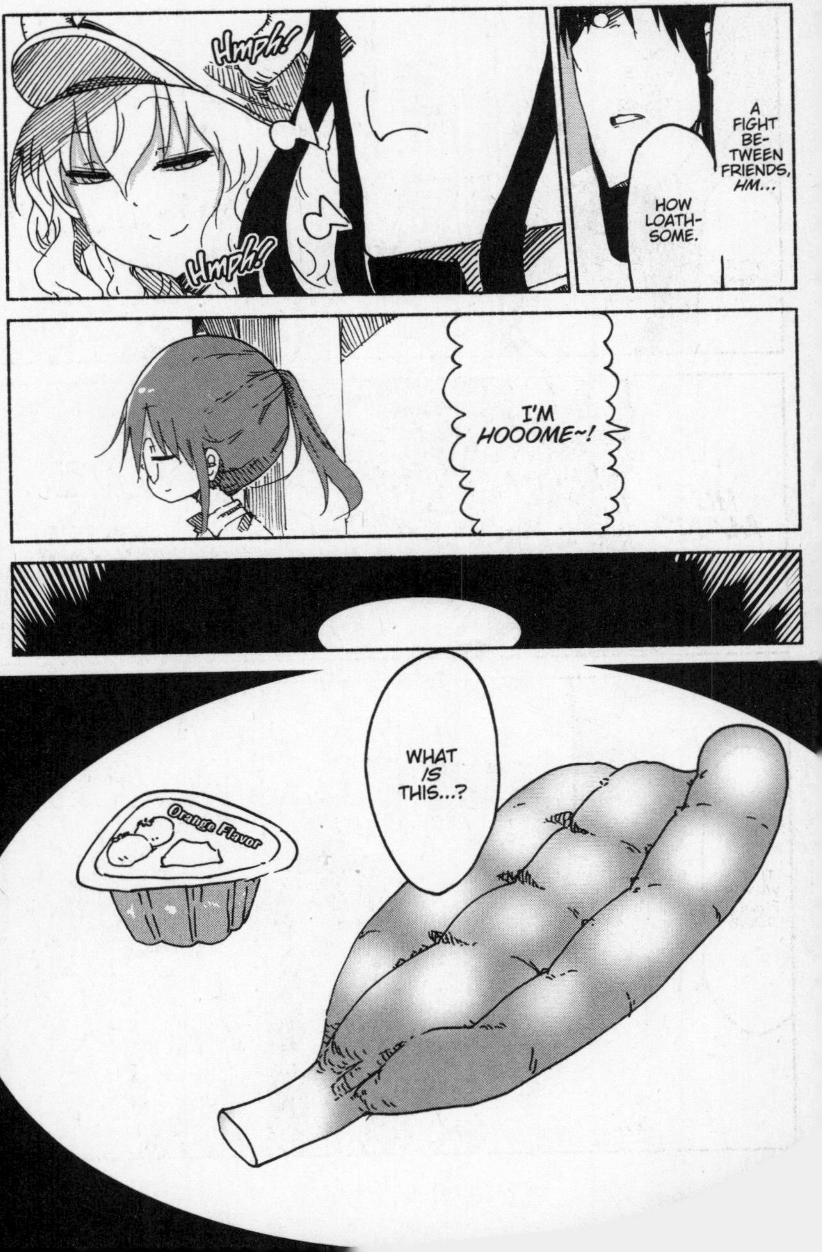
A FIGHT BE-TWEEN FRIENDS, HM...
HOW LOATH-SOME.
Hmph!
Hmph!
I'M HOOOME~!
WHAT IS THIS...?
Orange Flavor

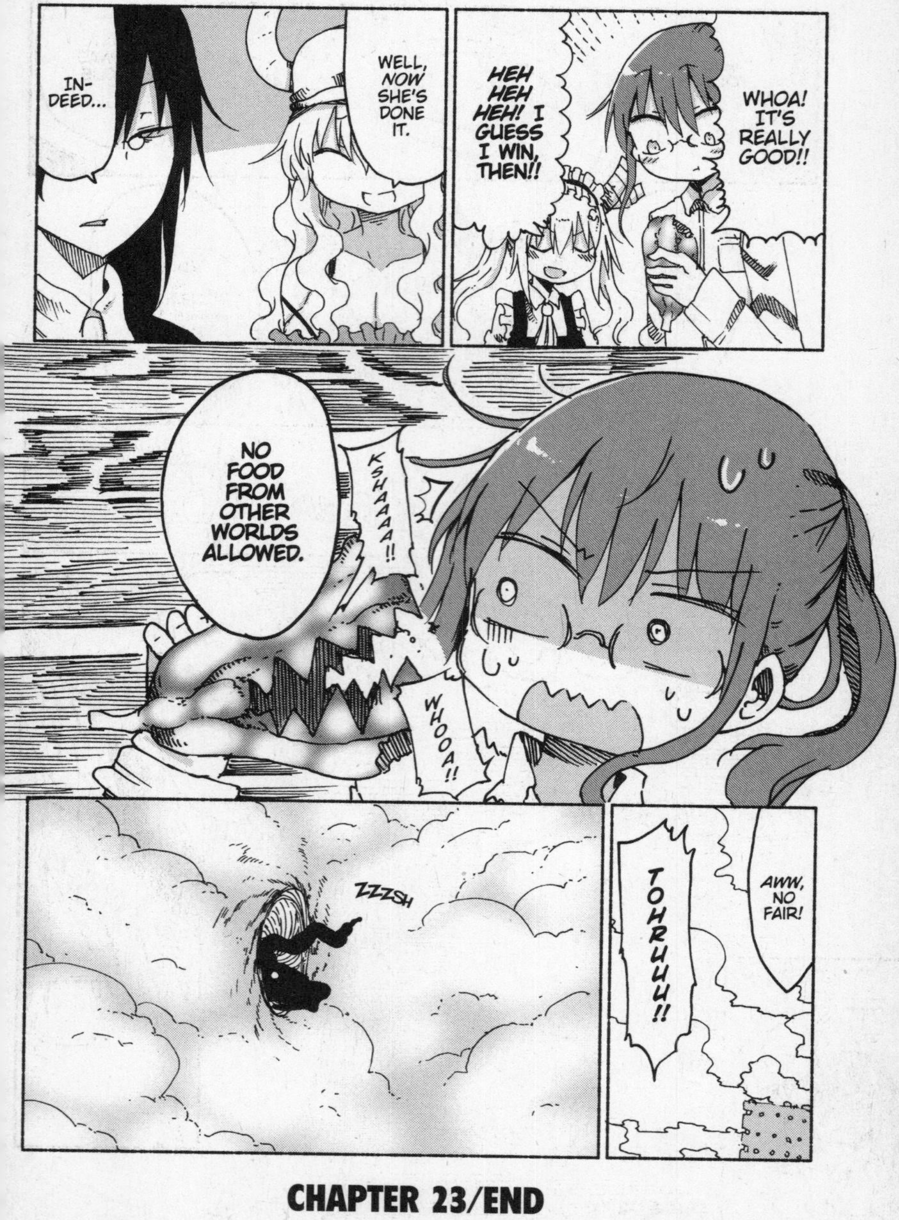
WHOA! IT'S REALLY GOOD!!
HEH HEH HEH! I GUESS I WIN, THEN!!
WELL, NOW SHE'S DONE IT.
IN-DEED...
KSHAAAAA!!
NO FOOD FROM OTHER WORLDS ALLOWED.
WHOOA!!
AWW, NO FAIR!
TOHRUUUU!!
ZZZSH

CHAPTER 23/END

CHAPTER 24

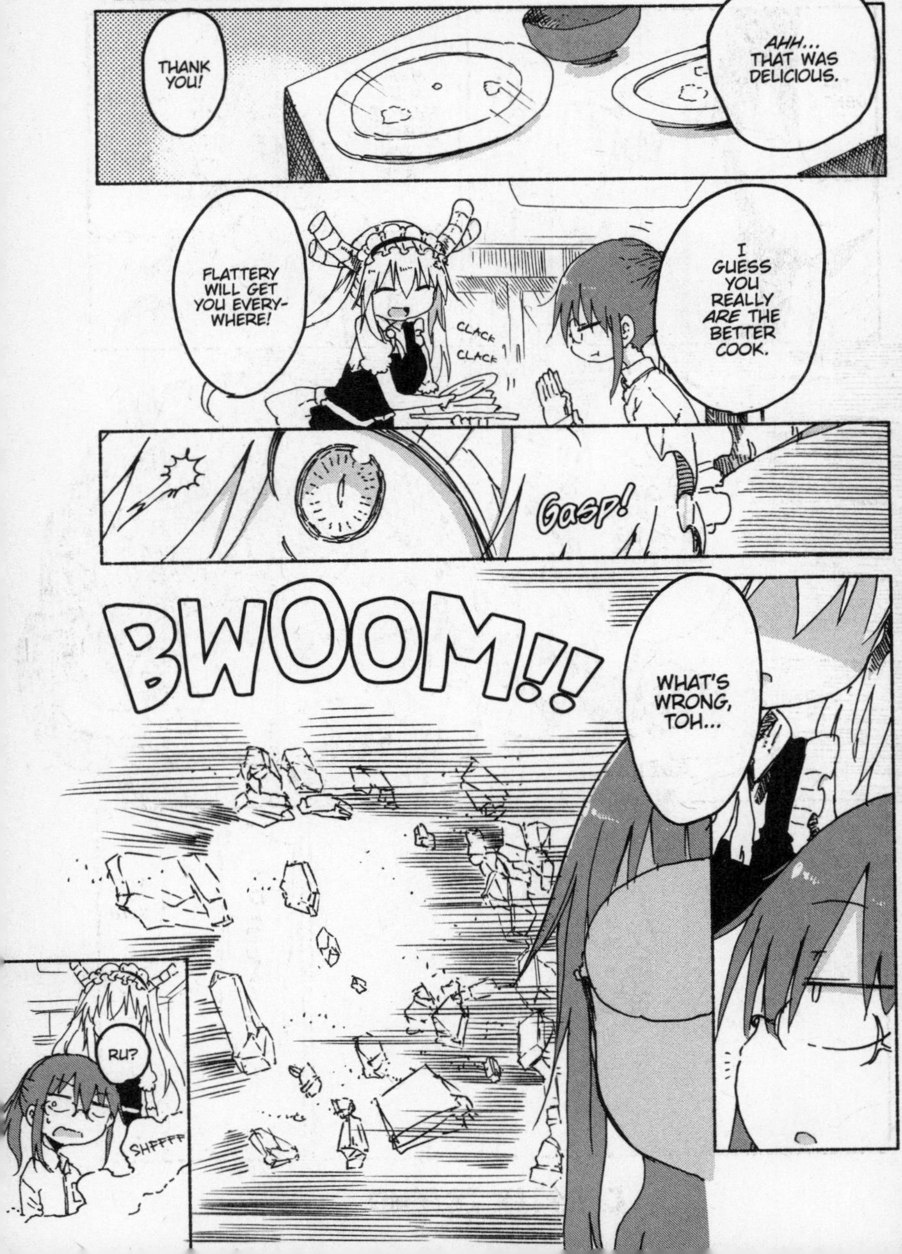
AHH... THAT WAS DELICIOUS.
THANK YOU!
I GUESS YOU REALLY *ARE* THE BETTER COOK.
FLATTERY WILL GET YOU EVERY-WHERE!
CLACK
CLACK
Gasp!
WHAT'S WRONG, TOH...
BWOOM!!
RU?
SHFFFF

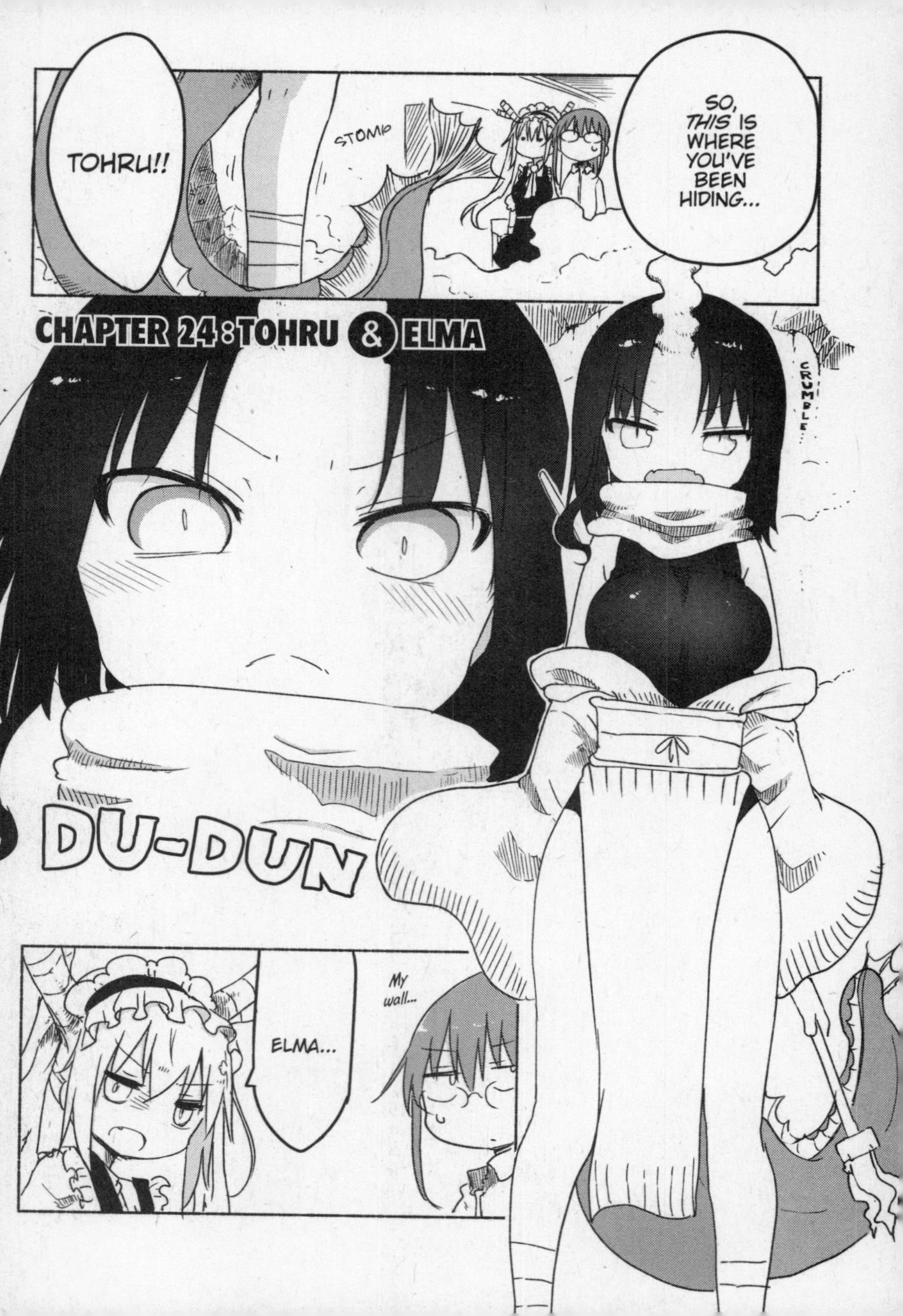
SO, THIS IS WHERE YOU'VE BEEN HIDING...
STOMP
TOHRU!!
CHAPTER 24: TOHRU & ELMA
CRUMBLE...
DU-DUN
My wall...
ELMA...

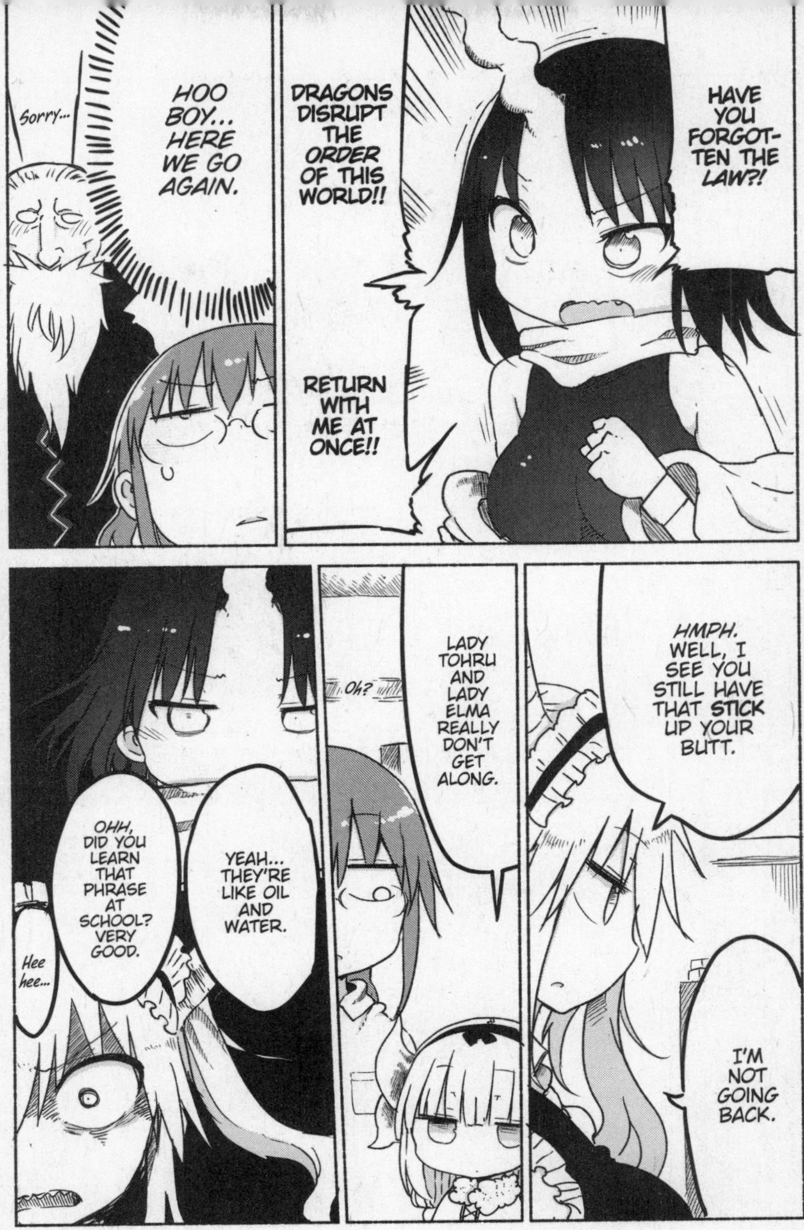
HAVE YOU FORGOT-TEN THE LAW?!
DRAGONS DISRUPT THE ORDER OF THIS WORLD!!
RETURN WITH ME AT ONCE!!
HOO BOY... HERE WE GO AGAIN.
Sorry...
HMPH. WELL, I SEE YOU STILL HAVE THAT STICK UP YOUR BUTT.
I'M NOT GOING BACK.
LADY TOHRU AND LADY ELMA REALLY DON'T GET ALONG.
Oh?
YEAH... THEY'RE LIKE OIL AND WATER.
OHH, DID YOU LEARN THAT PHRASE AT SCHOOL? VERY GOOD.
Hee hee...

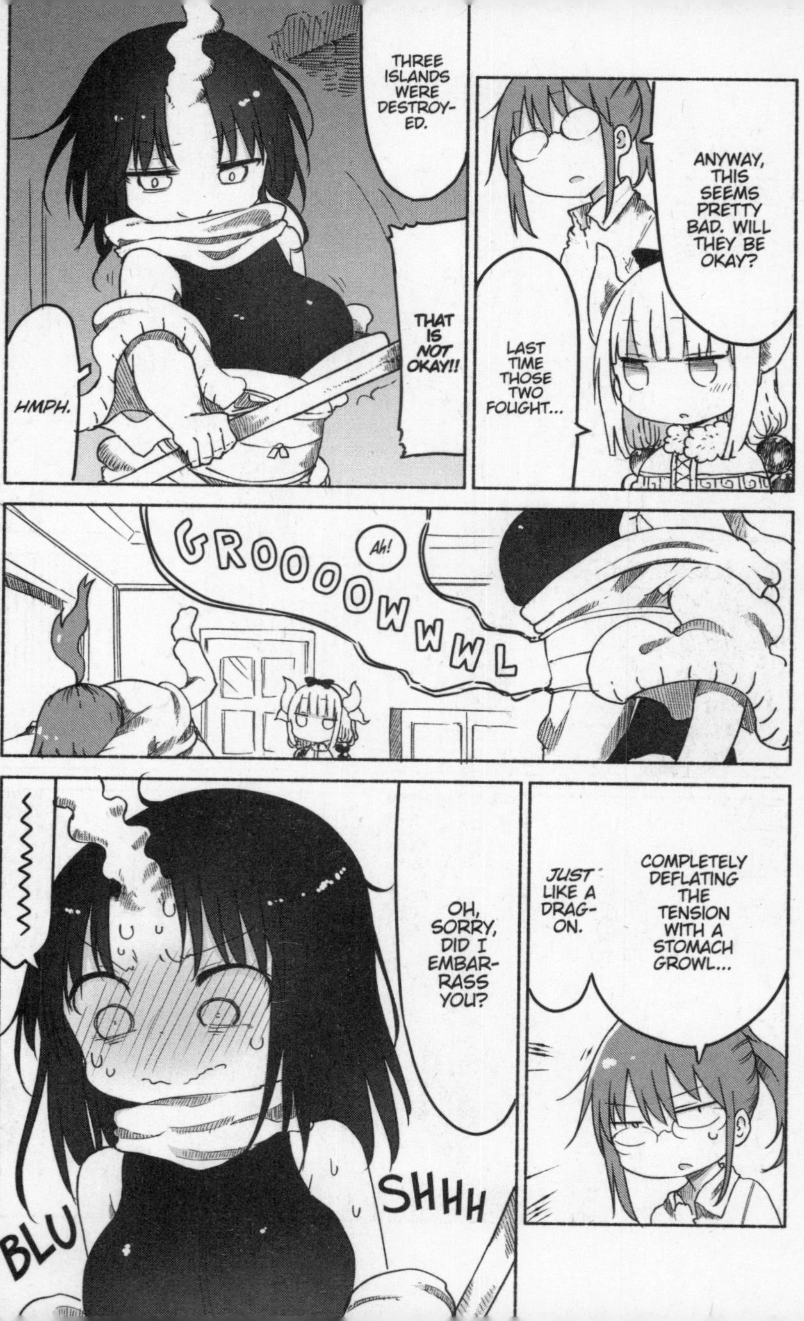

ANYWAY, THIS SEEMS PRETTY BAD. WILL THEY BE OKAY?
LAST TIME THOSE TWO FOUGHT...
THREE ISLANDS WERE DESTROY-ED.
THAT IS *NOT* OKAY!!
HMPH.
Ah!
GROOOOOWWWL
COMPLETELY DEFLATING THE TENSION WITH A STOMACH GROWL...
JUST LIKE A DRAG-ON.
OH, SORRY, DID I EMBAR-RASS YOU?
BLU
SHHH

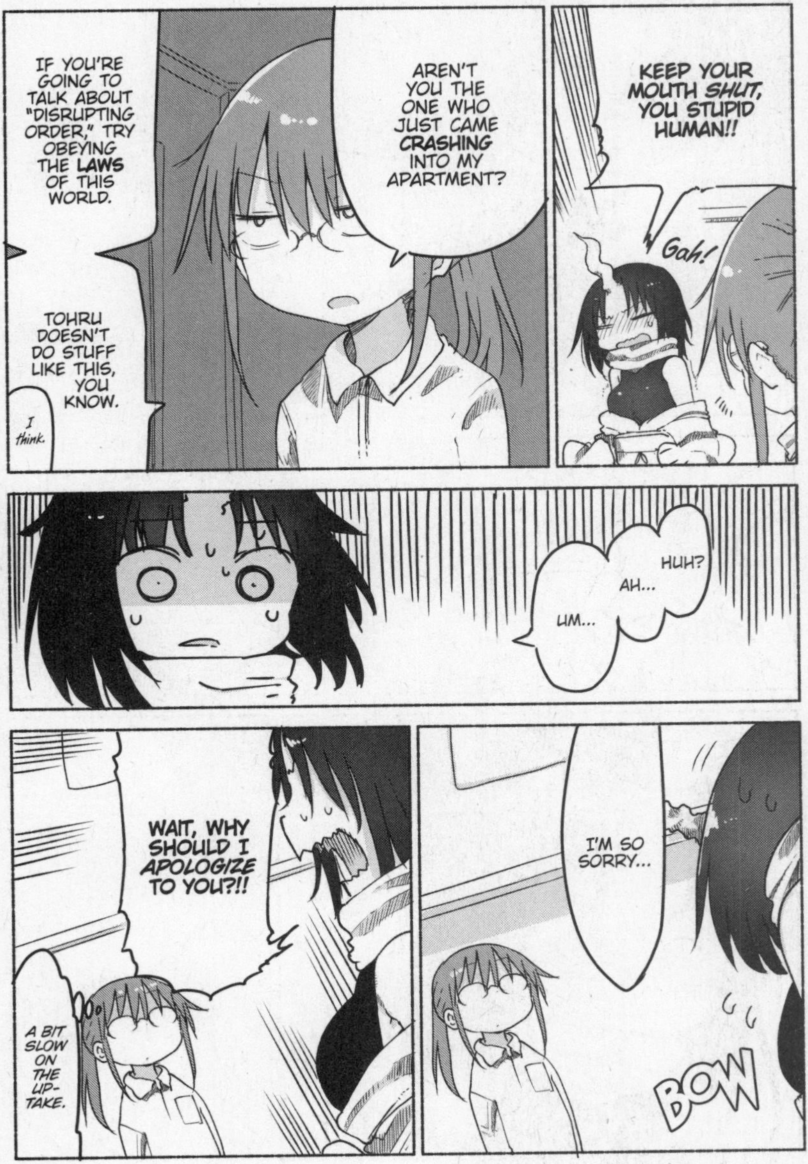

KEEP YOUR MOUTH SHUT, YOU STUPID HUMAN!!
Gah!
AREN'T YOU THE ONE WHO JUST CAME CRASHING INTO MY APARTMENT?
IF YOU'RE GOING TO TALK ABOUT "DISRUPTING ORDER," TRY OBEYING THE LAWS OF THIS WORLD.
TOHRU DOESN'T DO STUFF LIKE THIS, YOU KNOW.
I think.
HUH? AH... UM...
I'M SO SORRY...
BOW
WAIT, WHY SHOULD I APOLOGIZE TO YOU?!!
A BIT SLOW ON THE UP-TAKE.

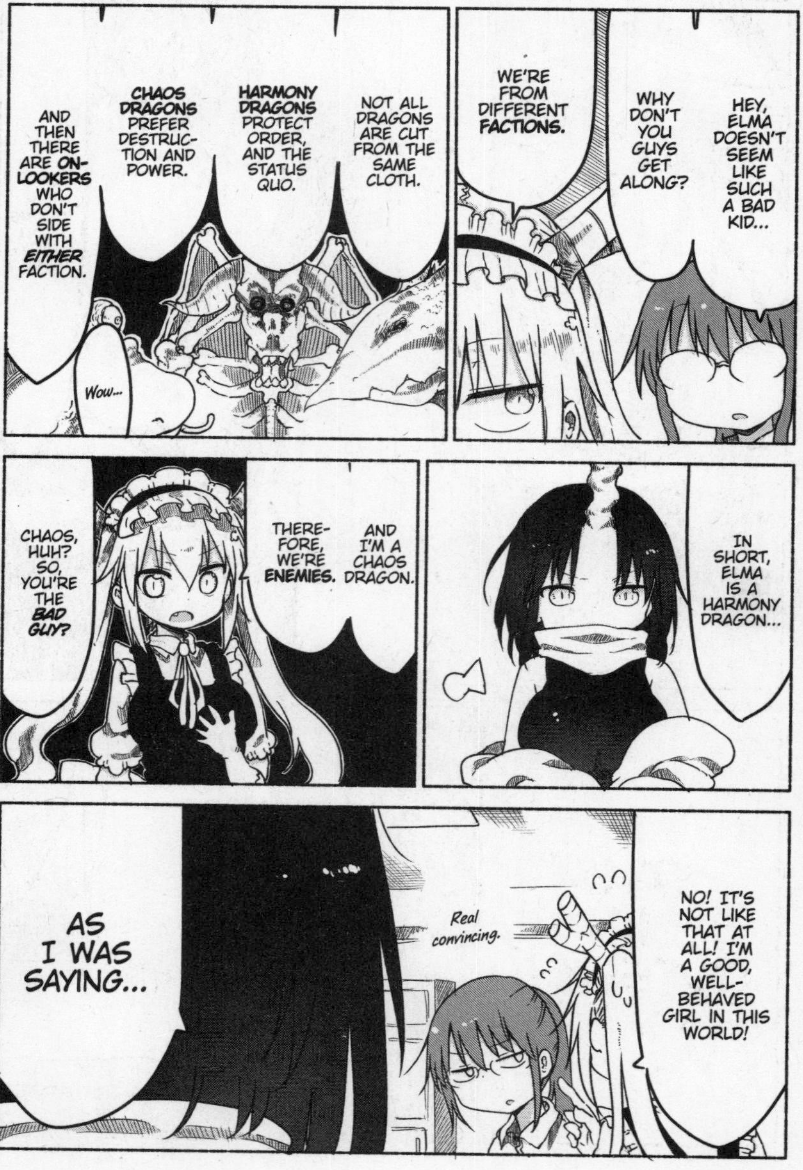
HEY, ELMA DOESN'T SEEM LIKE SUCH A BAD KID...
WHY DON'T YOU GUYS GET ALONG?
WE'RE FROM DIFFERENT FACTIONS.
NOT ALL DRAGONS ARE CUT FROM THE SAME CLOTH.
HARMONY DRAGONS PROTECT ORDER, AND THE STATUS QUO.
CHAOS DRAGONS PREFER DESTRUCTION AND POWER.
AND THEN THERE ARE ON-LOOKERS WHO DON'T SIDE WITH EITHER FACTION.
Wow...
IN SHORT, ELMA IS A HARMONY DRAGON...
AND I'M A CHAOS DRAGON.
THEREFORE, WE'RE ENEMIES.
CHAOS, HUH? SO, YOU'RE THE BAD GUY?
NO! IT'S NOT LIKE THAT AT ALL! I'M A GOOD, WELL-BEHAVED GIRL IN THIS WORLD!
Real convincing.
AS I WAS SAYING...

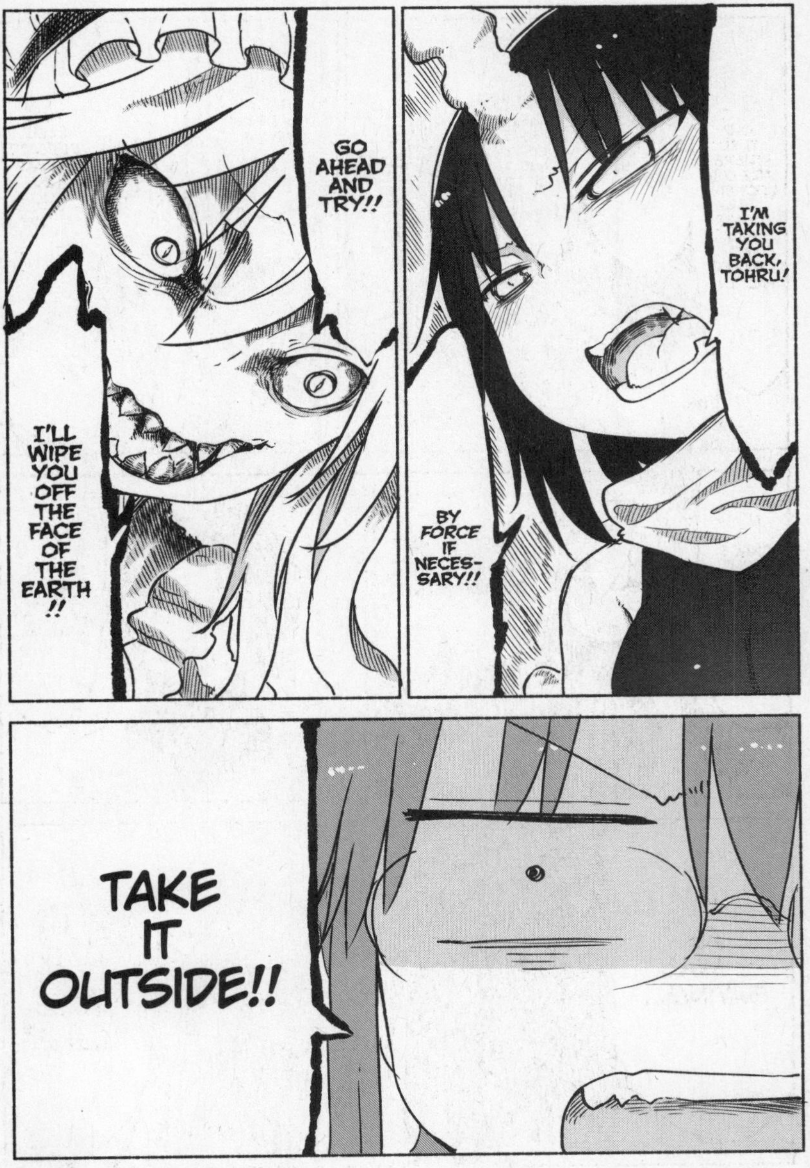
I'M TAKING YOU BACK, TOHRU!
BY FORCE IF NECES-SARY!!
GO AHEAD AND TRY!!
I'LL WIPE YOU OFF THE FACE OF THE EARTH!!
TAKE IT OUTSIDE!!

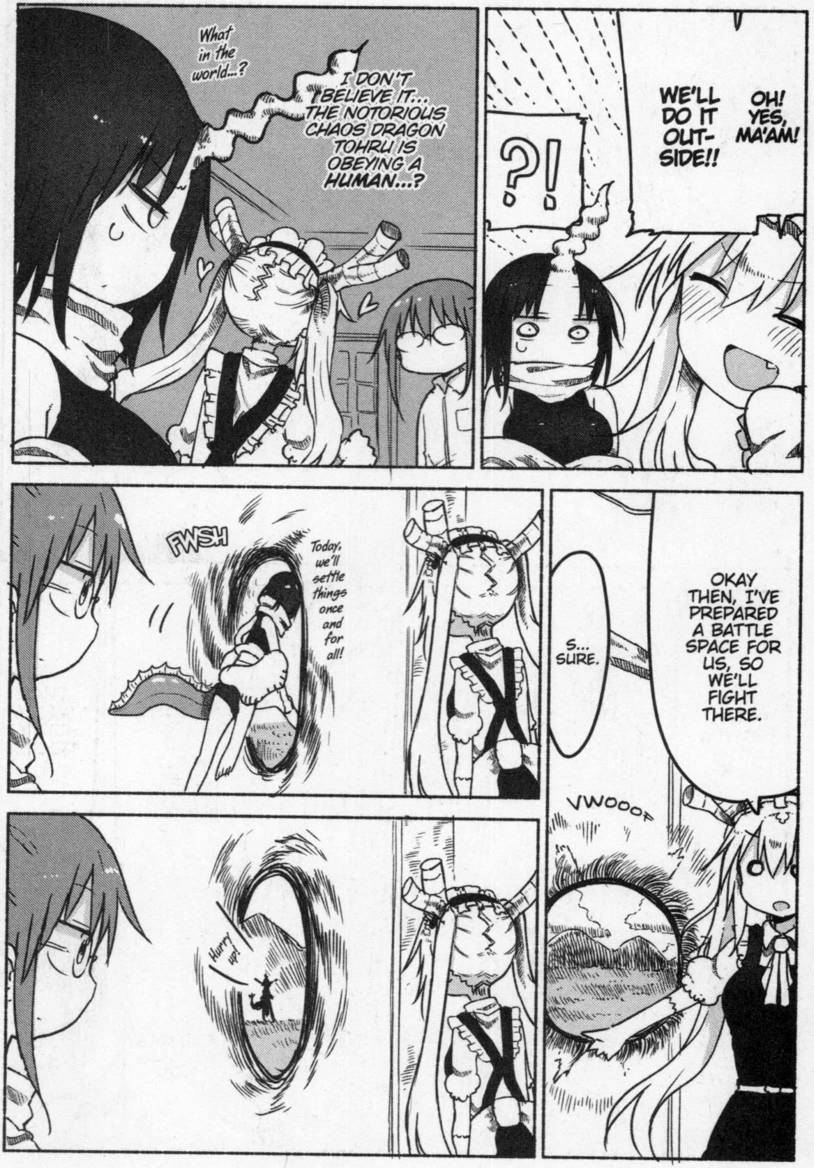
OH! YES, MA'AM!
WE'LL DO IT OUT-SIDE!!
?!
I DON'T BELIEVE IT... THE NOTORIOUS CHAOS DRAGON TOHRU IS OBEYING A HUMAN...?
What in the world...?
OKAY THEN, I'VE PREPARED A BATTLE SPACE FOR US, SO WE'LL FIGHT THERE.
S... SURE.
VWOOOF
Today, we'll settle things once and for all!
FWSH
Hurry up!

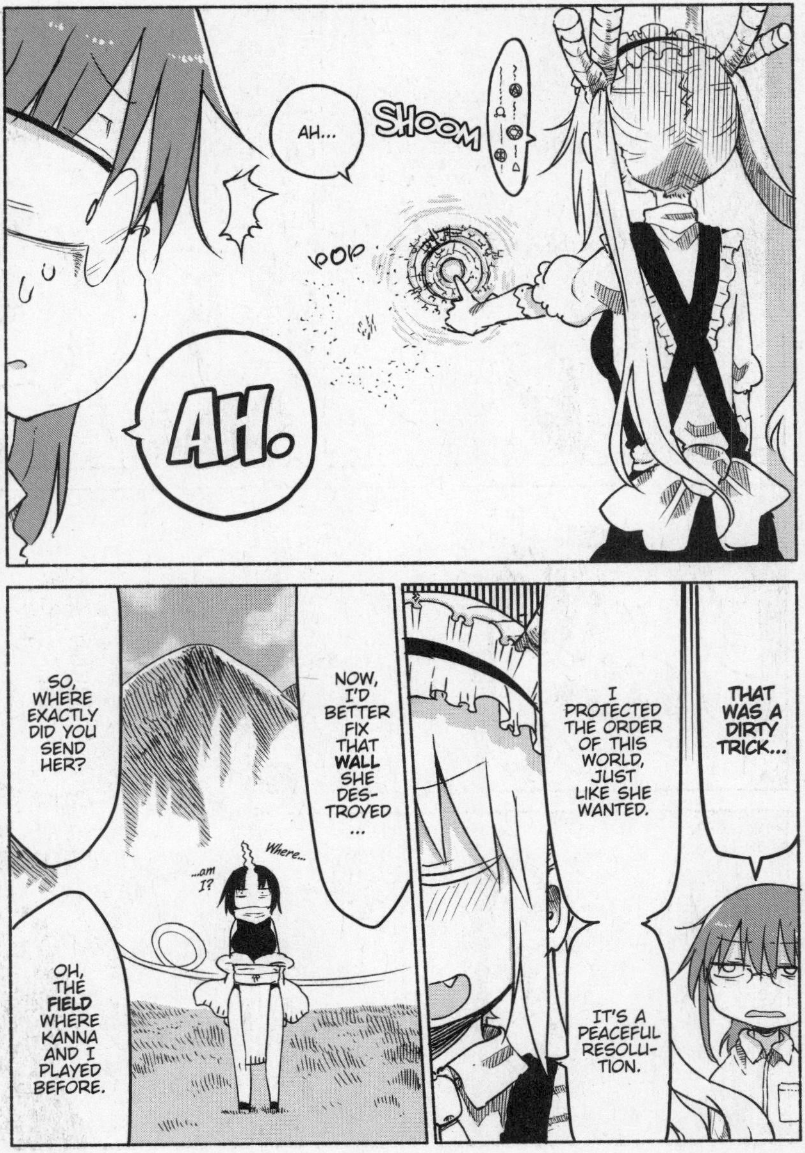
SHOOM
AH...
POP
AH.
THAT WAS A DIRTY TRICK...
I PROTECTED THE ORDER OF THIS WORLD, JUST LIKE SHE WANTED.
IT'S A PEACEFUL RESOLUTION.
NOW, I'D BETTER FIX THAT WALL SHE DESTROYED...
SO, WHERE EXACTLY DID YOU SEND HER?
Where...
...am I?
OH, THE FIELD WHERE KANNA AND I PLAYED BEFORE.

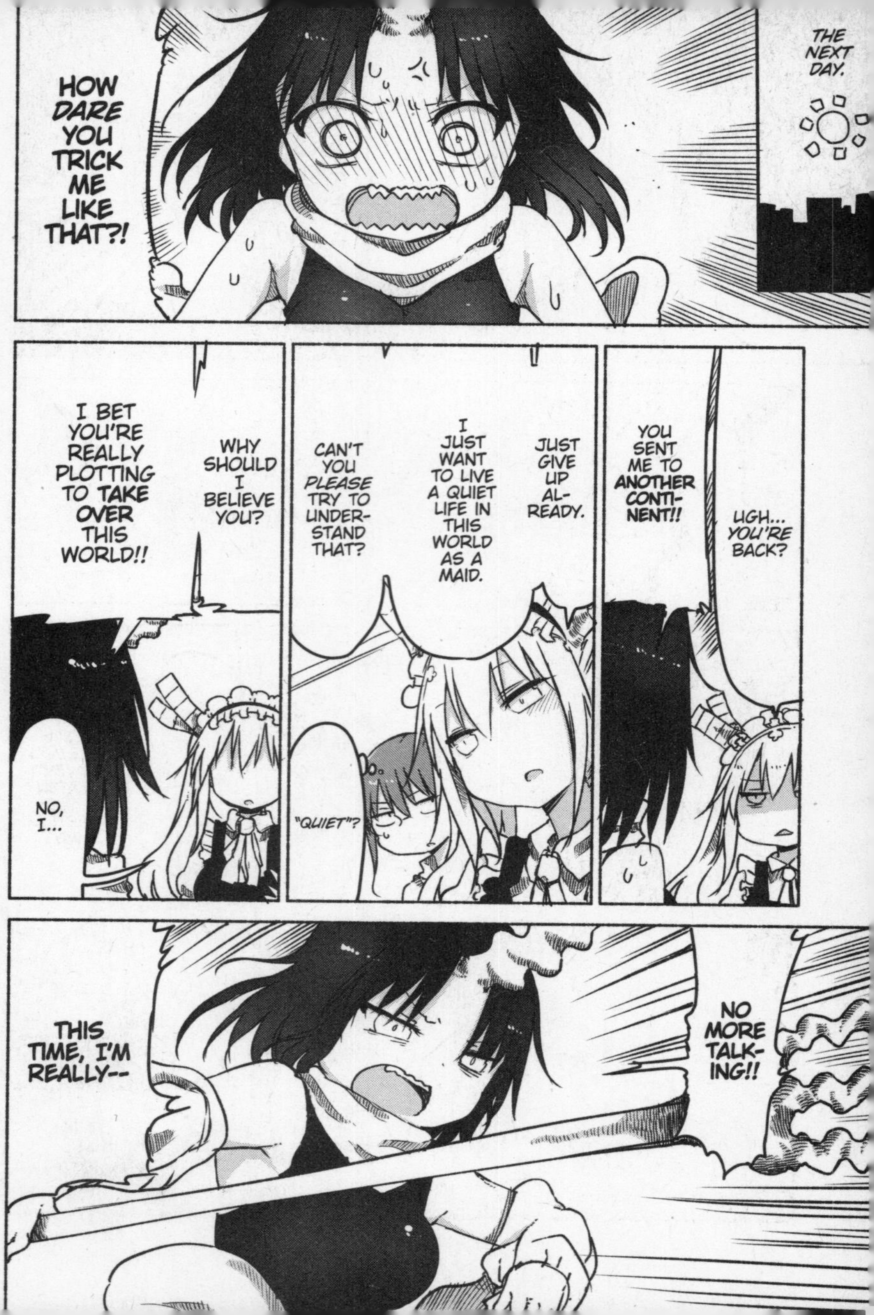
THE NEXT DAY.
HOW *DARE* YOU TRICK ME LIKE THAT?!
UGH... *YOU'RE* BACK?
YOU SENT ME TO **ANOTHER CONTINENT!!**
JUST GIVE UP AL-READY.
I JUST WANT TO LIVE A QUIET LIFE IN THIS WORLD AS A MAID.
CAN'T YOU *PLEASE* TRY TO UNDER-STAND THAT?
"*QUIET*"?
WHY SHOULD I BELIEVE YOU?
I BET YOU'RE REALLY PLOTTING TO **TAKE OVER** THIS WORLD!!
NO, I...
NO MORE TALK-ING!!
THIS TIME, I'M REALLY--

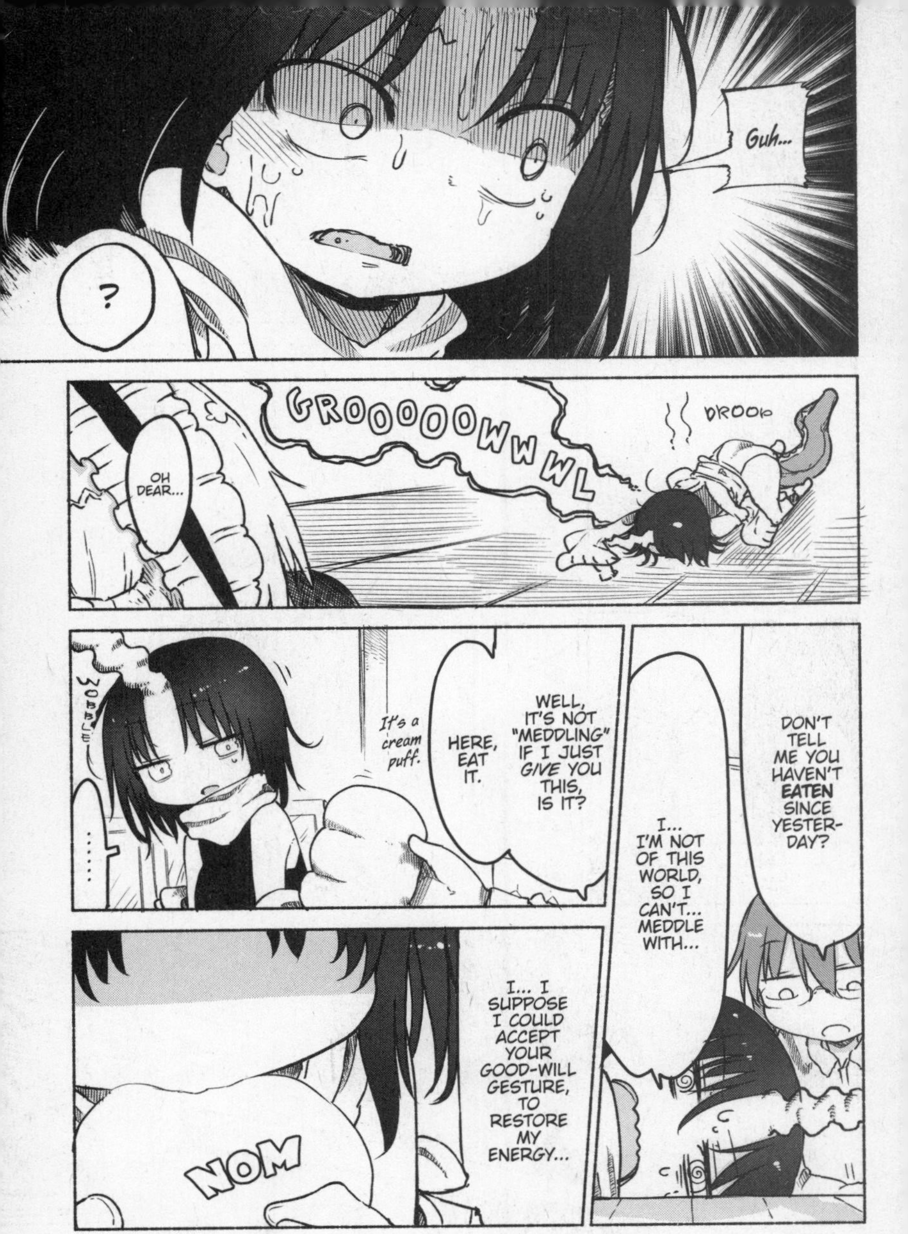
Guh...
?
DROOP
GROOOOOOWWWL
OH DEAR...
DON'T TELL ME YOU HAVEN'T EATEN SINCE YESTER-DAY?
I... I'M NOT OF THIS WORLD, SO I CAN'T... MEDDLE WITH...
WELL, IT'S NOT "MEDDLING" IF I JUST GIVE YOU THIS, IS IT?
HERE, EAT IT.
It's a cream puff.
WOBBLE
......
I... I SUPPOSE I COULD ACCEPT YOUR GOOD-WILL GESTURE, TO RESTORE MY ENERGY...
NOM

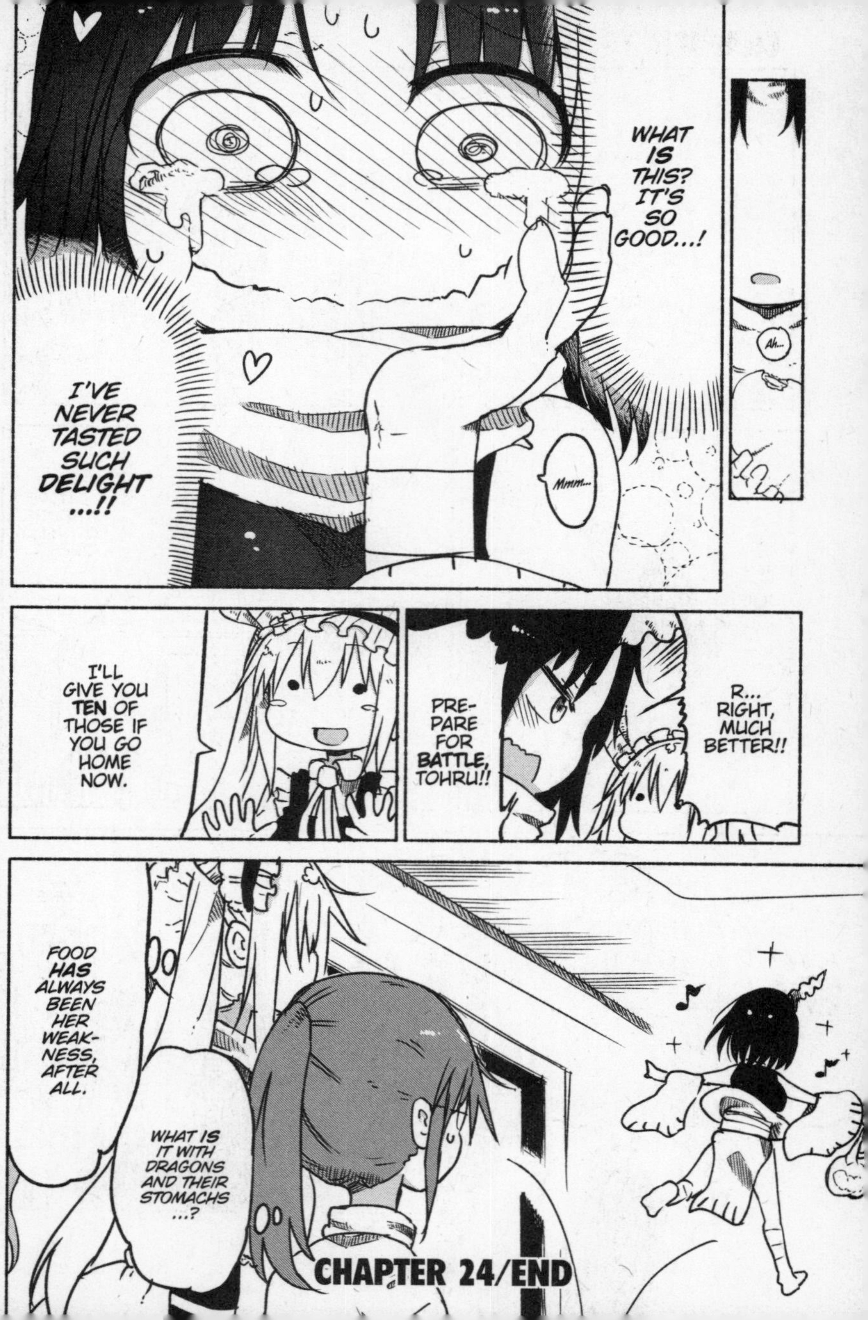
Ah...
WHAT IS THIS? IT'S SO GOOD...!
Mmm...
I'VE NEVER TASTED SUCH DELIGHT...!!
R... RIGHT, MUCH BETTER!!
PREPARE FOR BATTLE, TOHRU!!
I'LL GIVE YOU TEN OF THOSE IF YOU GO HOME NOW.
FOOD HAS ALWAYS BEEN HER WEAKNESS, AFTER ALL.
WHAT IS IT WITH DRAGONS AND THEIR STOMACHS...?
CHAPTER 24/END

CHAPTER 25

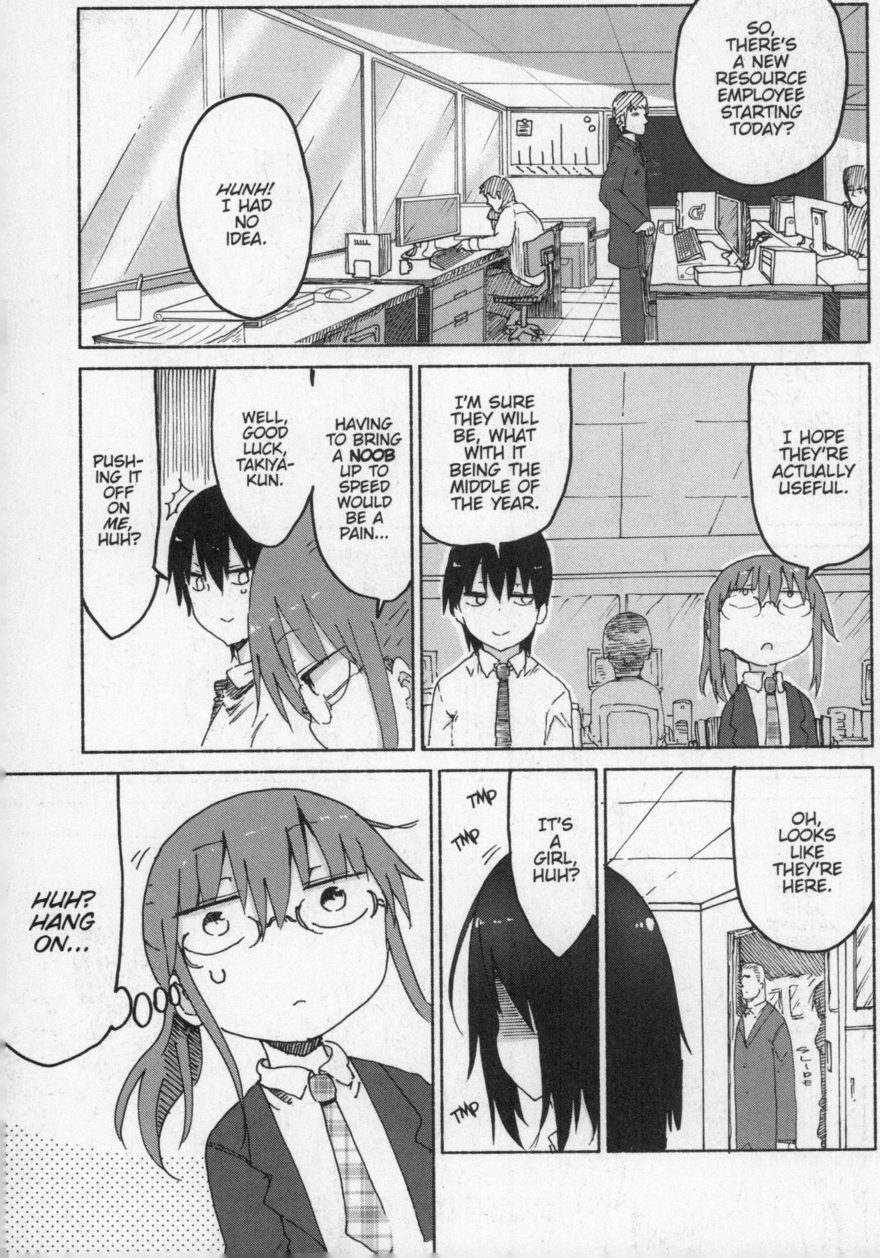
SO, THERE'S A NEW RESOURCE EMPLOYEE STARTING TODAY?
HUNH! I HAD NO IDEA.
I HOPE THEY'RE ACTUALLY USEFUL.
I'M SURE THEY WILL BE, WHAT WITH IT BEING THE MIDDLE OF THE YEAR.
HAVING TO BRING A NOOB UP TO SPEED WOULD BE A PAIN...
WELL, GOOD LUCK, TAKIYA-KUN.
PUSHING IT OFF ON ME, HUH?
OH, LOOKS LIKE THEY'RE HERE.
SLIDE
TMP
TMP
IT'S A GIRL, HUH?
TMP
HUH? HANG ON...

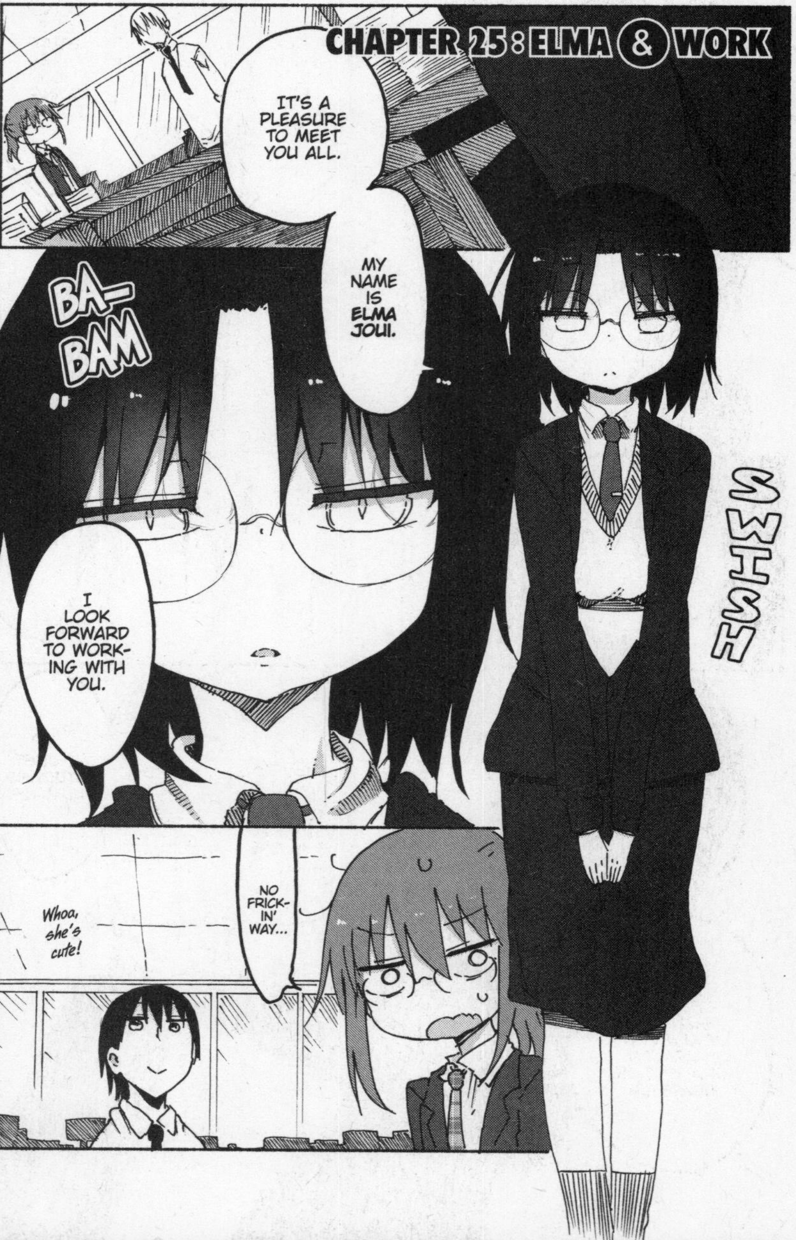
CHAPTER 25 : ELMA & WORK
IT'S A PLEASURE TO MEET YOU ALL.
MY NAME IS ELMA JOUI.
BA-BAM
I LOOK FORWARD TO WORK-ING WITH YOU.
SWISH
NO FRICK-IN' WAY...
Whoa, she's cute!

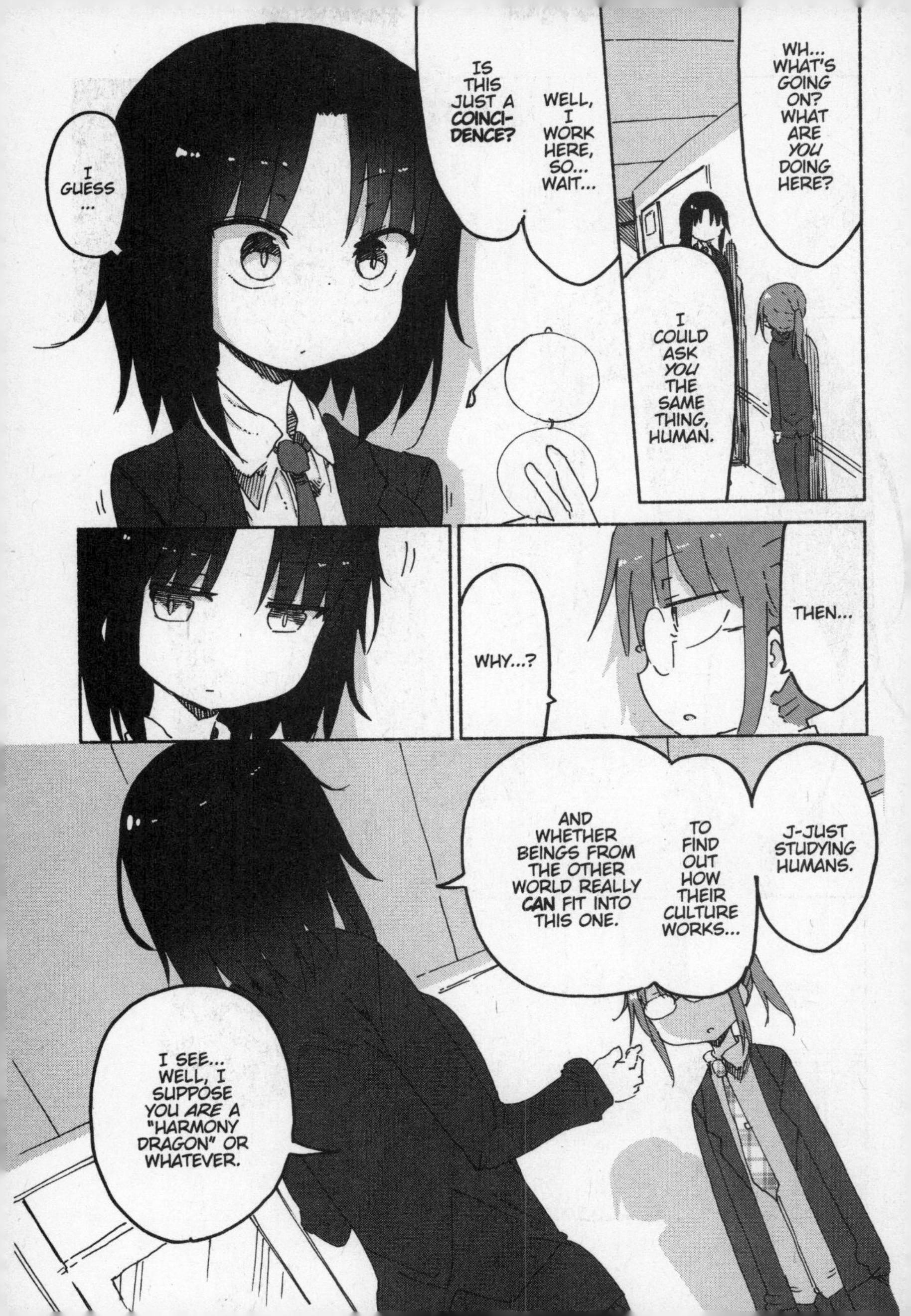
WH... WHAT'S GOING ON? WHAT ARE *YOU* DOING HERE?
I COULD ASK *YOU* THE SAME THING, HUMAN.
WELL, I WORK HERE, SO... WAIT...
IS THIS JUST A **COINCIDENCE?**
I GUESS...
THEN...
WHY...?
J-JUST STUDYING HUMANS.
TO FIND OUT HOW THEIR CULTURE WORKS...
AND WHETHER BEINGS FROM THE OTHER WORLD REALLY **CAN** FIT INTO THIS ONE.
I SEE... WELL, I SUPPOSE YOU *ARE* A "HARMONY DRAGON" OR WHATEVER.

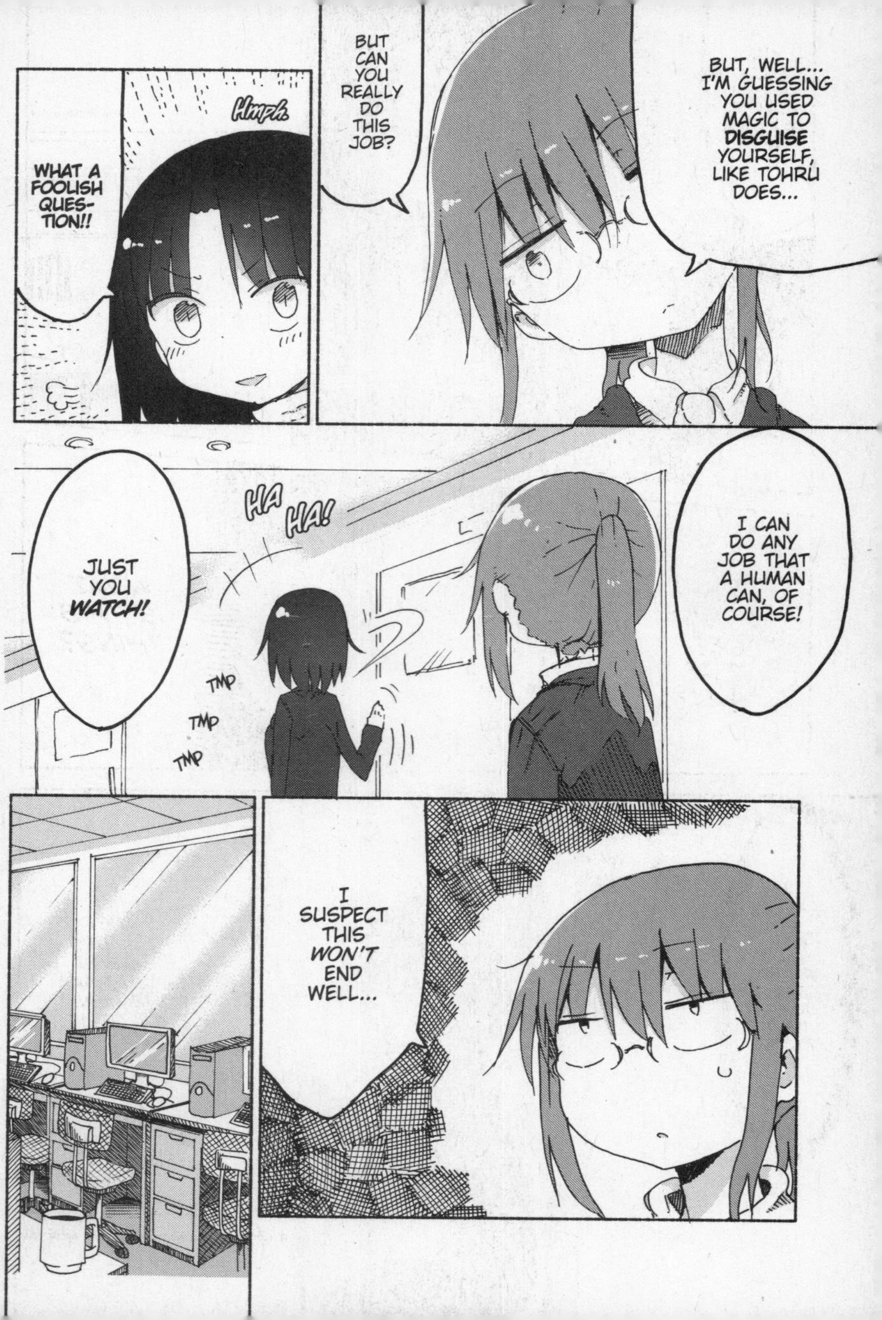
BUT, WELL... I'M GUESSING YOU USED MAGIC TO **DISGUISE** YOURSELF, LIKE TOHRU DOES...
BUT CAN YOU REALLY DO THIS JOB?
Hmph.
WHAT A FOOLISH QUES-TION!!
I CAN DO ANY JOB THAT A HUMAN CAN, OF COURSE!
HA HA!
JUST YOU *WATCH!*
TMP
TMP
TMP
I SUSPECT THIS *WON'T* END WELL...

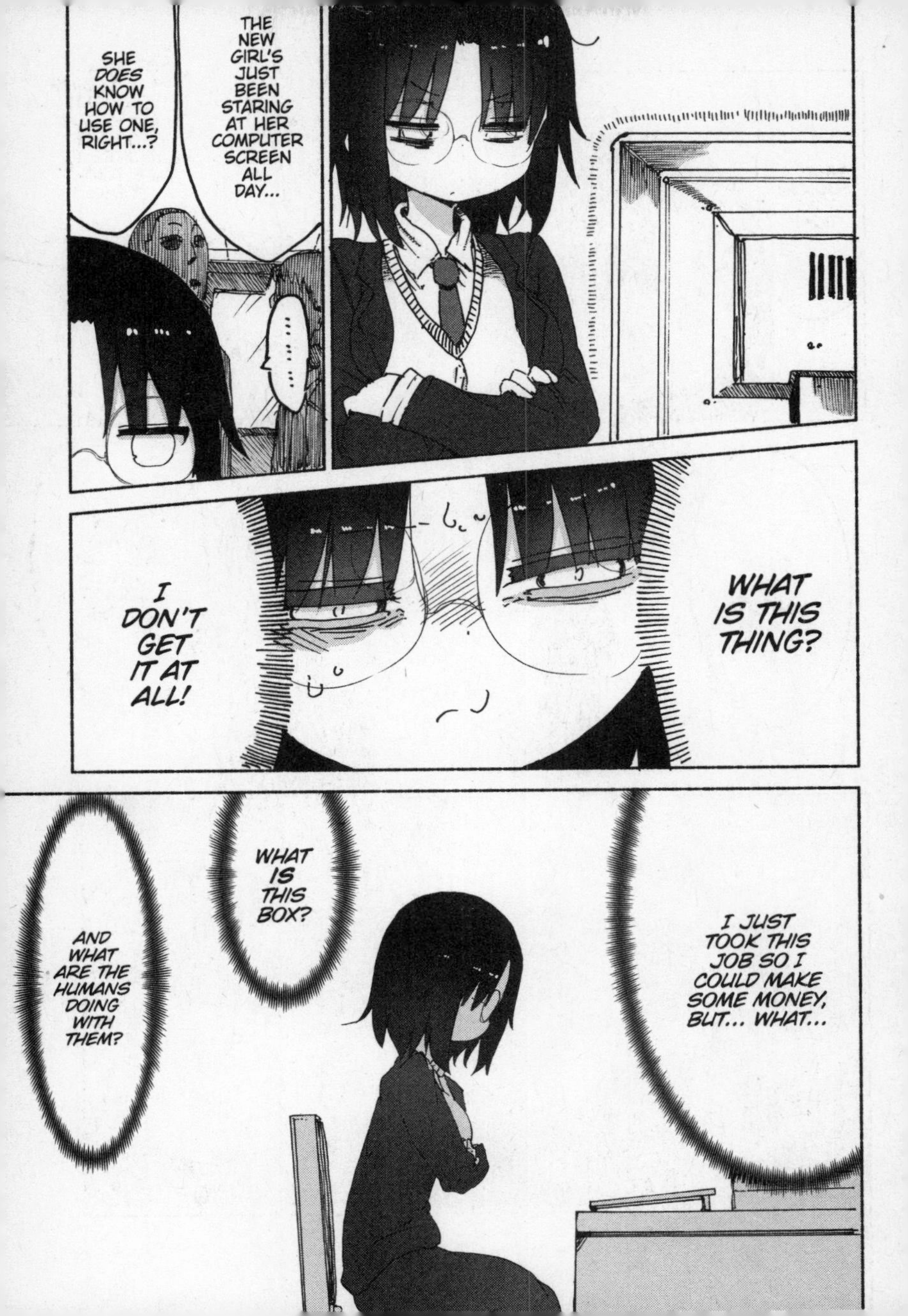
THE NEW GIRL'S JUST BEEN STARING AT HER COMPUTER SCREEN ALL DAY...
SHE *DOES* KNOW HOW TO USE ONE, RIGHT...?
......
WHAT IS THIS THING?
I DON'T GET IT AT ALL!
I JUST TOOK THIS JOB SO I COULD MAKE SOME MONEY, BUT... WHAT...
WHAT IS THIS BOX?
AND WHAT ARE THE HUMANS DOING WITH THEM?

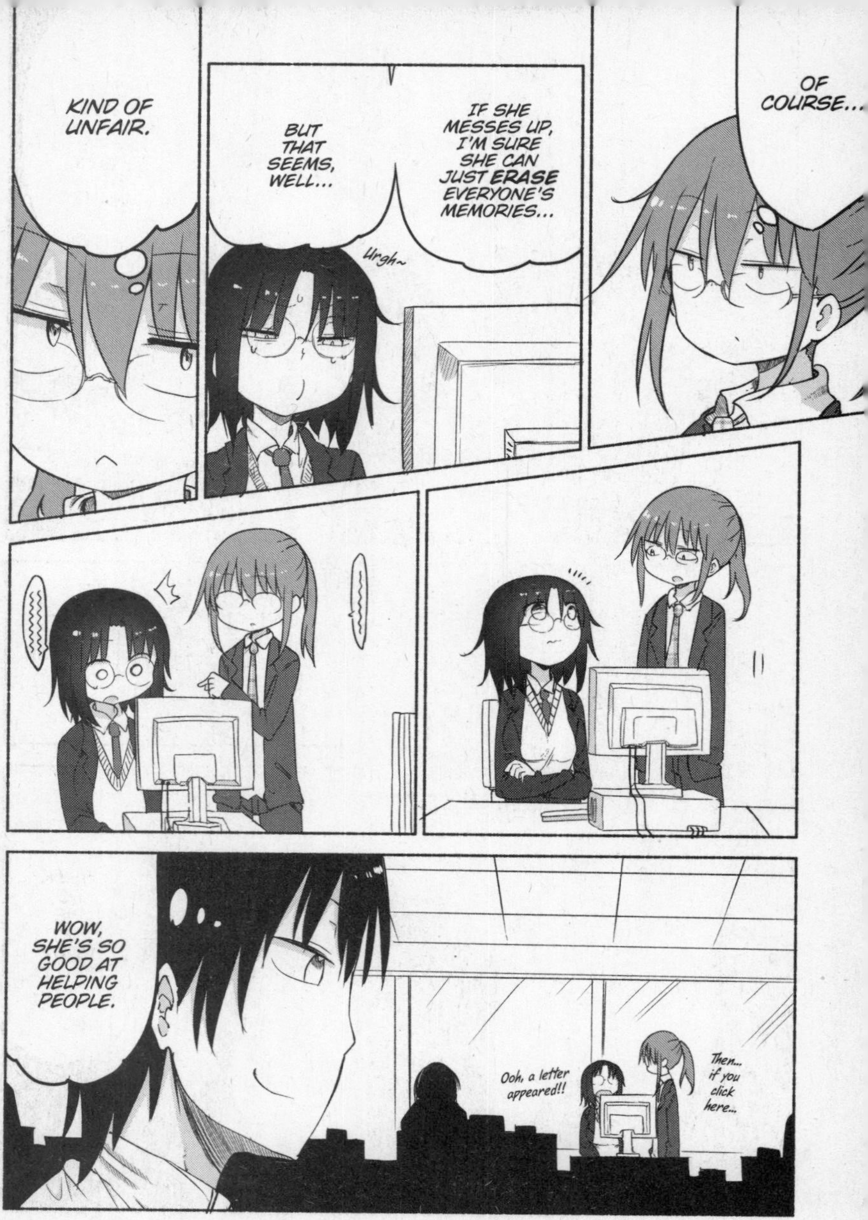
OF COURSE...
IF SHE MESSES UP, I'M SURE SHE CAN JUST ERASE EVERYONE'S MEMORIES...
BUT THAT SEEMS, WELL...
Urgh~
KIND OF UNFAIR.
WOW, SHE'S SO GOOD AT HELPING PEOPLE.
Then... if you click here...
Ooh, a letter appeared!!

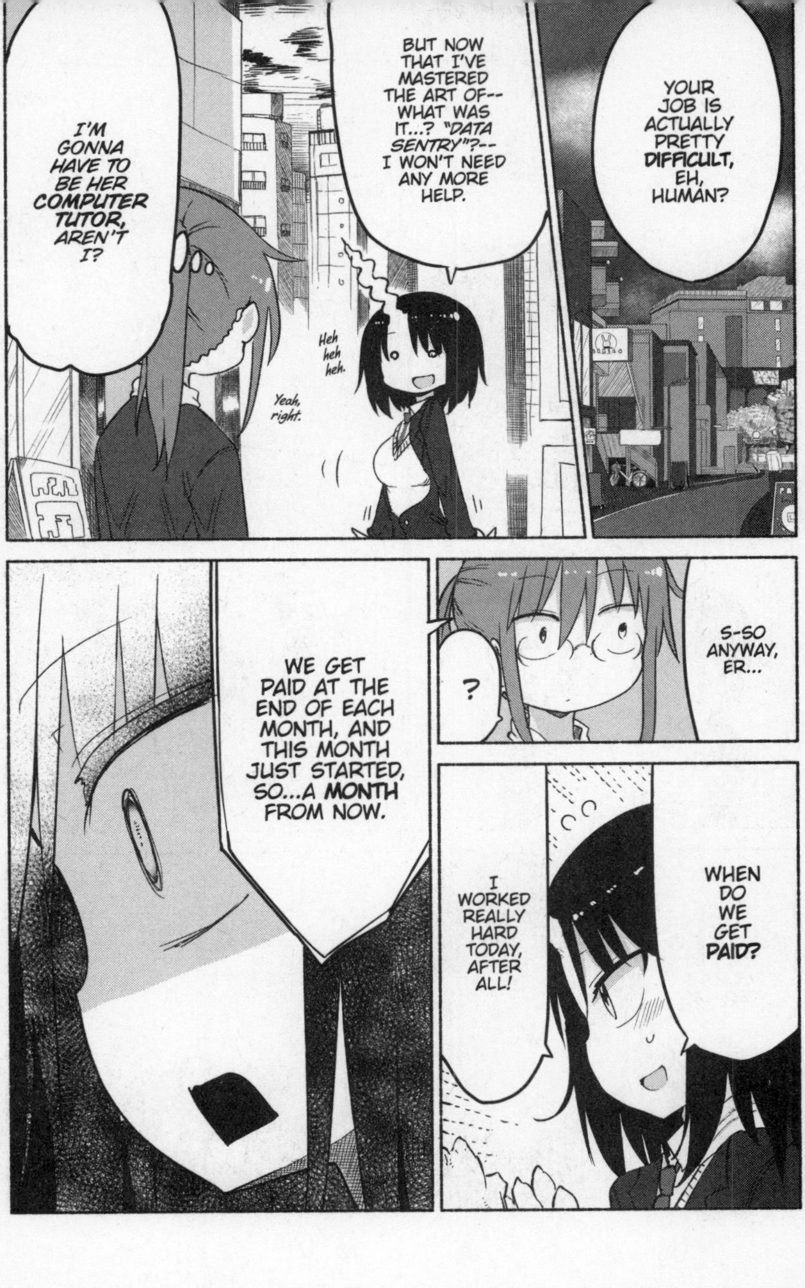
YOUR JOB IS ACTUALLY PRETTY DIFFICULT, EH, HUMAN?
BUT NOW THAT I'VE MASTERED THE ART OF-- WHAT WAS IT...? "DATA SENTRY"?-- I WON'T NEED ANY MORE HELP.
I'M GONNA HAVE TO BE HER COMPUTER TUTOR, AREN'T I?
Heh heh heh.
Yeah, right.
S-SO ANYWAY, ER...
?
WHEN DO WE GET PAID?
I WORKED REALLY HARD TODAY, AFTER ALL!
WE GET PAID AT THE END OF EACH MONTH, AND THIS MONTH JUST STARTED, SO...A MONTH FROM NOW.

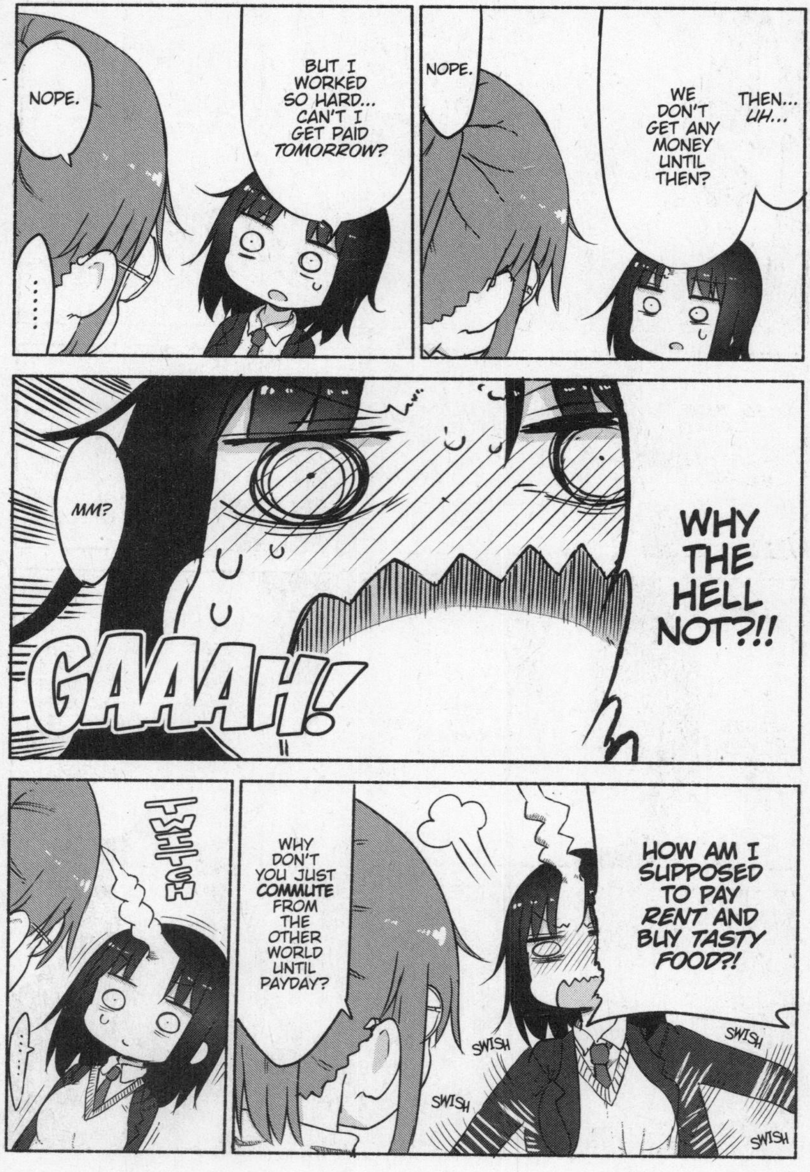

THEN... UH...
WE DON'T GET ANY MONEY UNTIL THEN?
NOPE.
BUT I WORKED SO HARD... CAN'T I GET PAID TOMORROW?
NOPE.
......
WHY THE HELL NOT?!!
GAAAH!
MM?
HOW AM I SUPPOSED TO PAY RENT AND BUY TASTY FOOD?!
SWISH
SWISH
SWISH
SWISH
WHY DON'T YOU JUST COMMUTE FROM THE OTHER WORLD UNTIL PAYDAY?
TWITCH
......

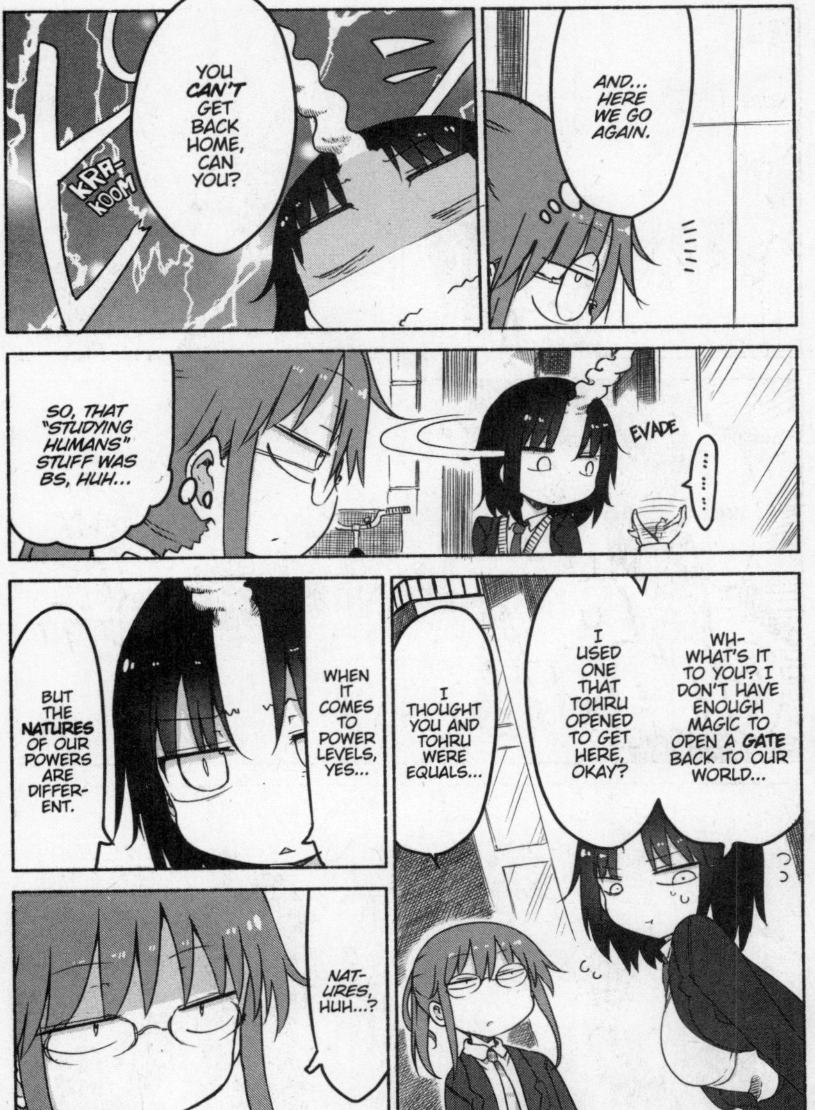
AND... HERE WE GO AGAIN.
YOU CAN'T GET BACK HOME, CAN YOU?
KRA-KOOM
EVADE
......
SO, THAT "STUDYING HUMANS" STUFF WAS BS, HUH...
WH-WHAT'S IT TO YOU? I DON'T HAVE ENOUGH MAGIC TO OPEN A GATE BACK TO OUR WORLD...
I USED ONE THAT TOHRU OPENED TO GET HERE, OKAY?
I THOUGHT YOU AND TOHRU WERE EQUALS...
WHEN IT COMES TO POWER LEVELS, YES...
BUT THE NATURES OF OUR POWERS ARE DIFFER-ENT.
NAT-URES, HUH...?

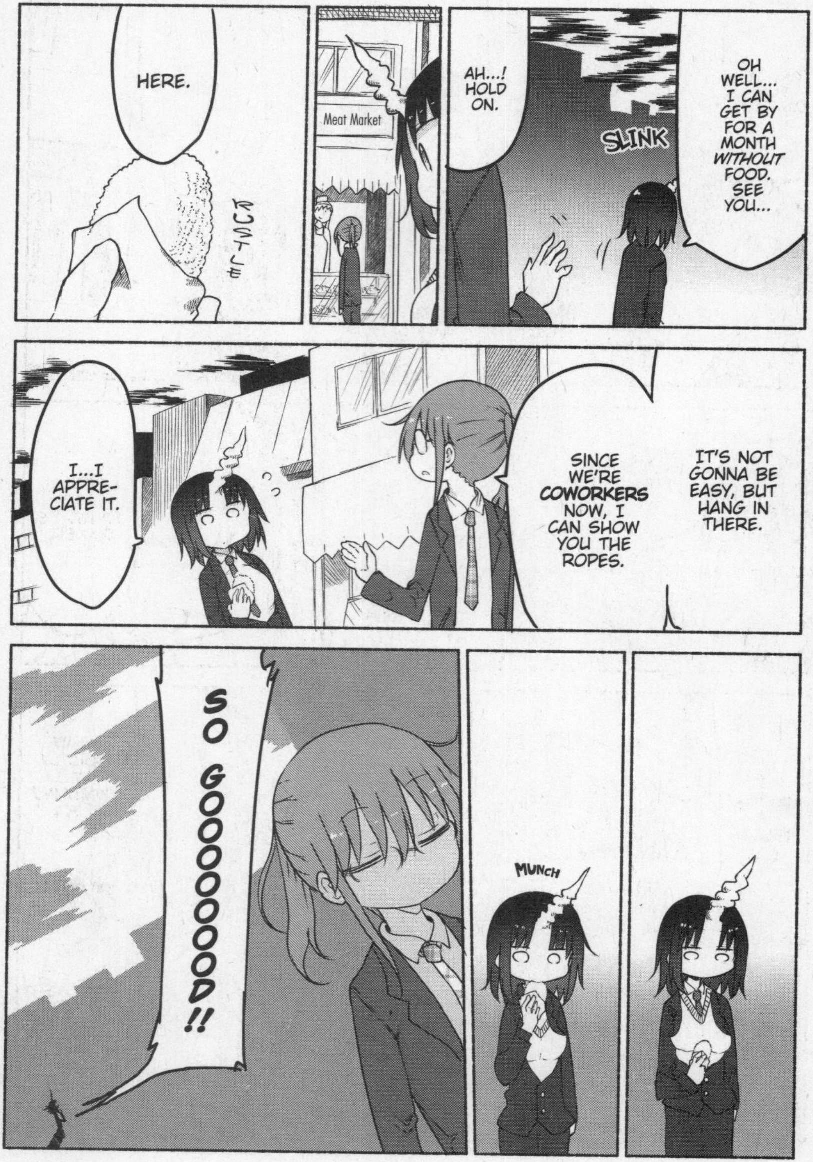
OH WELL... I CAN GET BY FOR A MONTH WITHOUT FOOD. SEE YOU...
AH...! HOLD ON.
SLINK
Meat Market
HERE.
RUSTLE
IT'S NOT GONNA BE EASY, BUT HANG IN THERE.
SINCE WE'RE COWORKERS NOW, I CAN SHOW YOU THE ROPES.
I...I APPRECIATE IT.
MUNCH
SO GOOOOOOOOD!!

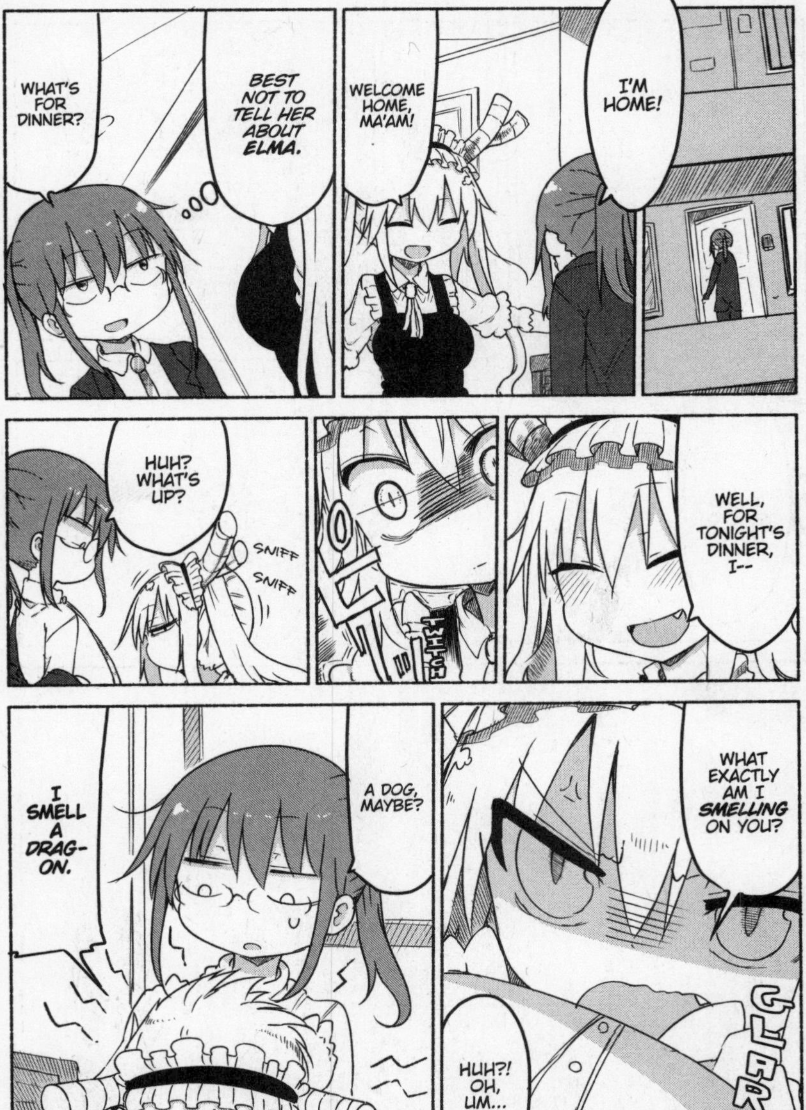
I'M HOME!
WELCOME HOME, MA'AM!
BEST NOT TO TELL HER ABOUT ELMA.
WHAT'S FOR DINNER?
WELL, FOR TONIGHT'S DINNER, I--
TWITCH
HUH? WHAT'S UP?
SNIFF
SNIFF
WHAT EXACTLY AM I SMELLING ON YOU?
GLARE
HUH?! OH, UM...
A DOG, MAYBE?
I SMELL A DRAG-ON.

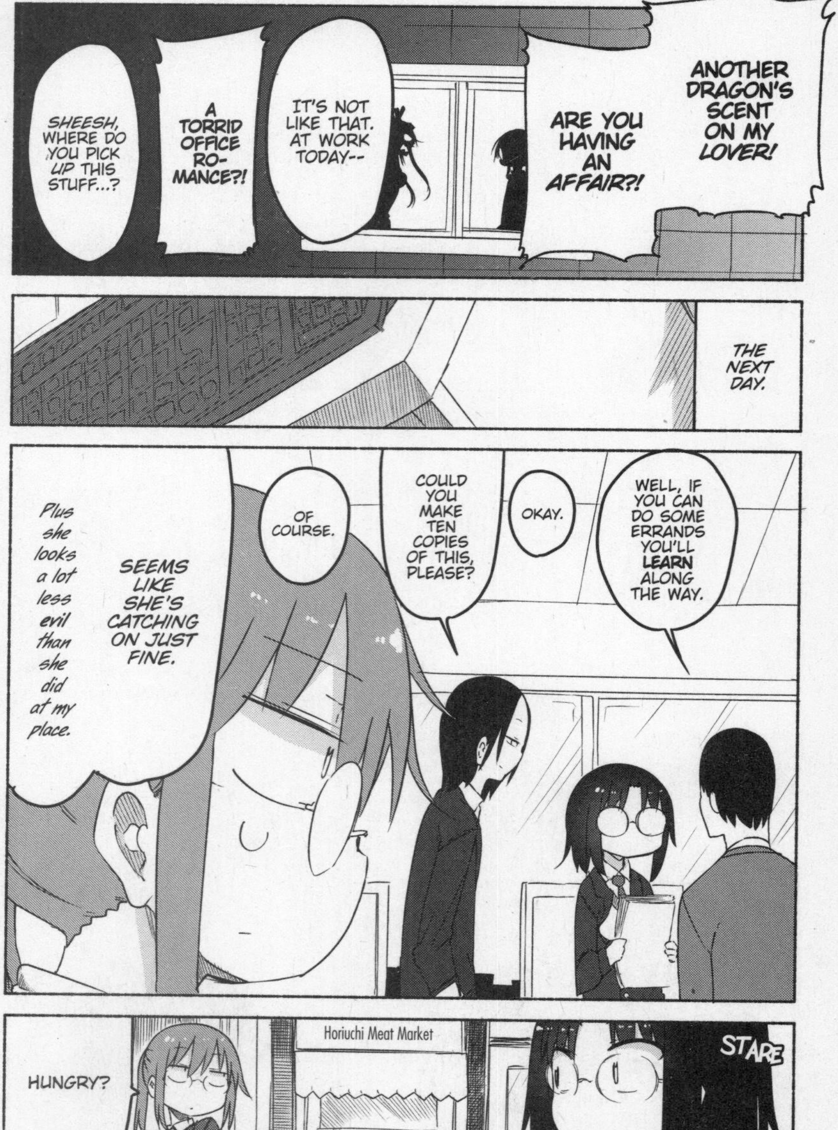
ANOTHER DRAGON'S SCENT ON MY LOVER!
ARE YOU HAVING AN AFFAIR?!
IT'S NOT LIKE THAT. AT WORK TODAY--
A TORRID OFFICE RO-MANCE?!
SHEESH, WHERE DO YOU PICK UP THIS STUFF...?
THE NEXT DAY.
WELL, IF YOU CAN DO SOME ERRANDS YOU'LL **LEARN** ALONG THE WAY.
OKAY.
COULD YOU MAKE TEN COPIES OF THIS, PLEASE?
OF COURSE.
SEEMS LIKE SHE'S CATCHING ON JUST FINE.
Plus she looks a lot less evil than she did at my place.
STARE
Horiuchi Meat Market
HUNGRY?

CHAPTER 25/END

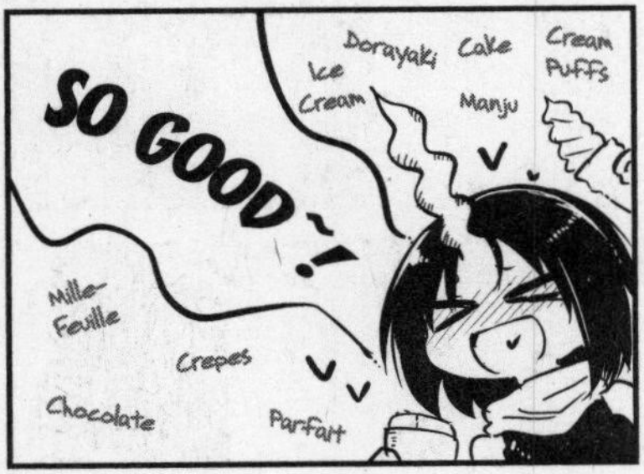
SO GOOD~!
Dorayaki
Cake
Cream Puffs
Ice Cream
Manju
Mille-Feuille
Crepes
Chocolate
Parfait

Miss Kobayashi's
DRAGON MAID

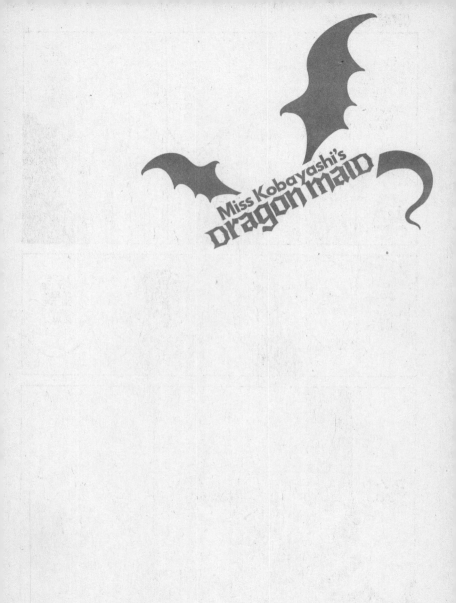

CHAPTER 26

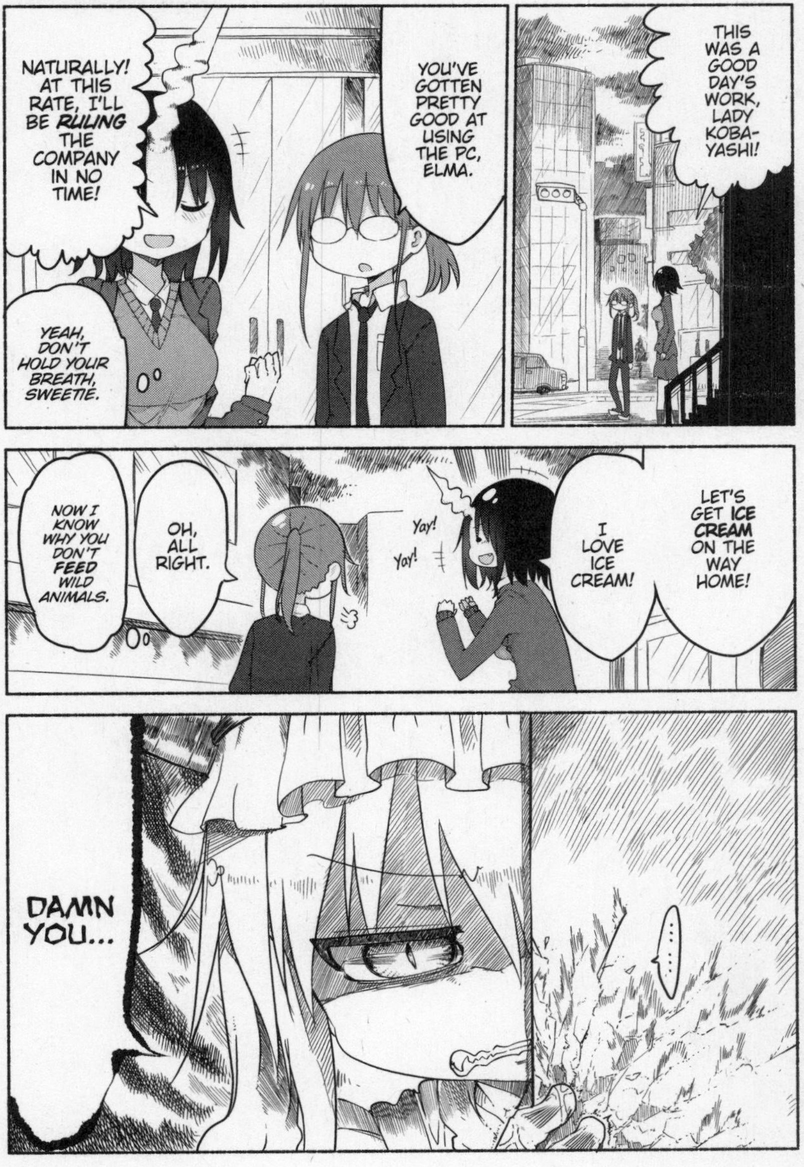
THIS WAS A GOOD DAY'S WORK, LADY KOBAYASHI!
YOU'VE GOTTEN PRETTY GOOD AT USING THE PC, ELMA.
NATURALLY! AT THIS RATE, I'LL BE RULING THE COMPANY IN NO TIME!
YEAH, DON'T HOLD YOUR BREATH, SWEETIE.
LET'S GET ICE CREAM ON THE WAY HOME!
I LOVE ICE CREAM!
Yay!
Yay!
OH, ALL RIGHT.
NOW I KNOW WHY YOU DON'T FEED WILD ANIMALS.
……
DAMN YOU...

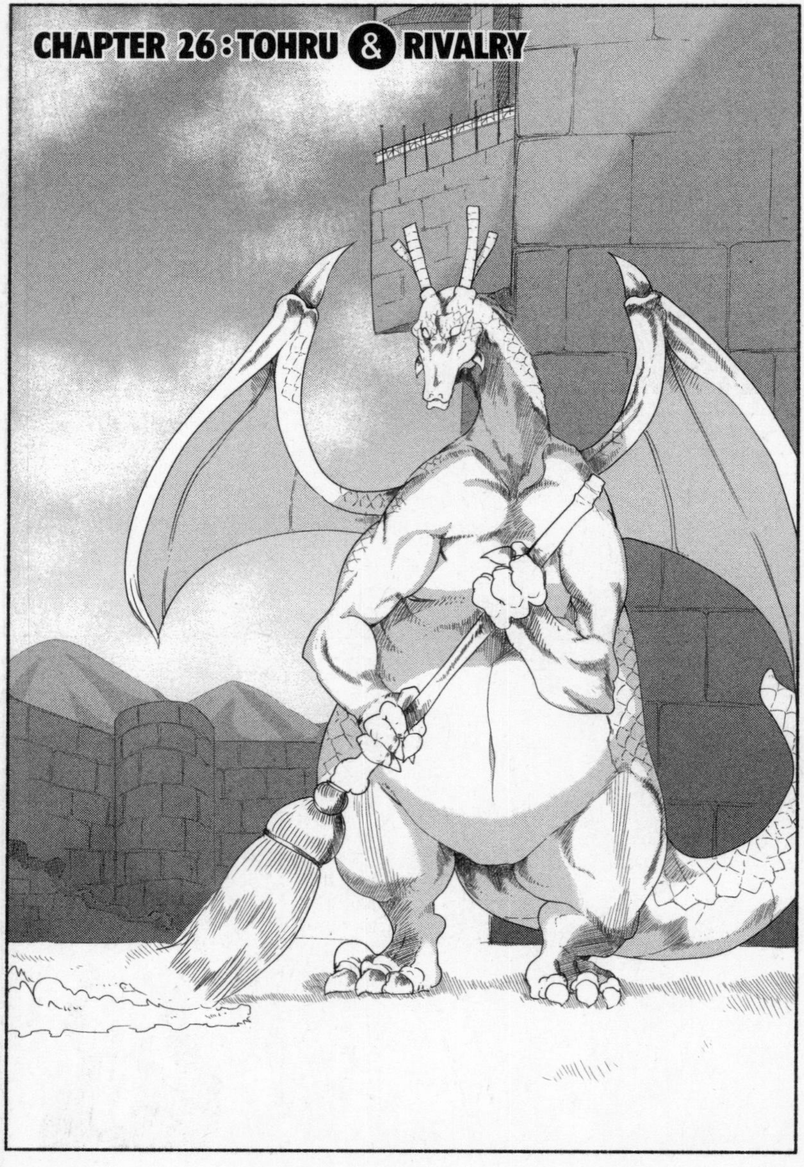
CHAPTER 26: TOHRU & RIVALRY

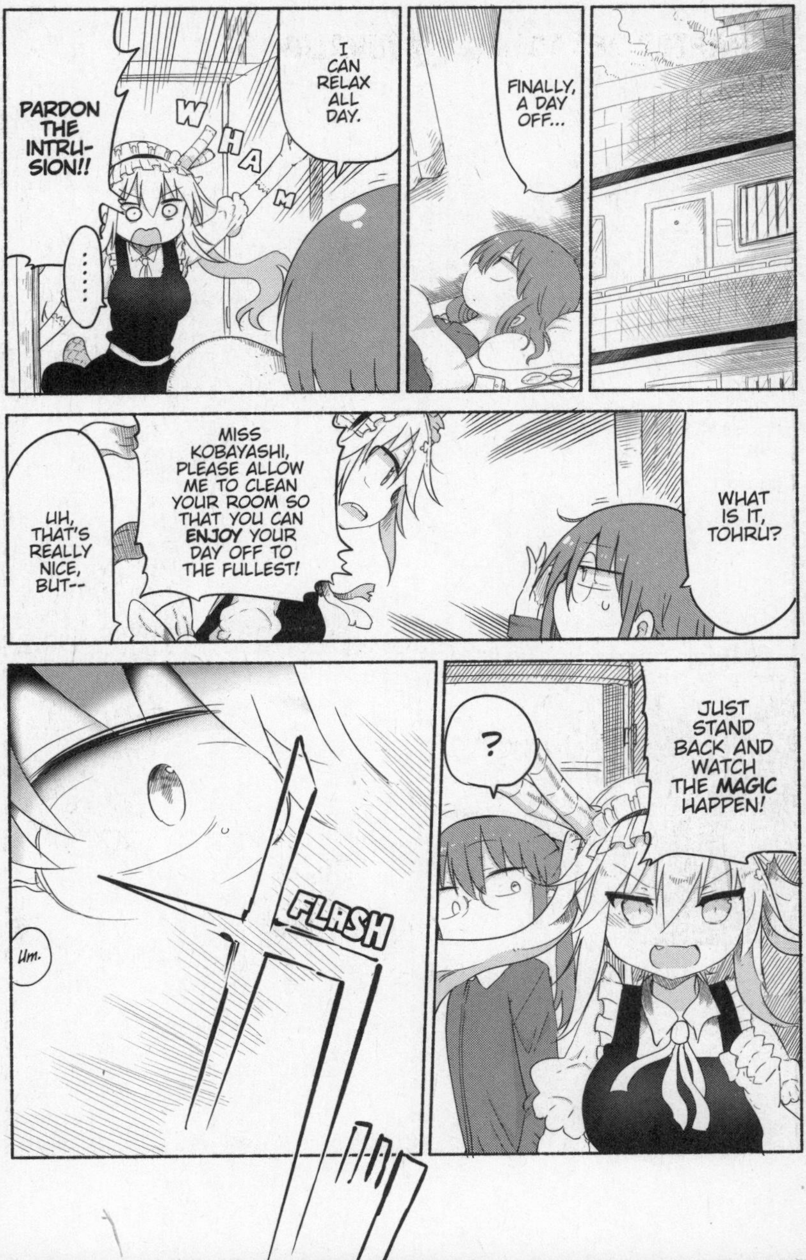
FINALLY, A DAY OFF...
I CAN RELAX ALL DAY.
WHAM
PARDON THE INTRUSION!!
......
WHAT IS IT, TOHRU?
MISS KOBAYASHI, PLEASE ALLOW ME TO CLEAN YOUR ROOM SO THAT YOU CAN ENJOY YOUR DAY OFF TO THE FULLEST!
UH, THAT'S REALLY NICE, BUT--
JUST STAND BACK AND WATCH THE MAGIC HAPPEN!
?
FLASH
Um.

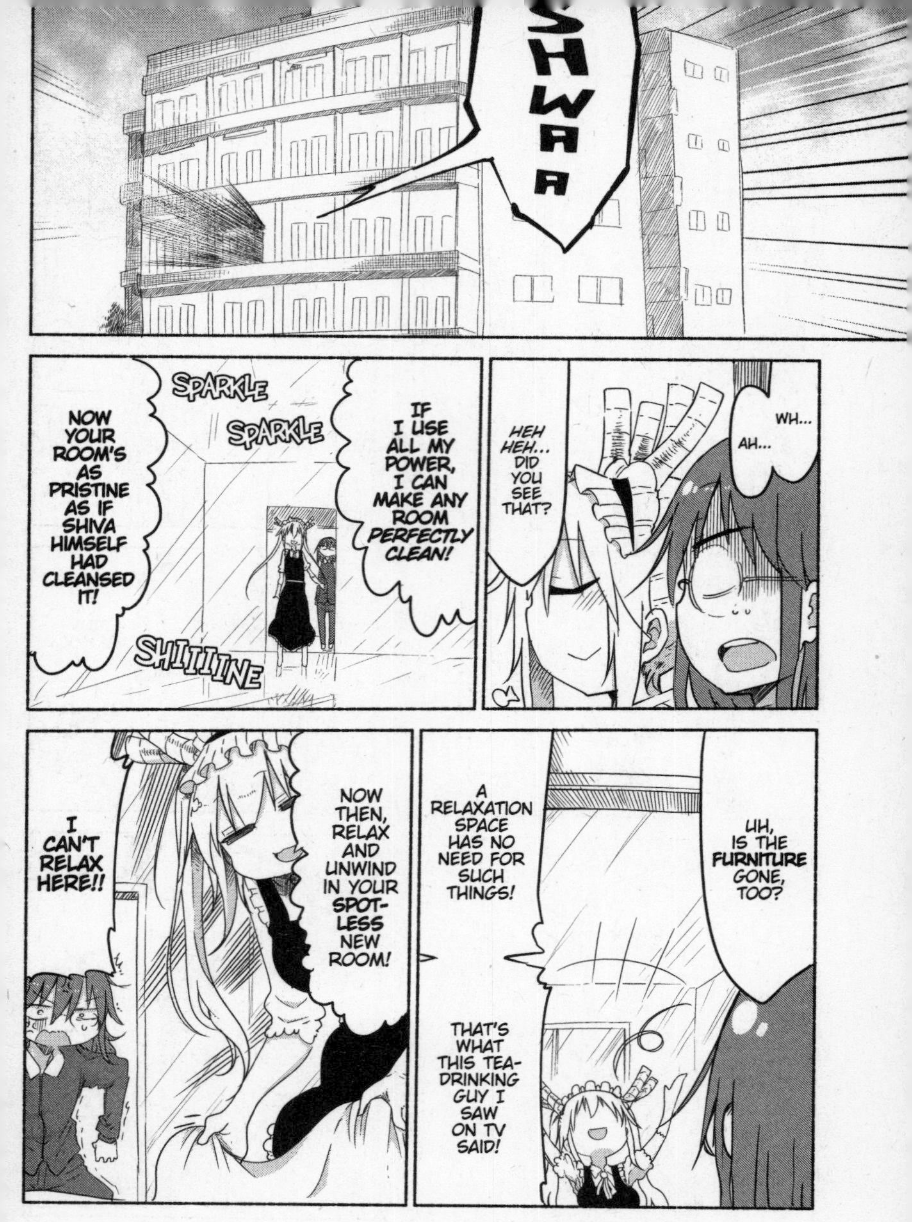
SHWA
WH... AH...
HEH HEH... DID YOU SEE THAT?
IF I USE ALL MY POWER, I CAN MAKE ANY ROOM PERFECTLY CLEAN!
SPARKLE
SPARKLE
NOW YOUR ROOM'S AS PRISTINE AS IF SHIVA HIMSELF HAD CLEANSED IT!
SHIIIIINE
UH, IS THE FURNITURE GONE, TOO?
A RELAXATION SPACE HAS NO NEED FOR SUCH THINGS!
THAT'S WHAT THIS TEA-DRINKING GUY I SAW ON TV SAID!
NOW THEN, RELAX AND UNWIND IN YOUR SPOTLESS NEW ROOM!
I CAN'T RELAX HERE!!

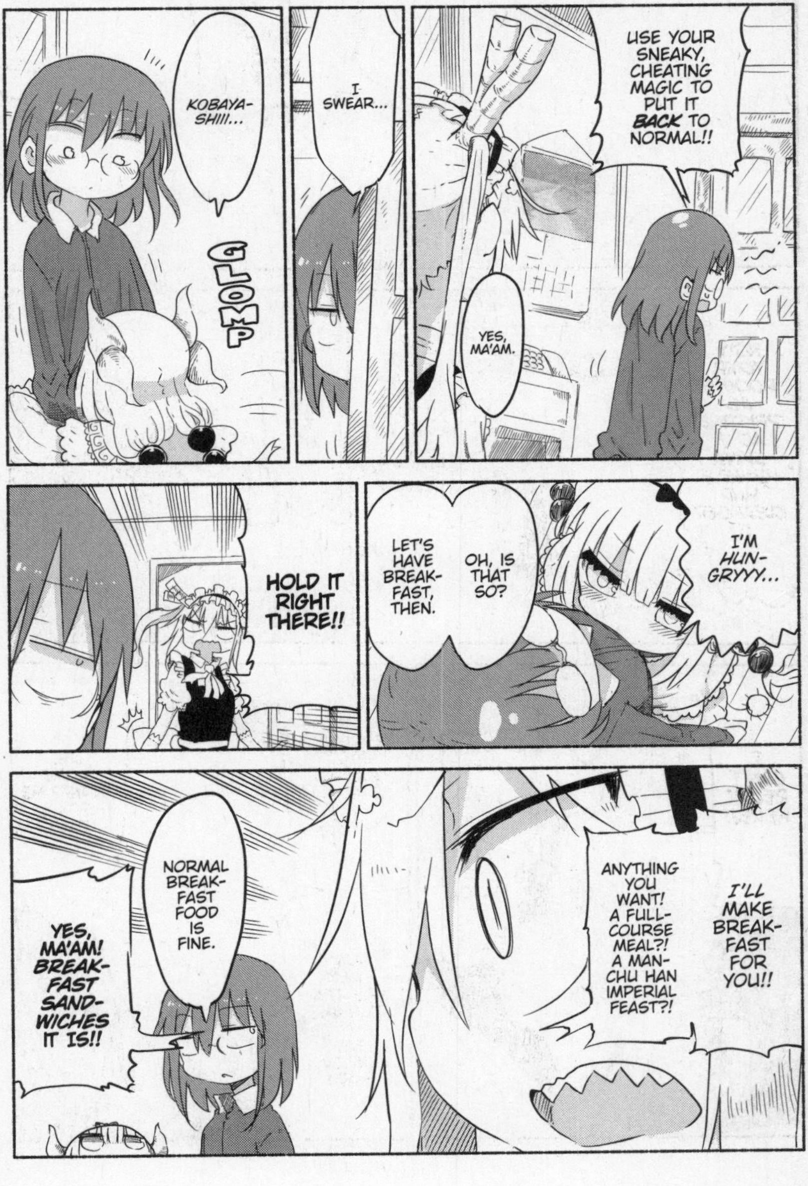
USE YOUR SNEAKY, CHEATING MAGIC TO PUT IT *BACK* TO NORMAL!!
YES, MA'AM.
I SWEAR...
KOBAYA-SHIII...
GLOMP
I'M HUN-GRYYY...
OH, IS THAT SO?
LET'S HAVE BREAK-FAST, THEN.
HOLD IT RIGHT THERE!!
I'LL MAKE BREAK-FAST FOR YOU!!
ANYTHING YOU WANT! A FULL-COURSE MEAL?! A MAN-CHU HAN IMPERIAL FEAST?!
NORMAL BREAK-FAST FOOD IS FINE.
YES, MA'AM! BREAK-FAST SAND-WICHES IT IS!!

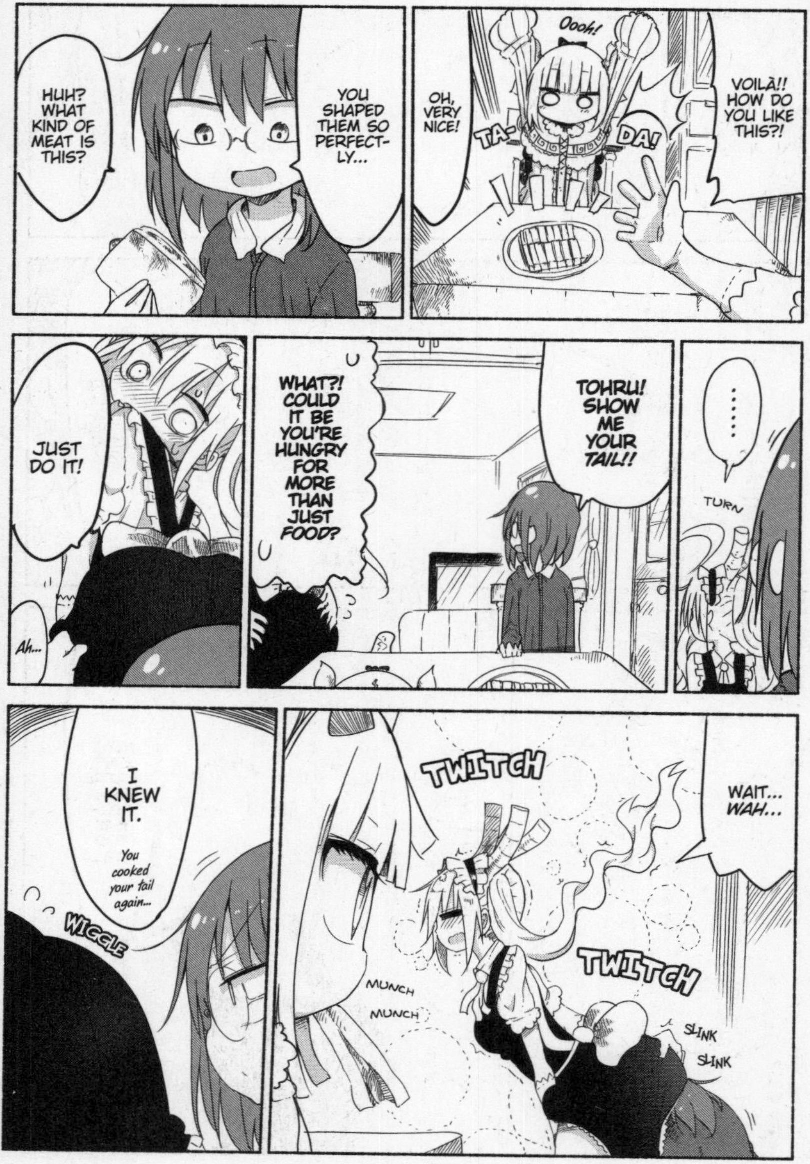
VOILÀ!! HOW DO YOU LIKE THIS?!
Oooh!
TA-
DA!
OH, VERY NICE!
YOU SHAPED THEM SO PERFECT-LY...
HUH? WHAT KIND OF MEAT IS THIS?
......
TURN
TOHRU! SHOW ME YOUR TAIL!!
WHAT?! COULD IT BE YOU'RE HUNGRY FOR MORE THAN JUST FOOD?
JUST DO IT!
Ah...
WAIT... WAH...
TWITCH
TWITCH
SLINK
SLINK
MUNCH
MUNCH
I KNEW IT.
You cooked your tail again...
WIGGLE

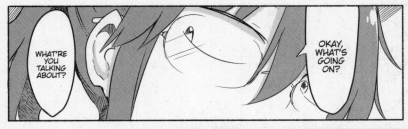

OKAY, WHAT'S GOING ON?
WHAT'RE YOU TALKING ABOUT?
YOU'RE WEIRDLY OVER-ENTHUSIASTIC TODAY...
YOU REALLY DON'T GET IT?
NO, I DON'T! YOU'RE TAKING THINGS WAY TOO FAR...
IT'S LIKE YOU'RE BACK TO THE WAY YOU BEHAVED WHEN YOU FIRST CAME HERE!
D-ZG DOZG

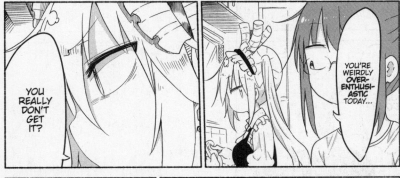

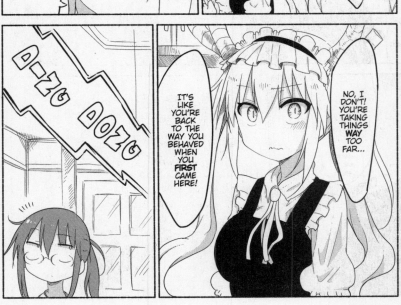

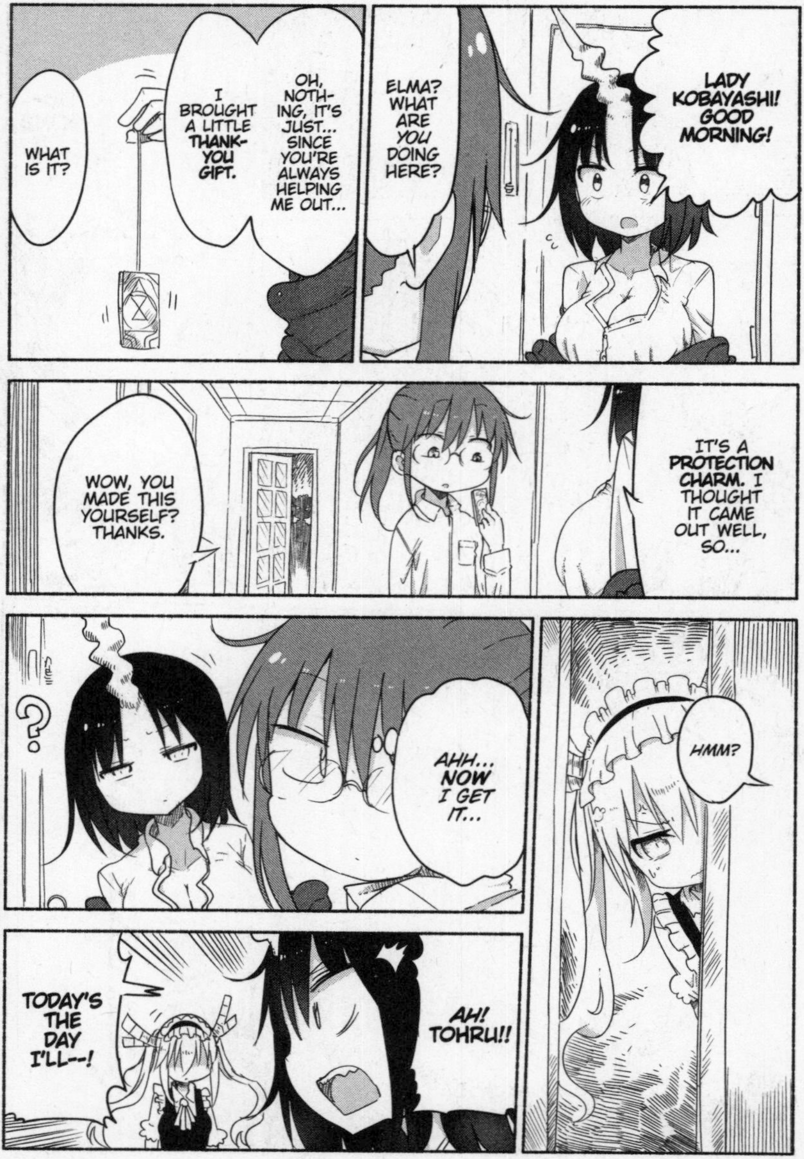
LADY KOBAYASHI! GOOD MORNING!
ELMA? WHAT ARE YOU DOING HERE?
OH, NOTHING, IT'S JUST... SINCE YOU'RE ALWAYS HELPING ME OUT...
I BROUGHT A LITTLE THANK-YOU GIFT.
WHAT IS IT?
IT'S A PROTECTION CHARM. I THOUGHT IT CAME OUT WELL, SO...
WOW, YOU MADE THIS YOURSELF? THANKS.
HMM?
AHH... NOW I GET IT...
AH! TOHRU!!
TODAY'S THE DAY I'LL--!

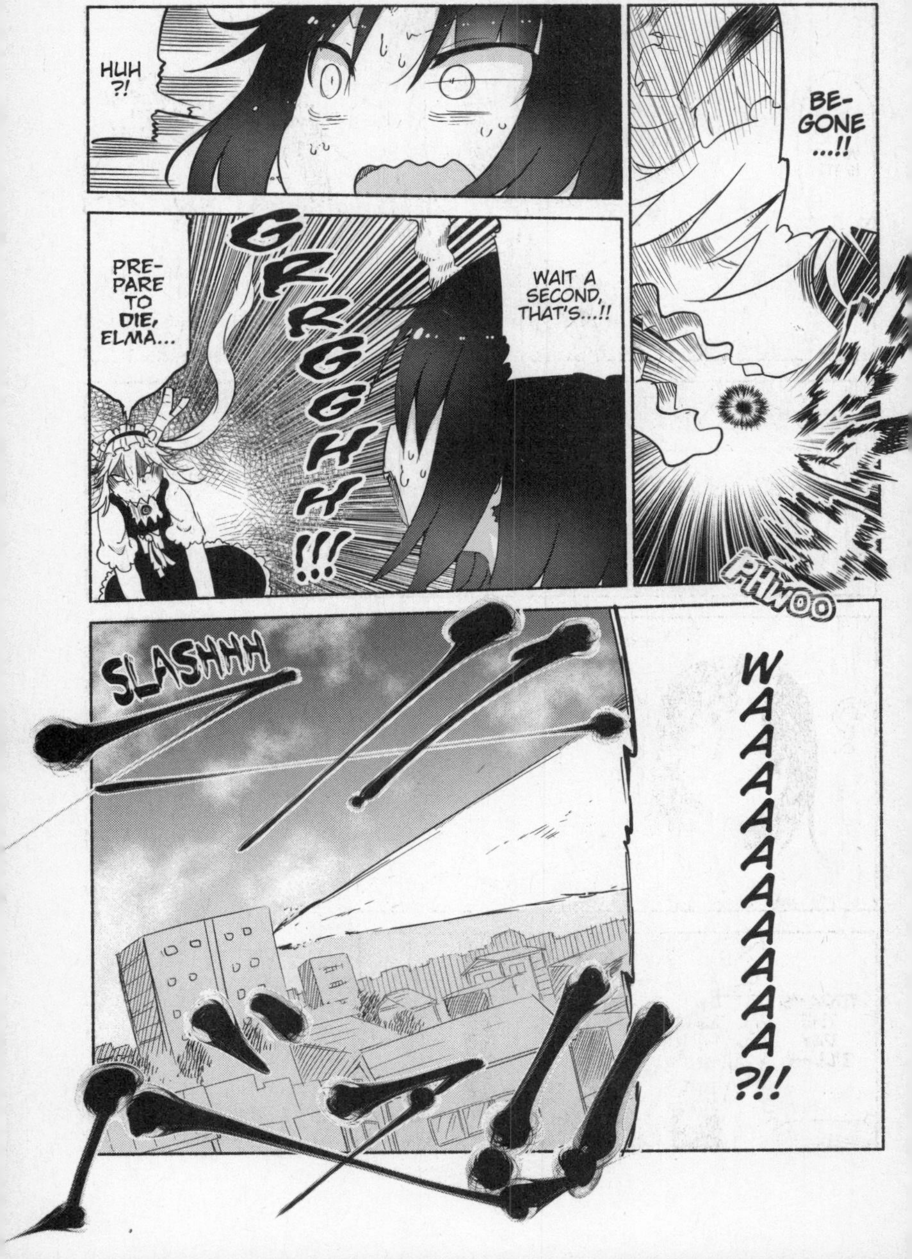
BE-
GONE
...!!
PHWOO
HUH
?!
WAIT A SECOND, THAT'S...!!
GRRGGHH!!!
PRE-
PARE
TO
DIE,
ELMA...
WAAAAAAAAAA?!!
SLASHHH

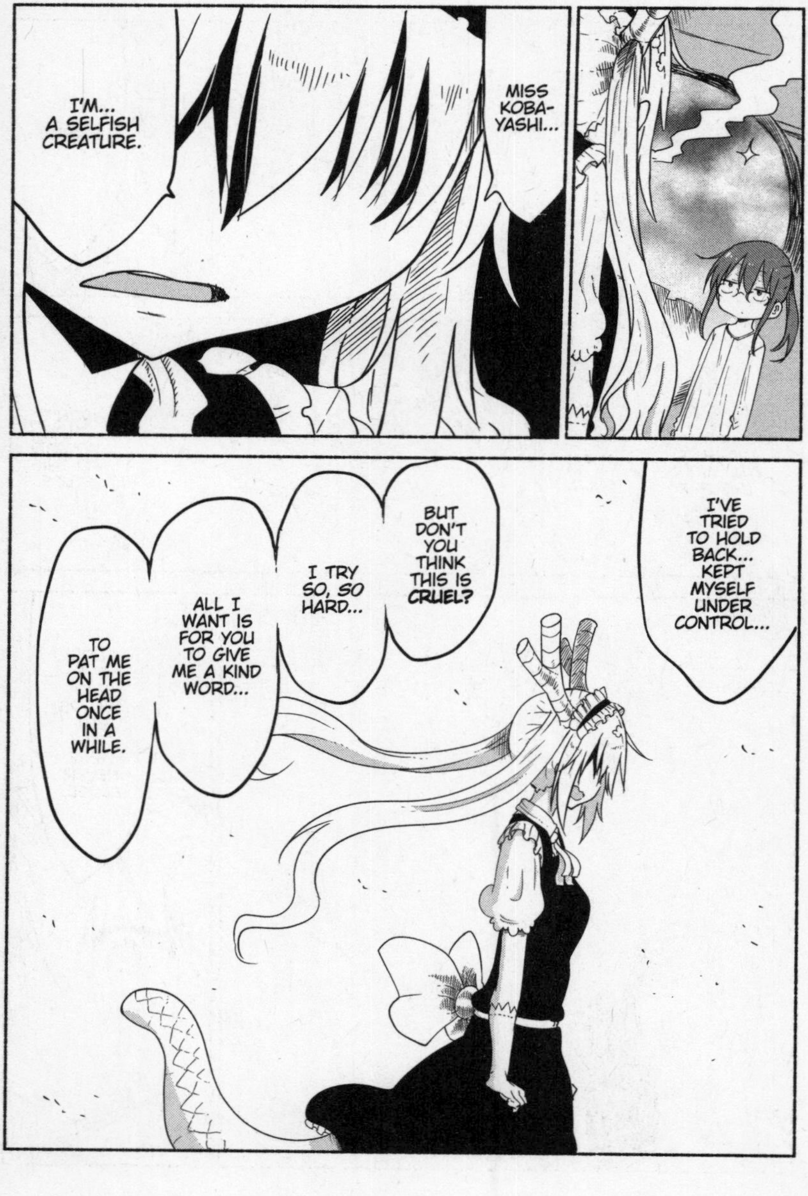
MISS KOBA-YASHI...
I'M... A SELFISH CREATURE.
I'VE TRIED TO HOLD BACK... KEPT MYSELF UNDER CONTROL...
BUT DON'T YOU THINK THIS IS CRUEL?
I TRY SO, SO HARD...
ALL I WANT IS FOR YOU TO GIVE ME A KIND WORD...
TO PAT ME ON THE HEAD ONCE IN A WHILE.

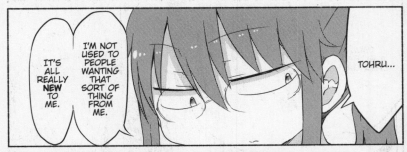

TOHRU...
I'M NOT USED TO PEOPLE WANTING THAT SORT OF THING FROM ME.
IT'S ALL REALLY NEW TO ME.
I DON'T KNOW HOW TO DO THIS STUFF.
I PUT UP WALLS, KEEP MY DISTANCE...
I'VE OFTEN THOUGHT THAT RELATION-SHIPS ARE MORE TROUBLE THAN THEY'RE WORTH.
SURE, I'VE HAD FRIENDS, BUT THEY WERE NEVER CLOSE.
BUT I GUESS IT'S TIME I GOT OVER ALL THAT.
PAT

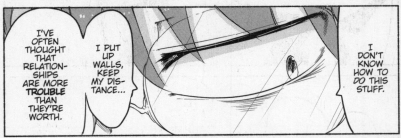

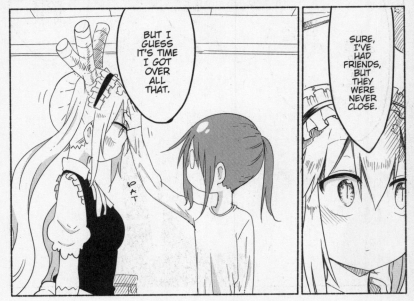

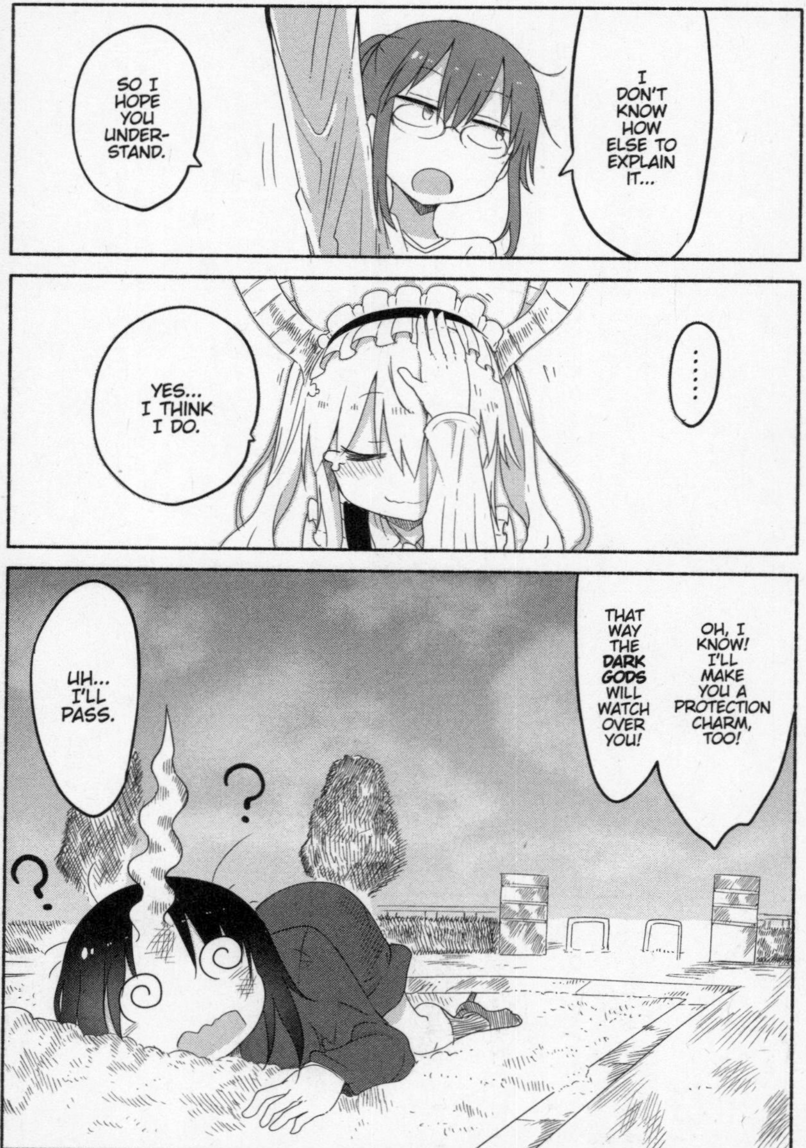
I DON'T KNOW HOW ELSE TO EXPLAIN IT...
SO I HOPE YOU UNDERSTAND.
......
YES... I THINK I DO.
OH, I KNOW! I'LL MAKE YOU A PROTECTION CHARM, TOO!
THAT WAY THE DARK GODS WILL WATCH OVER YOU!
?
?
UH... I'LL PASS.

CHAPTER 26/END

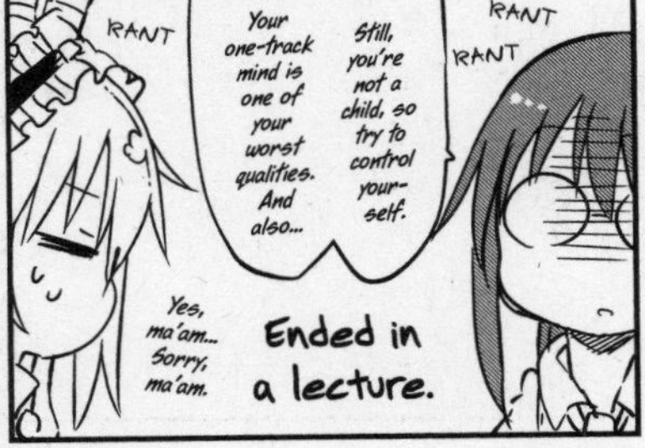
RANT
RANT
Your one-track mind is one of your worst qualities. And also...
Still, you're not a child, so try to control your-self.
RANT
Ended in a lecture.
Yes, ma'am... Sorry, ma'am.

Miss Kobayashi's Dragon Maid

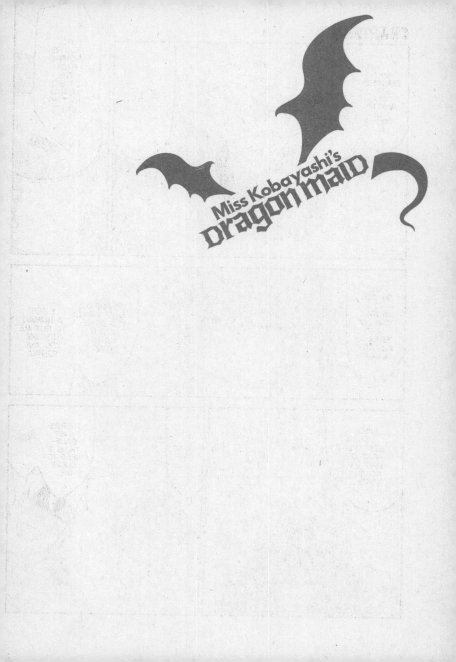

CHAPTER 27

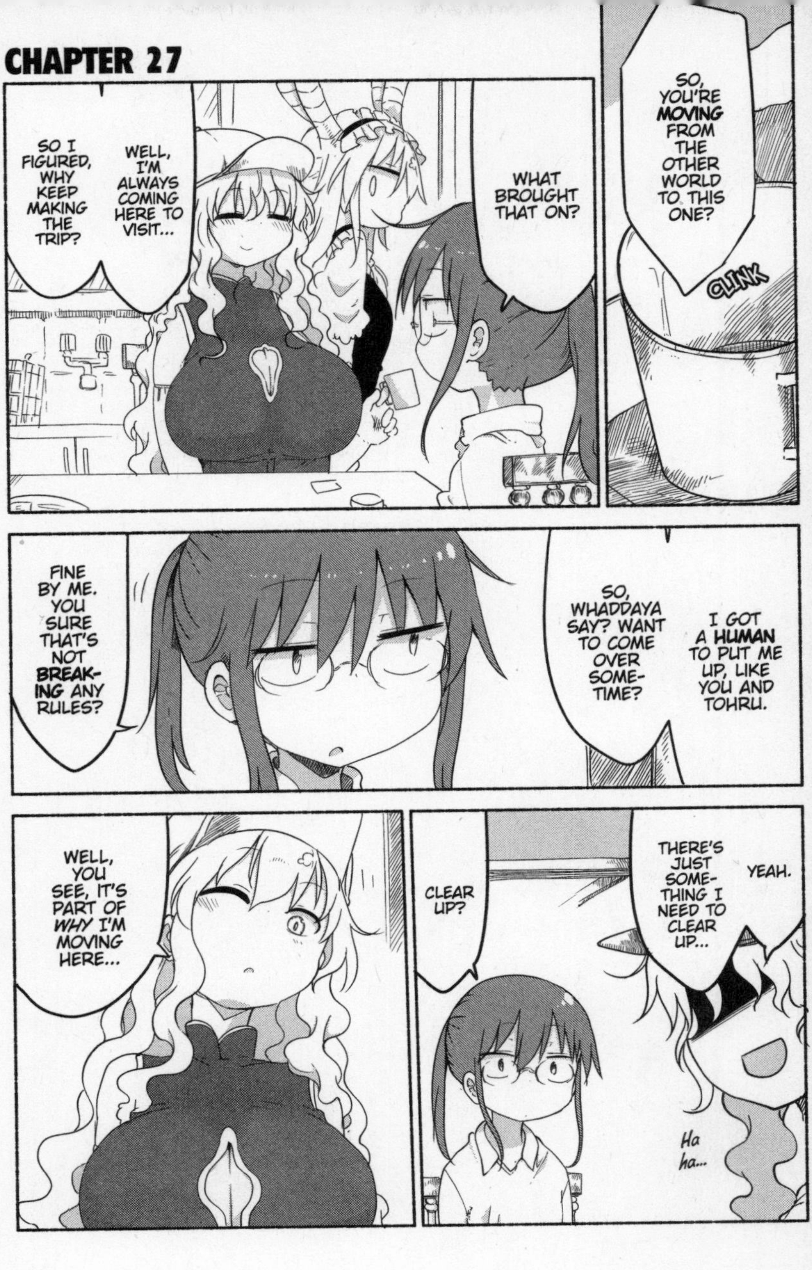
SO, YOU'RE **MOVING** FROM THE OTHER WORLD TO THIS ONE?
CLINK
WHAT BROUGHT THAT ON?
WELL, I'M ALWAYS COMING HERE TO VISIT...
SO I FIGURED, WHY KEEP MAKING THE TRIP?
I GOT A **HUMAN** TO PUT ME UP, LIKE YOU AND TOHRU.
SO, WHADDAYA SAY? WANT TO COME OVER SOME-TIME?
FINE BY ME. YOU SURE THAT'S NOT **BREAK-ING** ANY RULES?
YEAH.
THERE'S JUST SOME-THING I NEED TO CLEAR UP...
Ha ha...
CLEAR UP?
WELL, YOU SEE, IT'S PART OF *WHY* I'M MOVING HERE...

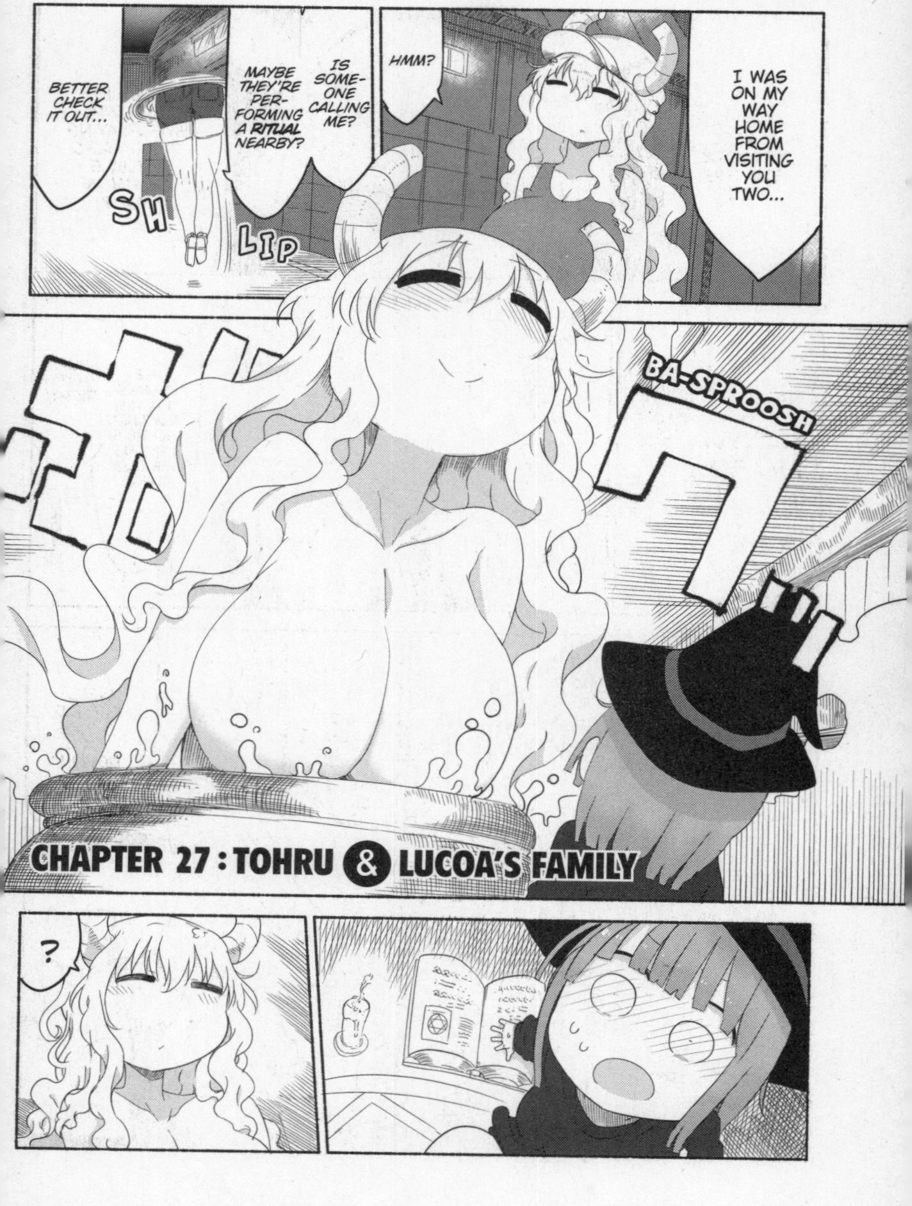
I WAS ON MY WAY HOME FROM VISITING YOU TWO...
HMM?
IS SOMEONE CALLING ME?
MAYBE THEY'RE PERFORMING A RITUAL NEARBY?
BETTER CHECK IT OUT...
SHLIP
BA-SPROOSH
CHAPTER 27 : TOHRU & LUCOA'S FAMILY
?

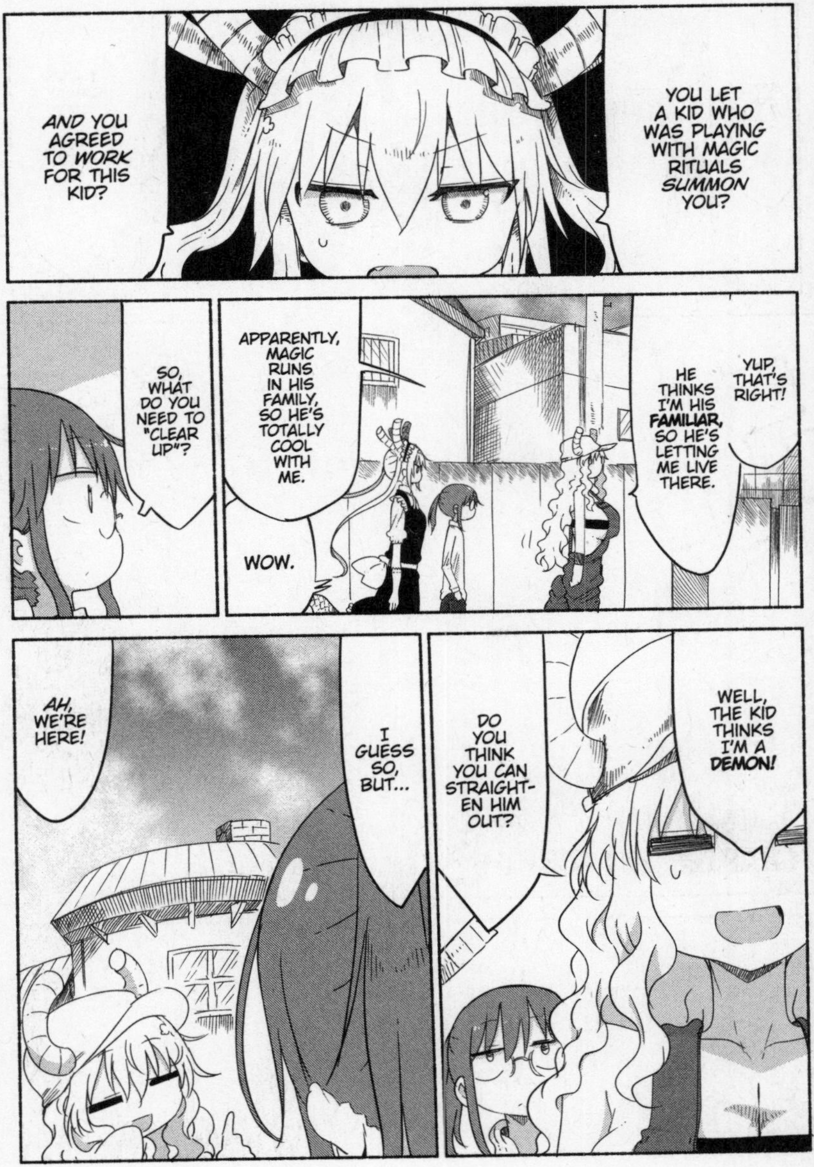
YOU LET A KID WHO WAS PLAYING WITH MAGIC RITUALS SUMMON YOU?
AND YOU AGREED TO WORK FOR THIS KID?
YUP, THAT'S RIGHT!
HE THINKS I'M HIS FAMILIAR, SO HE'S LETTING ME LIVE THERE.
APPARENTLY, MAGIC RUNS IN HIS FAMILY, SO HE'S TOTALLY COOL WITH ME.
WOW.
SO, WHAT DO YOU NEED TO "CLEAR UP"?
WELL, THE KID THINKS I'M A DEMON!
DO YOU THINK YOU CAN STRAIGHTEN HIM OUT?
I GUESS SO, BUT...
AH, WE'RE HERE!

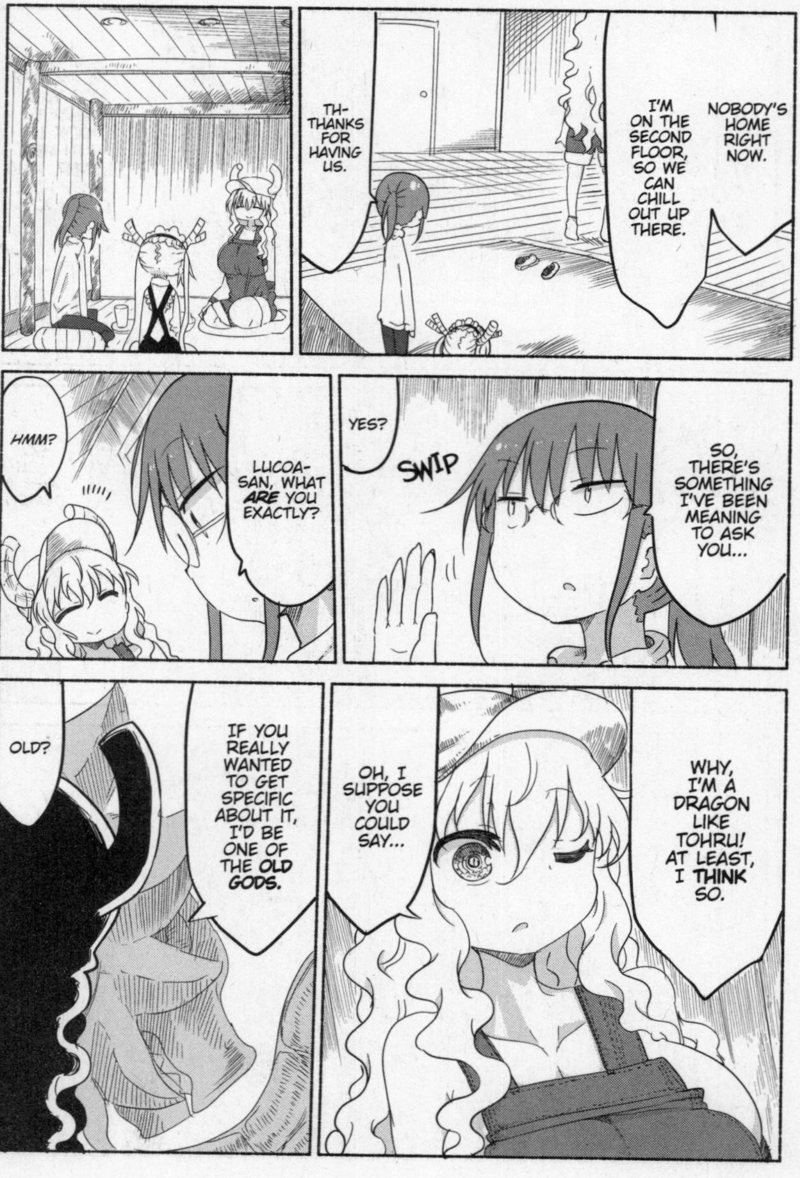
NOBODY'S HOME RIGHT NOW.
I'M ON THE SECOND FLOOR, SO WE CAN CHILL OUT UP THERE.
TH-THANKS FOR HAVING US.
SO, THERE'S SOMETHING I'VE BEEN MEANING TO ASK YOU...
SWIP
YES?
LUCOA-SAN, WHAT **ARE** YOU EXACTLY?
HMM?
WHY, I'M A DRAGON LIKE TOHRU! AT LEAST, I **THINK** SO.
OH, I SUPPOSE YOU COULD SAY...
IF YOU REALLY WANTED TO GET SPECIFIC ABOUT IT, I'D BE ONE OF THE **OLD GODS.**
OLD?

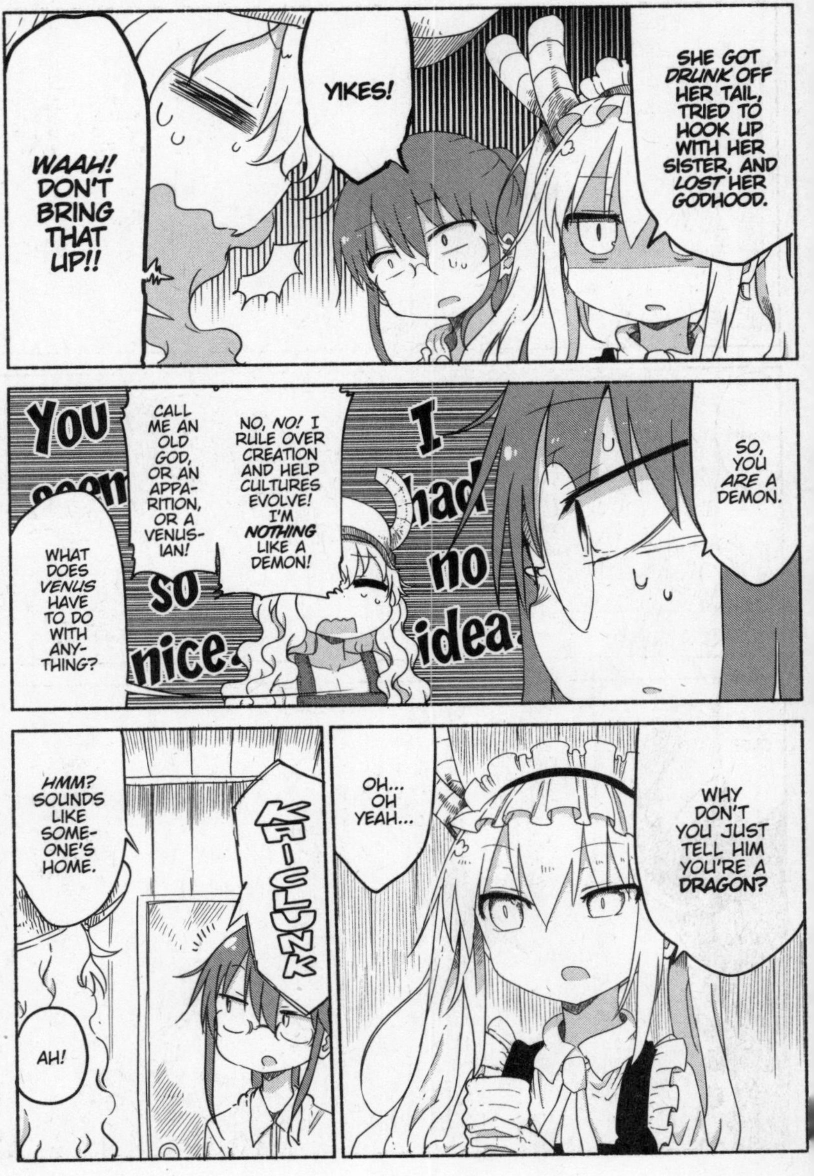
SHE GOT DRUNK OFF HER TAIL, TRIED TO HOOK UP WITH HER SISTER, AND LOST HER GODHOOD.
YIKES!
WAAH! DON'T BRING THAT UP!!
SO, YOU ARE A DEMON.
I had no idea.
NO, NO! I RULE OVER CREATION AND HELP CULTURES EVOLVE! I'M NOTHING LIKE A DEMON!
CALL ME AN OLD GOD, OR AN APPARITION, OR A VENUSIAN!
You seem so nice.
WHAT DOES VENUS HAVE TO DO WITH ANYTHING?
WHY DON'T YOU JUST TELL HIM YOU'RE A DRAGON?
OH... OH YEAH...
KA-CLUNK
HMM? SOUNDS LIKE SOMEONE'S HOME.
AH!

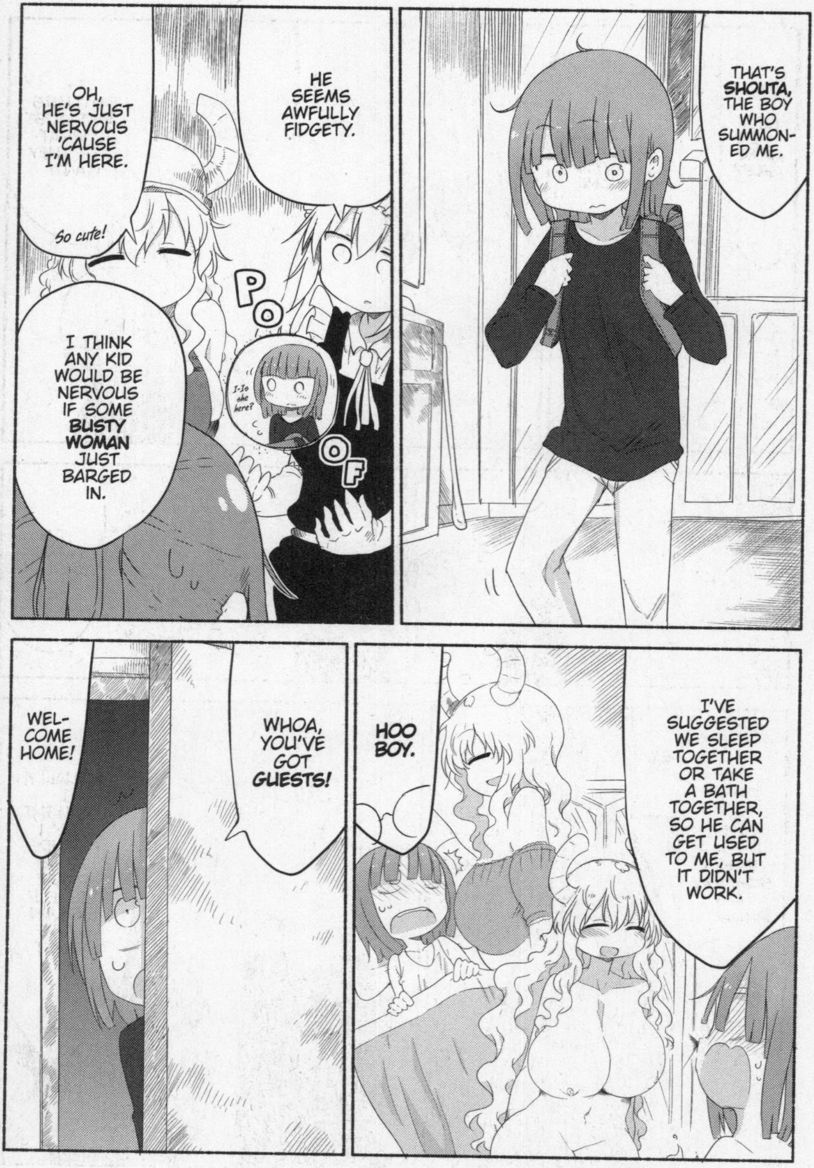
THAT'S SHOUTA, THE BOY WHO SUMMON-ED ME.
HE SEEMS AWFULLY FIDGETY.
OH, HE'S JUST NERVOUS 'CAUSE I'M HERE.
So cute!
POOF
I-Is she here?
I THINK ANY KID WOULD BE NERVOUS IF SOME BUSTY WOMAN JUST BARGED IN.
I'VE SUGGESTED WE SLEEP TOGETHER OR TAKE A BATH TOGETHER, SO HE CAN GET USED TO ME, BUT IT DIDN'T WORK.
HOO BOY.
WHOA, YOU'VE GOT GUESTS!
WEL-COME HOME!

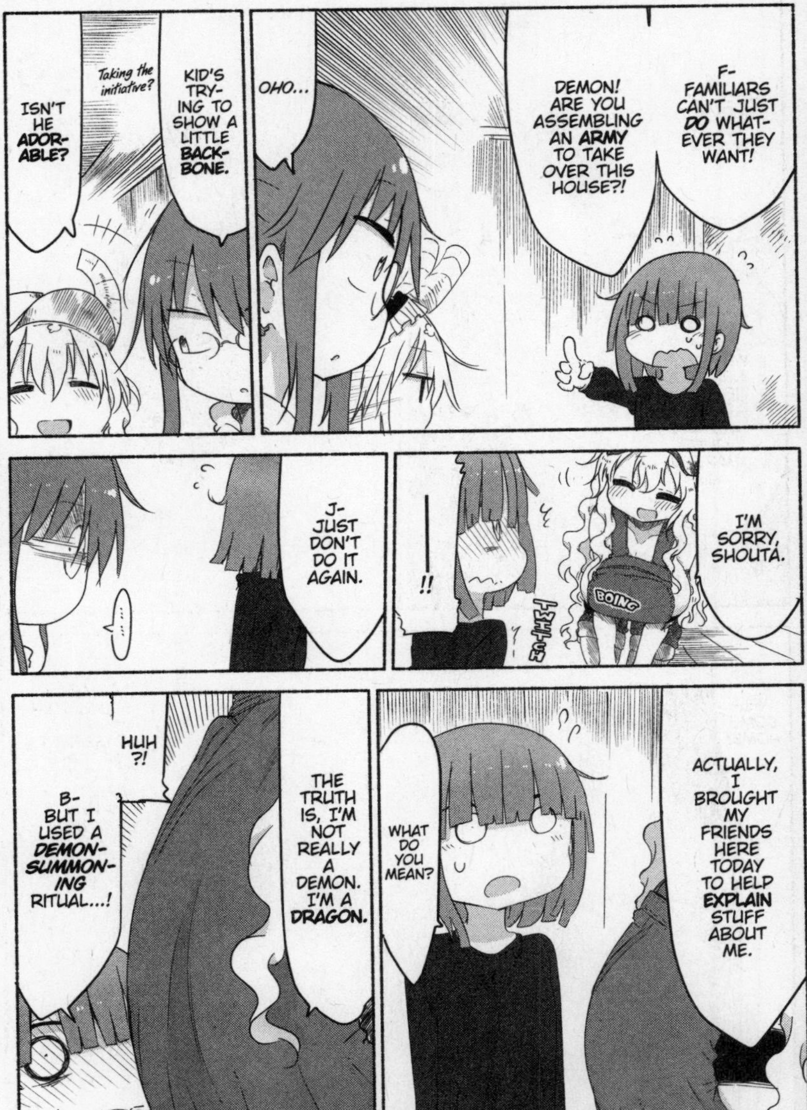
F-FAMILIARS CAN'T JUST DO WHATEVER THEY WANT!
DEMON! ARE YOU ASSEMBLING AN ARMY TO TAKE OVER THIS HOUSE?!
OHO...
KID'S TRYING TO SHOW A LITTLE BACKBONE.
Taking the initiative?
ISN'T HE ADORABLE?
I'M SORRY, SHOUTA.
BOING
TWITCH
!!
J-JUST DON'T DO IT AGAIN.
...
ACTUALLY, I BROUGHT MY FRIENDS HERE TODAY TO HELP EXPLAIN STUFF ABOUT ME.
WHAT DO YOU MEAN?
THE TRUTH IS, I'M NOT REALLY A DEMON. I'M A DRAGON.
HUH?!
B-BUT I USED A DEMON-SUMMONING RITUAL...!

SEE, AN EVIL DEMON COULD BE REALLY DANGEROUS, SO I FIGURED I'D PREEMPT ANY WHO TRIED TO SHOW UP.
B-BUT THERE'S NO WAY MY MAGIC IS STRONG ENOUGH TO SUMMON A DRAGON...
HEY!
YOU'RE MAKING THIS UP TO SCARE ME, AREN'T YOU?! YOU CAN'T FOOL ME, DEMON!!
DU-DUUUN
SEE, THIS IS HOW IT ALWAYS ENDS UP...
GOT-CHA.
SO, LUCOA TELLS ME THERE'S MAGIC IN YOUR BLOODLINE, SHOUTA. WHY WERE YOU SUMMONING A DEMON?
I-I THOUGHT IT'D PROVE THAT I'M AN ADULT...
WE SORCERERS ARE CURRENTLY LYING LOW IN THIS WORLD, BUT EVENTUALLY WE'LL HAVE TO GO BACK TO OUR WORLD.
WE NEED TO BE ABLE TO RETURN IMMEDIATELY WHEN THAT TIME COMES, SO WE HAVE TO KEEP OUR POWERS STRONG.
THAT'S WHY I MUST...

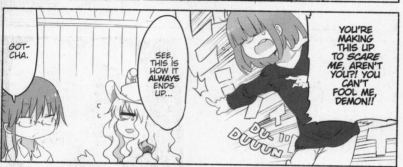

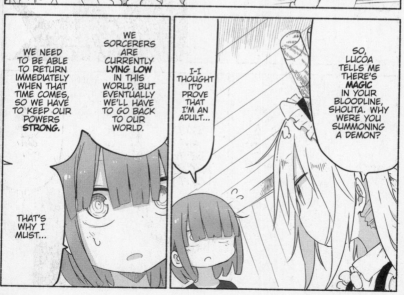

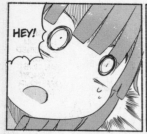

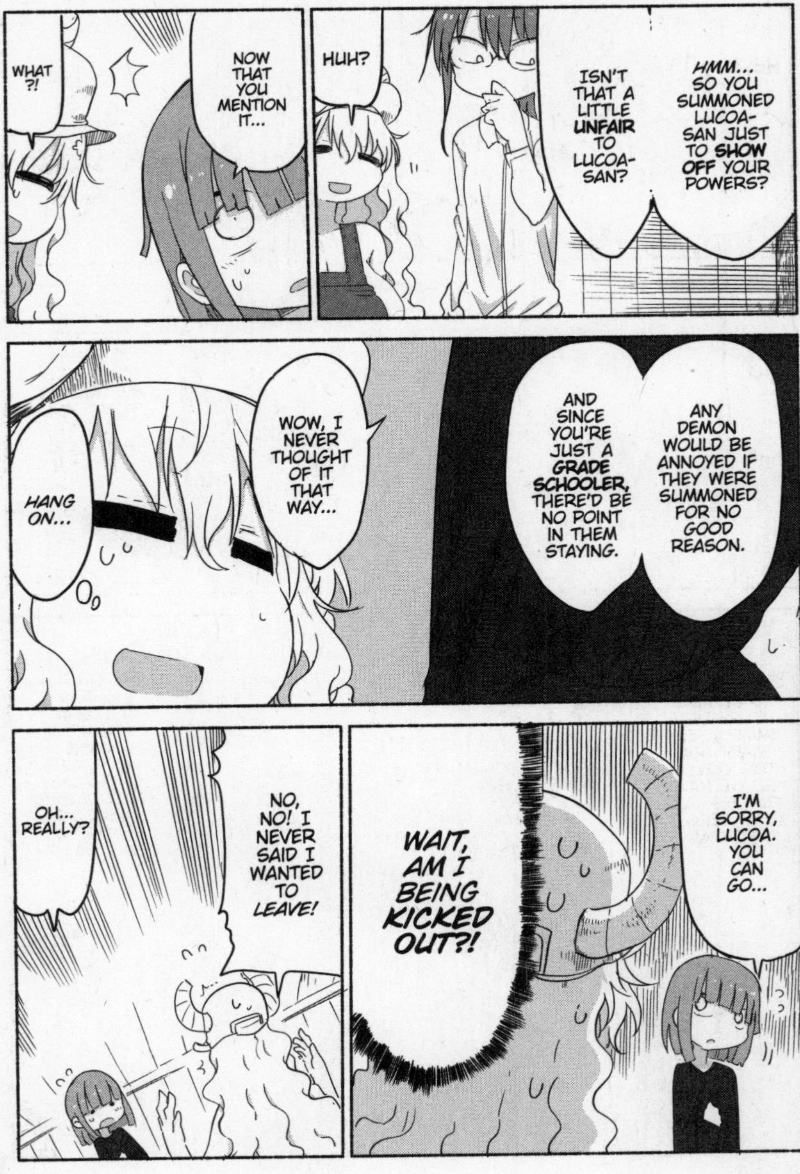
HMM... SO YOU SUMMONED LUCOA-SAN JUST TO SHOW OFF YOUR POWERS?
ISN'T THAT A LITTLE UNFAIR TO LUCOA-SAN?
HUH?
NOW THAT YOU MENTION IT...
WHAT ?!
ANY DEMON WOULD BE ANNOYED IF THEY WERE SUMMONED FOR NO GOOD REASON.
AND SINCE YOU'RE JUST A GRADE SCHOOLER, THERE'D BE NO POINT IN THEM STAYING.
WOW, I NEVER THOUGHT OF IT THAT WAY...
HANG ON...
I'M SORRY, LUCOA. YOU CAN GO...
WAIT, AM I BEING KICKED OUT?!
NO, NO! I NEVER SAID I WANTED TO LEAVE!
OH... REALLY?

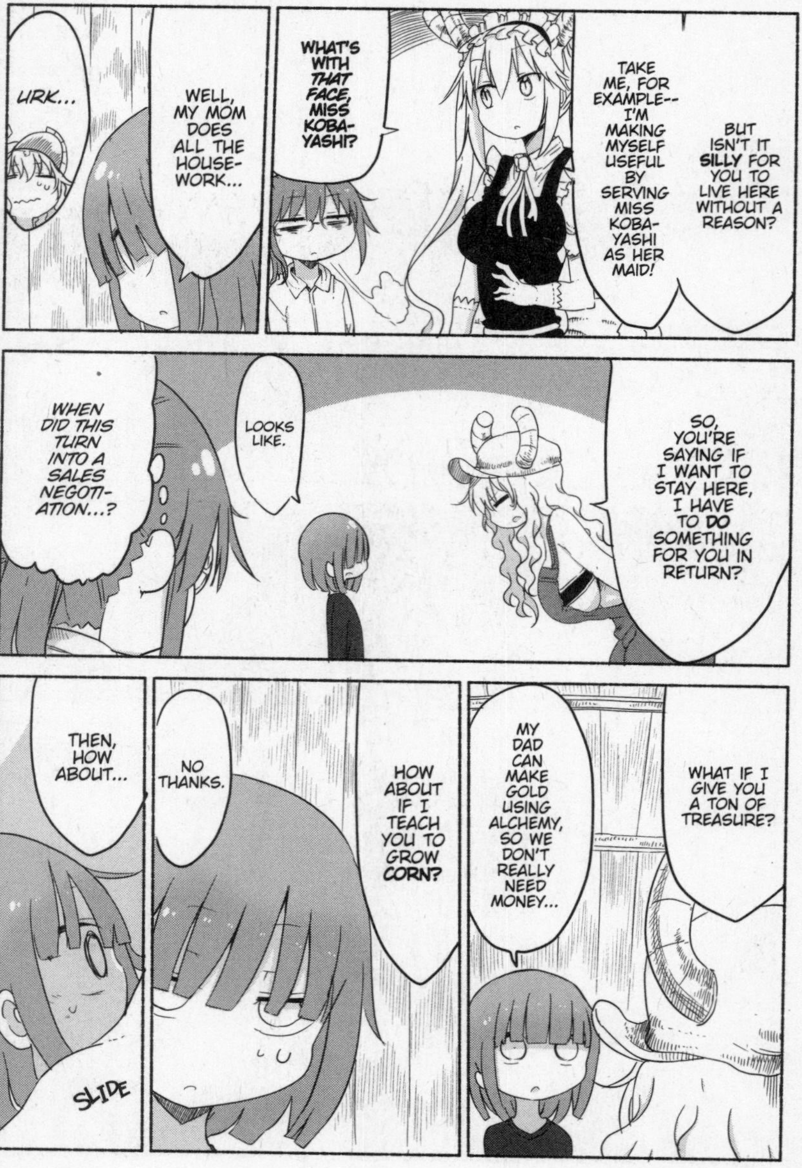
BUT ISN'T IT SILLY FOR YOU TO LIVE HERE WITHOUT A REASON?
TAKE ME, FOR EXAMPLE-- I'M MAKING MYSELF USEFUL BY SERVING MISS KOBAYASHI AS HER MAID!
WHAT'S WITH THAT FACE, MISS KOBAYASHI?
WELL, MY MOM DOES ALL THE HOUSEWORK...
URK...
SO, YOU'RE SAYING IF I WANT TO STAY HERE, I HAVE TO DO SOMETHING FOR YOU IN RETURN?
LOOKS LIKE.
WHEN DID THIS TURN INTO A SALES NEGOTIATION...?
WHAT IF I GIVE YOU A TON OF TREASURE?
MY DAD CAN MAKE GOLD USING ALCHEMY, SO WE DON'T REALLY NEED MONEY...
HOW ABOUT IF I TEACH YOU TO GROW CORN?
NO THANKS.
THEN, HOW ABOUT...
SLIDE

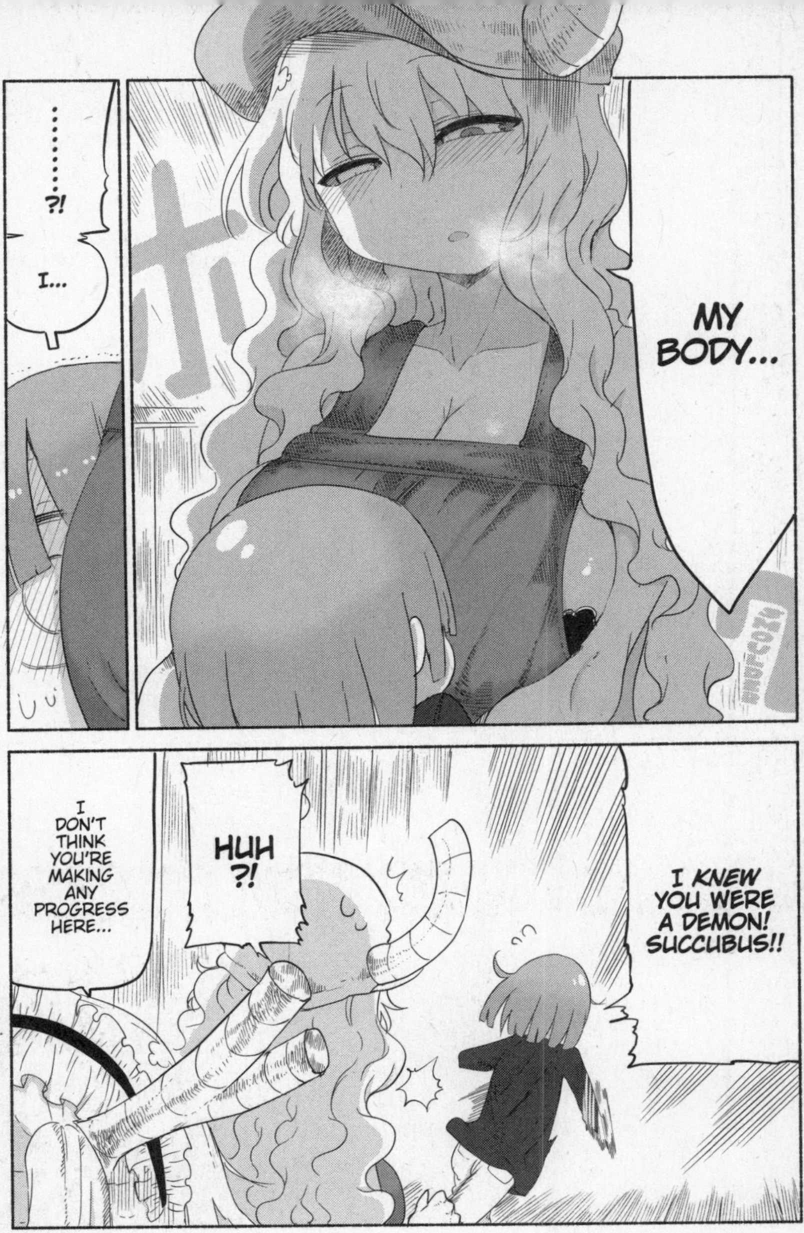
MY BODY...
......?!
I...
I KNEW YOU WERE A DEMON! SUCCUBUS!!
HUH ?!
I DON'T THINK YOU'RE MAKING ANY PROGRESS HERE...

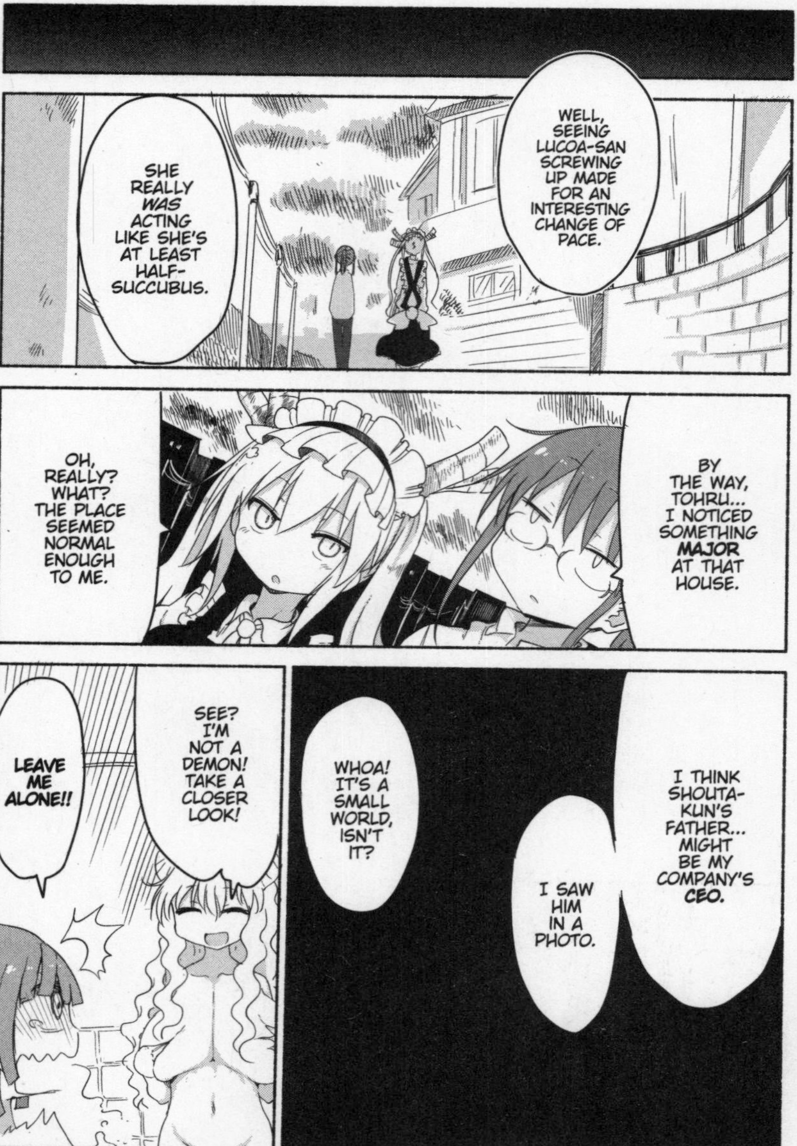
WELL, SEEING LUCOA-SAN SCREWING UP MADE FOR AN INTERESTING CHANGE OF PACE.
SHE REALLY WAS ACTING LIKE SHE'S AT LEAST HALF-SUCCUBUS.
BY THE WAY, TOHRU... I NOTICED SOMETHING MAJOR AT THAT HOUSE.
OH, REALLY? WHAT? THE PLACE SEEMED NORMAL ENOUGH TO ME.
I THINK SHOUTA-KUN'S FATHER... MIGHT BE MY COMPANY'S CEO.
I SAW HIM IN A PHOTO.
WHOA! IT'S A SMALL WORLD, ISN'T IT?
SEE? I'M NOT A DEMON! TAKE A CLOSER LOOK!
LEAVE ME ALONE!!

CHAPTER 27/END

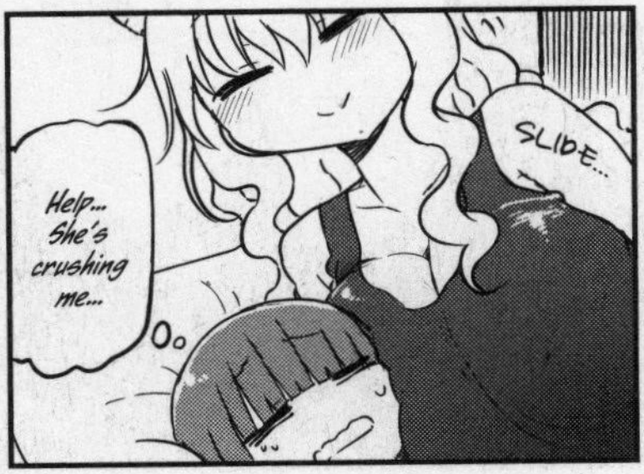
SLIDE...
Help... She's crushing me...

Miss Kobayashi's Dragon Maid

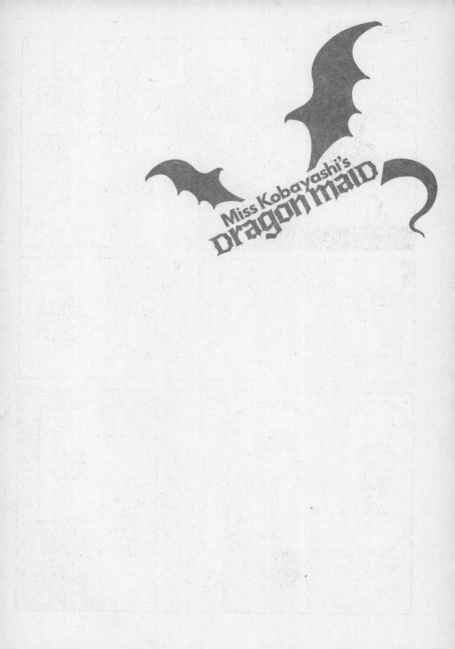

CHAPTER 28

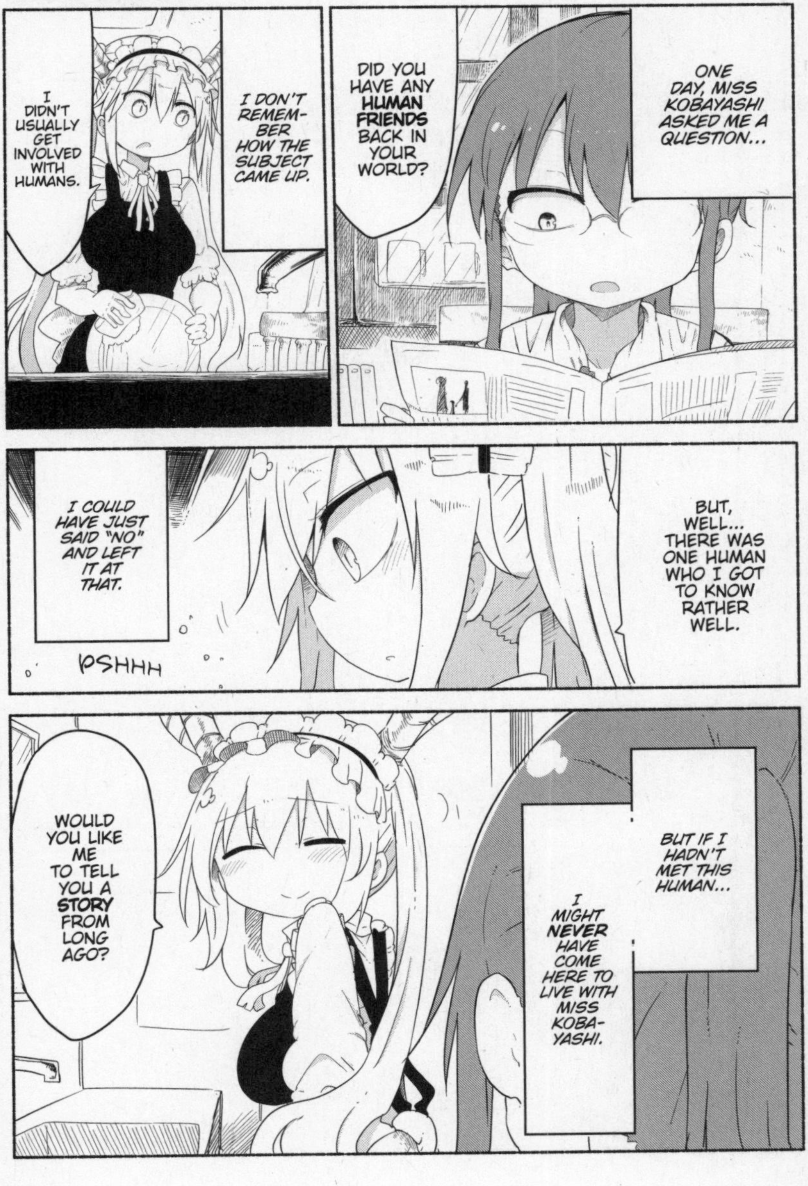
ONE DAY, MISS KOBAYASHI ASKED ME A QUESTION…
DID YOU HAVE ANY HUMAN FRIENDS BACK IN YOUR WORLD?
I DON'T REMEMBER HOW THE SUBJECT CAME UP.
I DIDN'T USUALLY GET INVOLVED WITH HUMANS.
BUT, WELL… THERE WAS ONE HUMAN WHO I GOT TO KNOW RATHER WELL.
I COULD HAVE JUST SAID "NO" AND LEFT IT AT THAT.
PSHHH
BUT IF I HADN'T MET THIS HUMAN…
I MIGHT NEVER HAVE COME HERE TO LIVE WITH MISS KOBAYASHI.
WOULD YOU LIKE ME TO TELL YOU A STORY FROM LONG AGO?

I FIRST MET THIS HUMAN IN THE **RUINS** OF A VILLAGE.

CHAPTER 28: TOHRU & TALES OF THE PAST 1

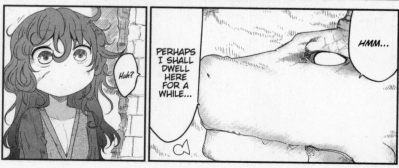

Huh?

PERHAPS I SHALL DWELL HERE FOR A WHILE...

HMM...

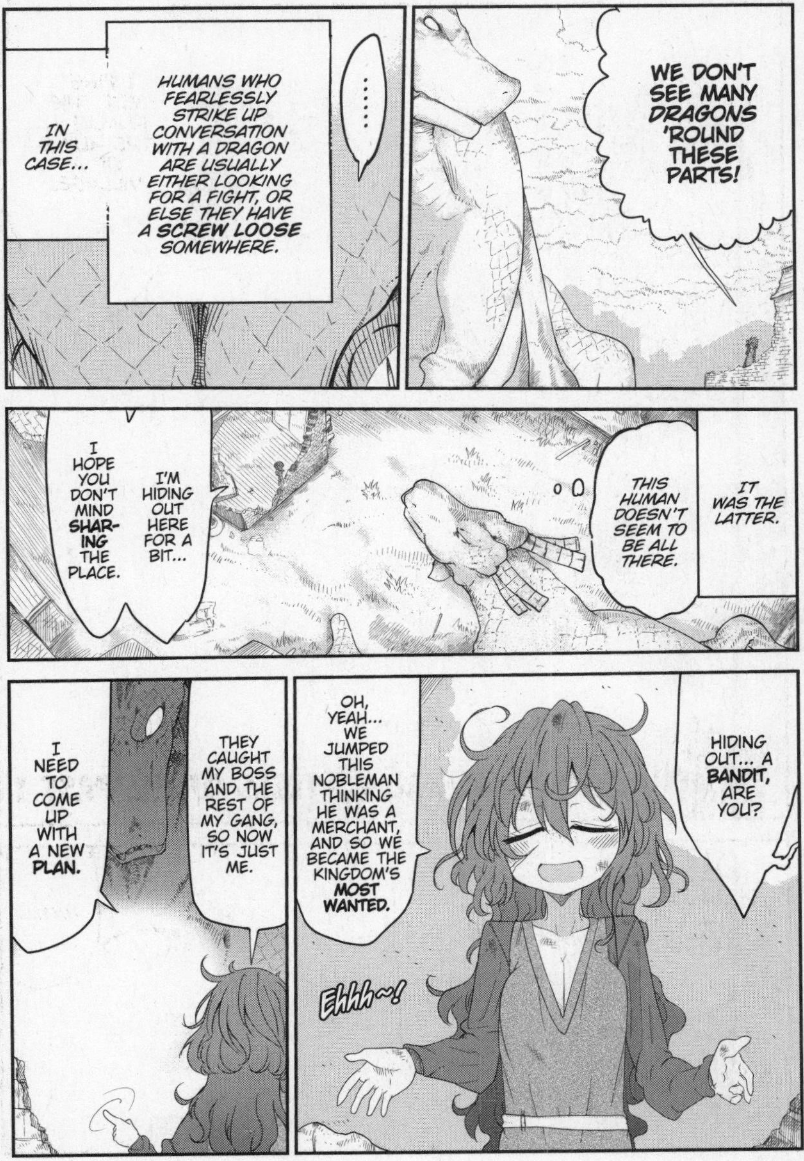
WE DON'T SEE MANY DRAGONS 'ROUND THESE PARTS!
......
HUMANS WHO FEARLESSLY STRIKE UP CONVERSATION WITH A DRAGON ARE USUALLY EITHER LOOKING FOR A FIGHT, OR ELSE THEY HAVE A SCREW LOOSE SOMEWHERE.
IN THIS CASE...
IT WAS THE LATTER.
THIS HUMAN DOESN'T SEEM TO BE ALL THERE.
I'M HIDING OUT HERE FOR A BIT...
I HOPE YOU DON'T MIND SHARING THE PLACE.
HIDING OUT... A BANDIT, ARE YOU?
OH, YEAH... WE JUMPED THIS NOBLEMAN THINKING HE WAS A MERCHANT, AND SO WE BECAME THE KINGDOM'S MOST WANTED.
Ehhh~!
THEY CAUGHT MY BOSS AND THE REST OF MY GANG, SO NOW IT'S JUST ME.
I NEED TO COME UP WITH A NEW PLAN.

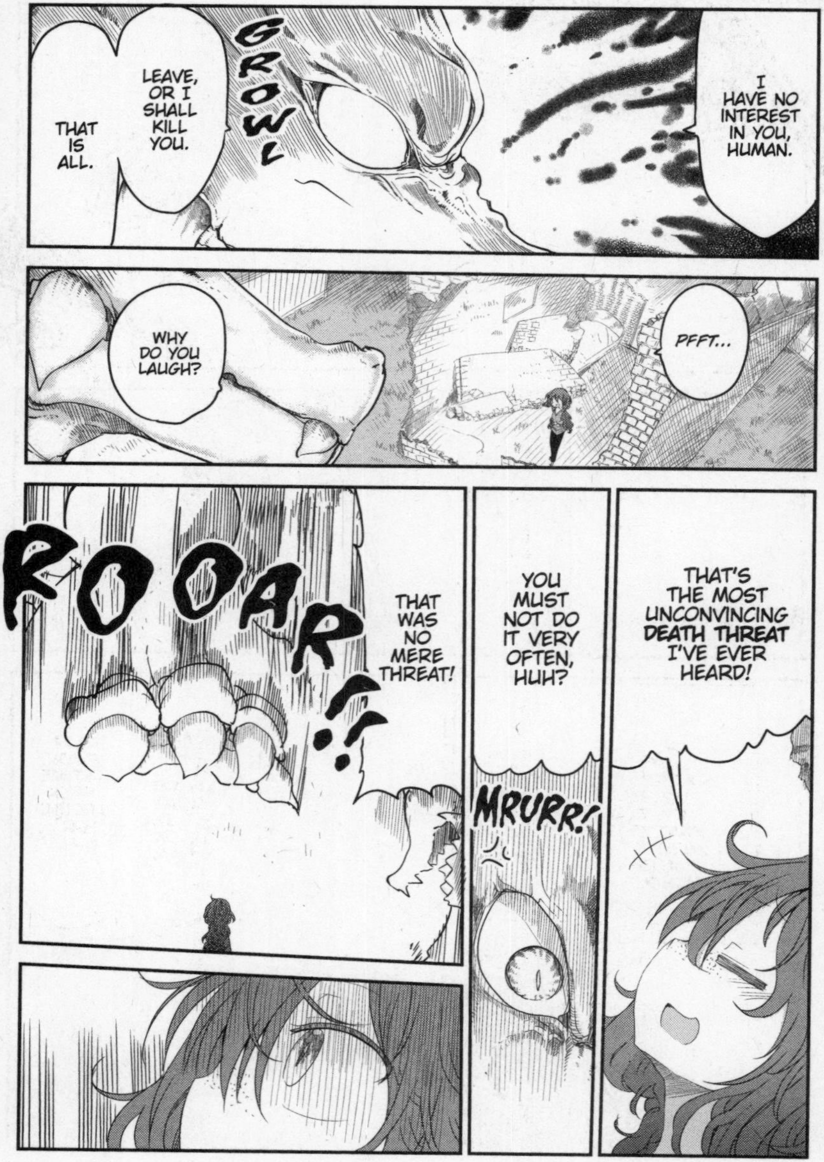
I HAVE NO INTEREST IN YOU, HUMAN.
GROWL
LEAVE, OR I SHALL KILL YOU.
THAT IS ALL.
PFFT...
WHY DO YOU LAUGH?
THAT'S THE MOST UNCONVINCING **DEATH THREAT** I'VE EVER HEARD!
YOU MUST NOT DO IT VERY OFTEN, HUH?
MRURR!
THAT WAS NO MERE THREAT!
ROOAR!!

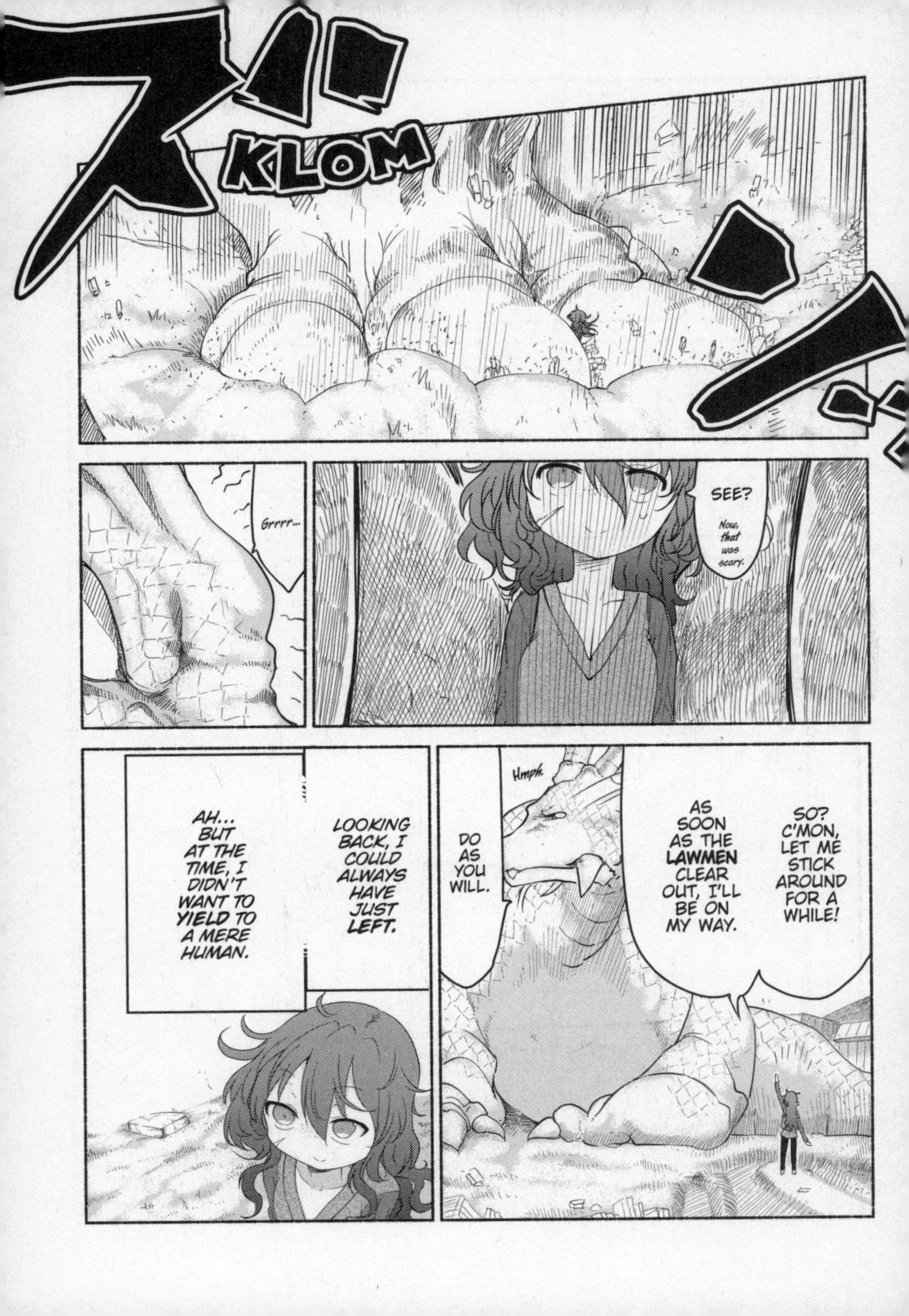
KLOM
SEE?
Now, that was scary.
Grrrr...
SO? C'MON, LET ME STICK AROUND FOR A WHILE!
AS SOON AS THE LAWMEN CLEAR OUT, I'LL BE ON MY WAY.
Hmph.
DO AS YOU WILL.
LOOKING BACK, I COULD ALWAYS HAVE JUST LEFT.
AH... BUT AT THE TIME, I DIDN'T WANT TO YIELD TO A MERE HUMAN.

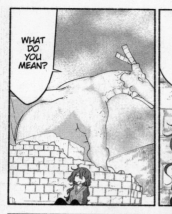

Hey...
Hey, you!
HOW DOES IT FEEL?
BEING A DRAGON.
WHAT DO YOU MEAN?
FLYING THROUGH THE SKY... BEING STRONG ENOUGH TO BEAT UP ANYBODY...
I WANNA KNOW... WHAT'S IT LIKE TO BE TRULY FREE IN THIS WORLD?
......
Hmph.
HEY, ARE YOU IGNORING ME?!
THIS HUMAN ENVIES DRAGONS FOR THE THINGS WE SEE AS NORMAL...
SHE HAS YET TO SEE THAT SHE IS FREE, TOO.

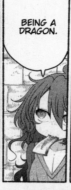

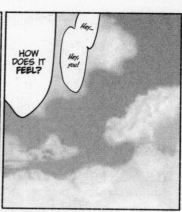

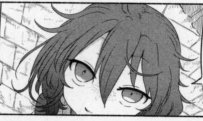

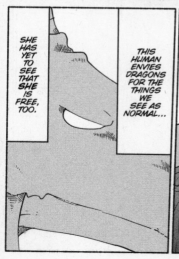

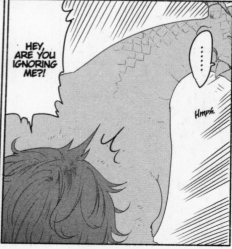

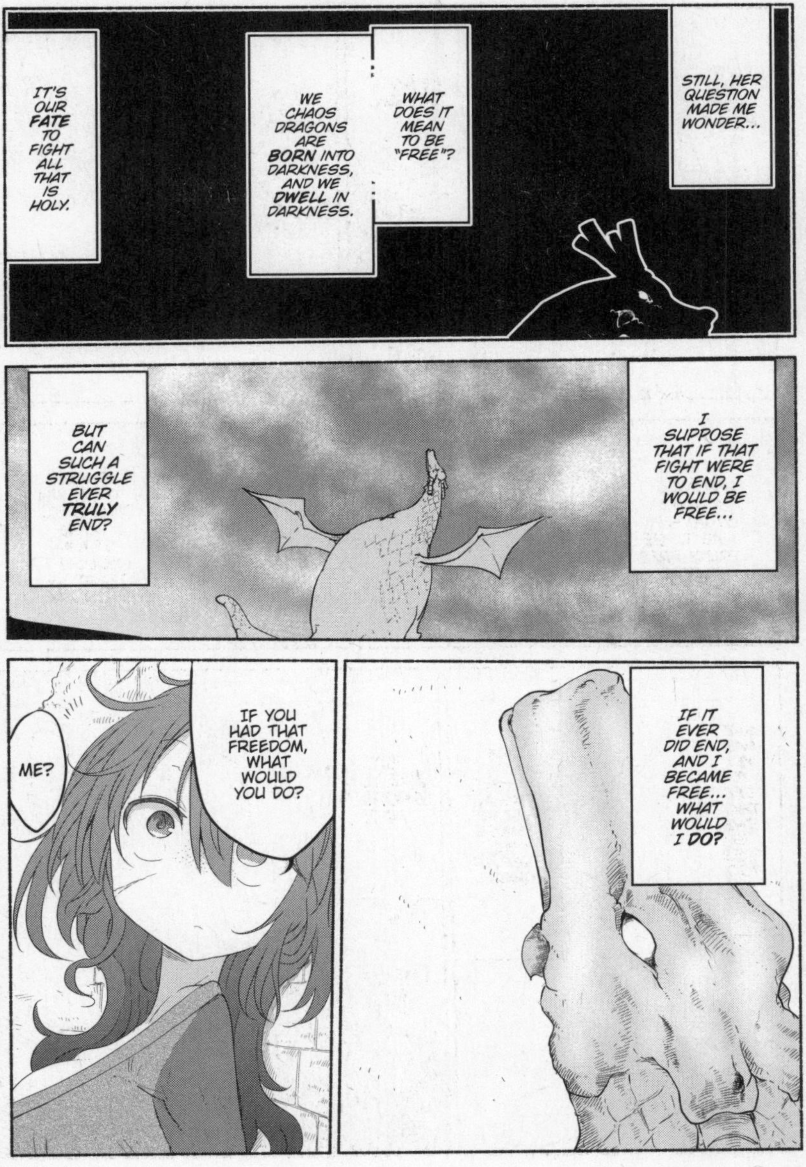
STILL, HER QUESTION MADE ME WONDER...
WHAT DOES IT MEAN TO BE "FREE"?
WE CHAOS DRAGONS ARE BORN INTO DARKNESS, AND WE DWELL IN DARKNESS.
IT'S OUR FATE TO FIGHT ALL THAT IS HOLY.
I SUPPOSE THAT IF THAT FIGHT WERE TO END, I WOULD BE FREE...
BUT CAN SUCH A STRUGGLE EVER TRULY END?
IF IT EVER DID END, AND I BECAME FREE... WHAT WOULD I DO?
IF YOU HAD THAT FREEDOM, WHAT WOULD YOU DO?
ME?

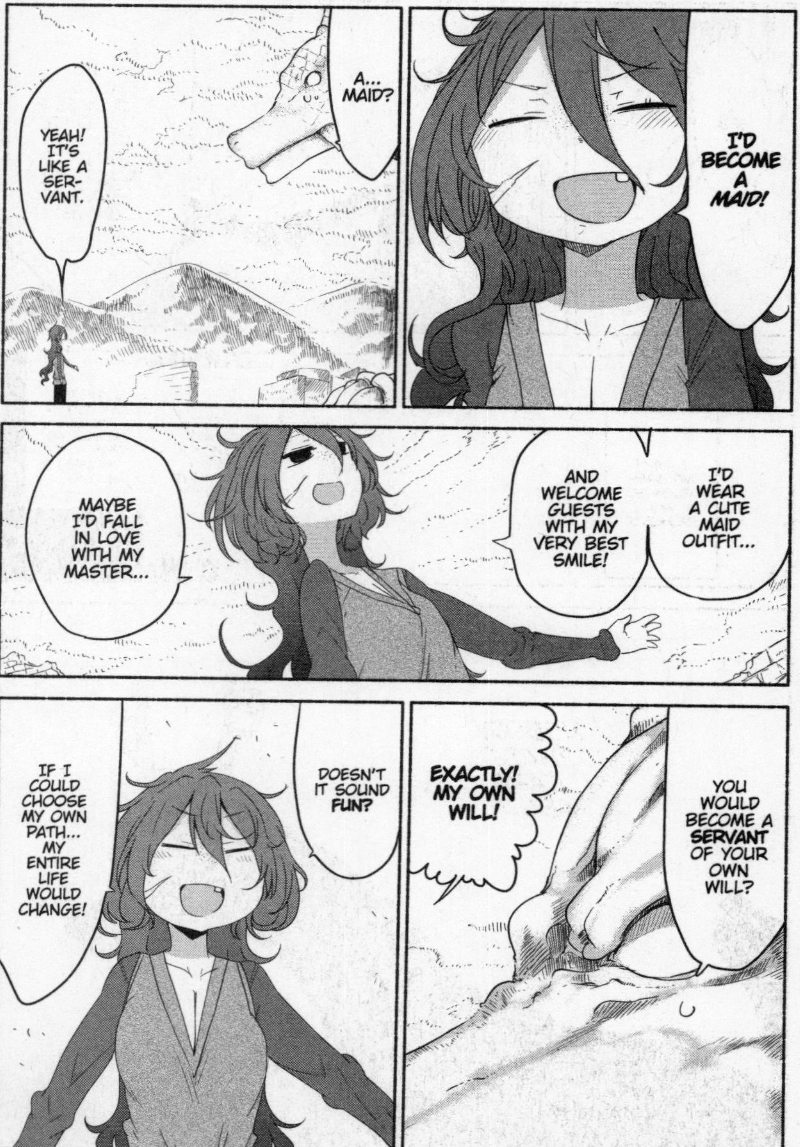
I'D BECOME A MAID!
A... MAID?
YEAH! IT'S LIKE A SER-VANT.
I'D WEAR A CUTE MAID OUTFIT...
AND WELCOME GUESTS WITH MY VERY BEST SMILE!
MAYBE I'D FALL IN LOVE WITH MY MASTER...
YOU WOULD BECOME A SERVANT OF YOUR OWN WILL?
EXACTLY! MY OWN WILL!
DOESN'T IT SOUND FUN?
IF I COULD CHOOSE MY OWN PATH... MY ENTIRE LIFE WOULD CHANGE!

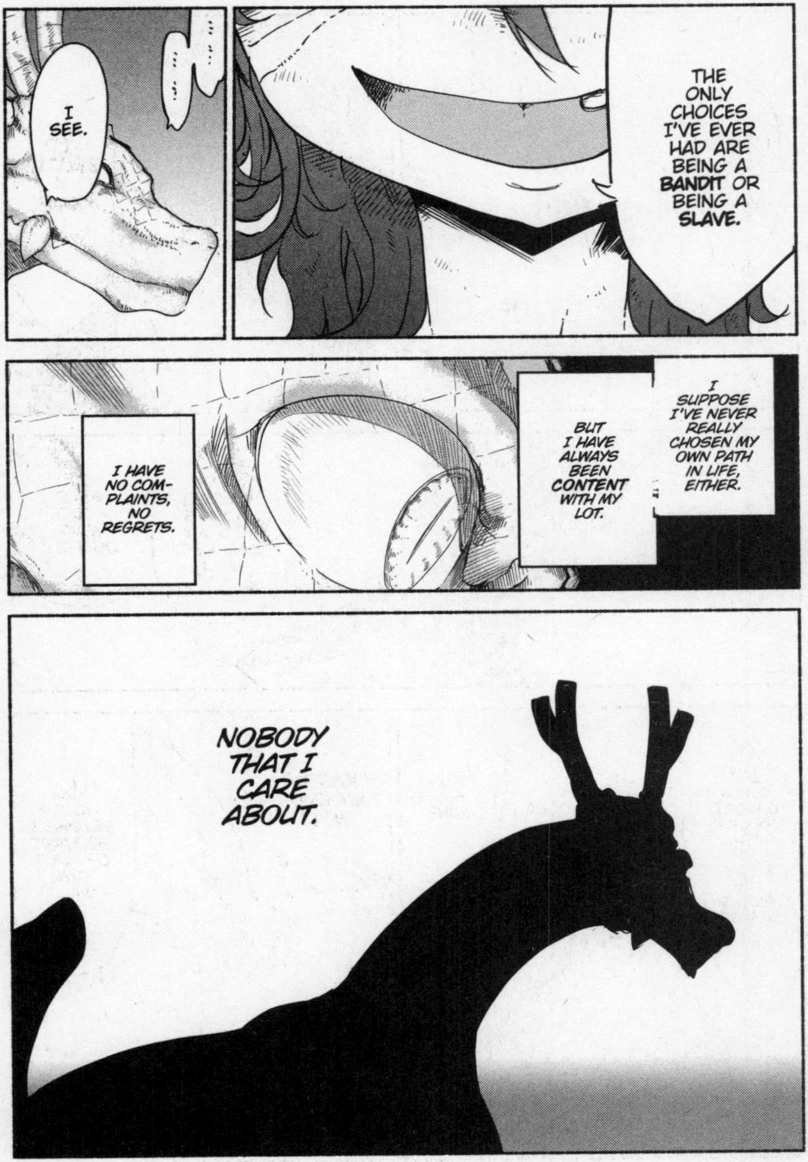
THE ONLY CHOICES I'VE EVER HAD ARE BEING A BANDIT OR BEING A SLAVE.
...
I SEE.
I SUPPOSE I'VE NEVER REALLY CHOSEN MY OWN PATH IN LIFE, EITHER.
BUT I HAVE ALWAYS BEEN CONTENT WITH MY LOT.
I HAVE NO COM-PLAINTS, NO REGRETS.
NOBODY THAT I CARE ABOUT.

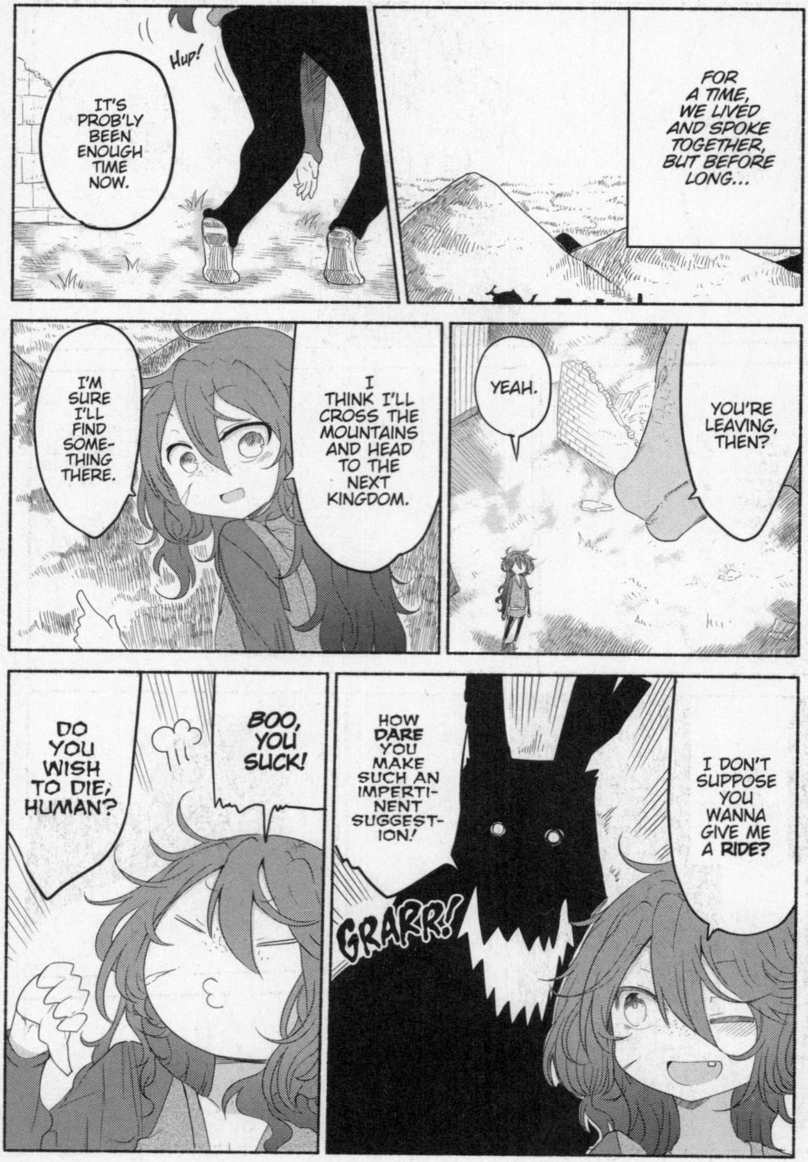
FOR A TIME, WE LIVED AND SPOKE TOGETHER, BUT BEFORE LONG...
Hup!
IT'S PROB'LY BEEN ENOUGH TIME NOW.
YOU'RE LEAVING, THEN?
YEAH.
I THINK I'LL CROSS THE MOUNTAINS AND HEAD TO THE NEXT KINGDOM.
I'M SURE I'LL FIND SOME-THING THERE.
I DON'T SUPPOSE YOU WANNA GIVE ME A RIDE?
HOW DARE YOU MAKE SUCH AN IMPERTI-NENT SUGGEST-ION!
GRARR!
BOO, YOU SUCK!
DO YOU WISH TO DIE, HUMAN?

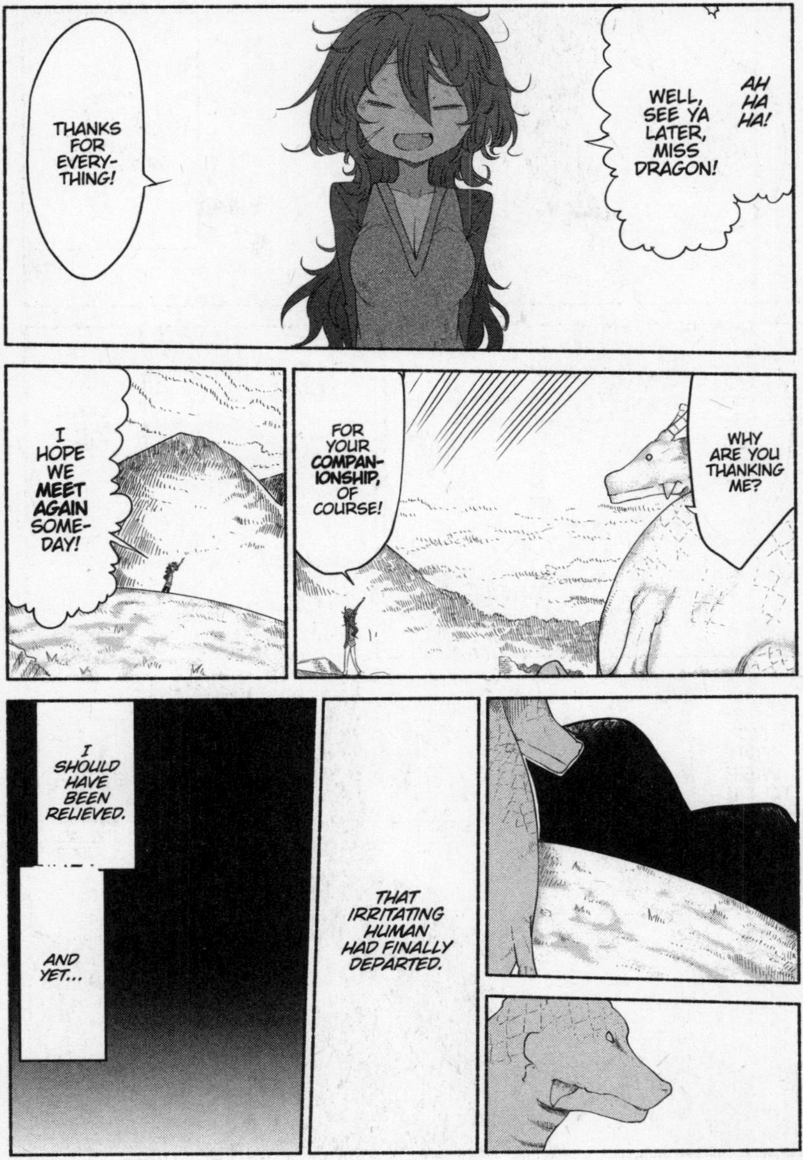
AH HA HA!
WELL, SEE YA LATER, MISS DRAGON!
THANKS FOR EVERYTHING!
WHY ARE YOU THANKING ME?
FOR YOUR COMPANIONSHIP, OF COURSE!
I HOPE WE MEET AGAIN SOMEDAY!
THAT IRRITATING HUMAN HAD FINALLY DEPARTED.
I SHOULD HAVE BEEN RELIEVED.
AND YET...

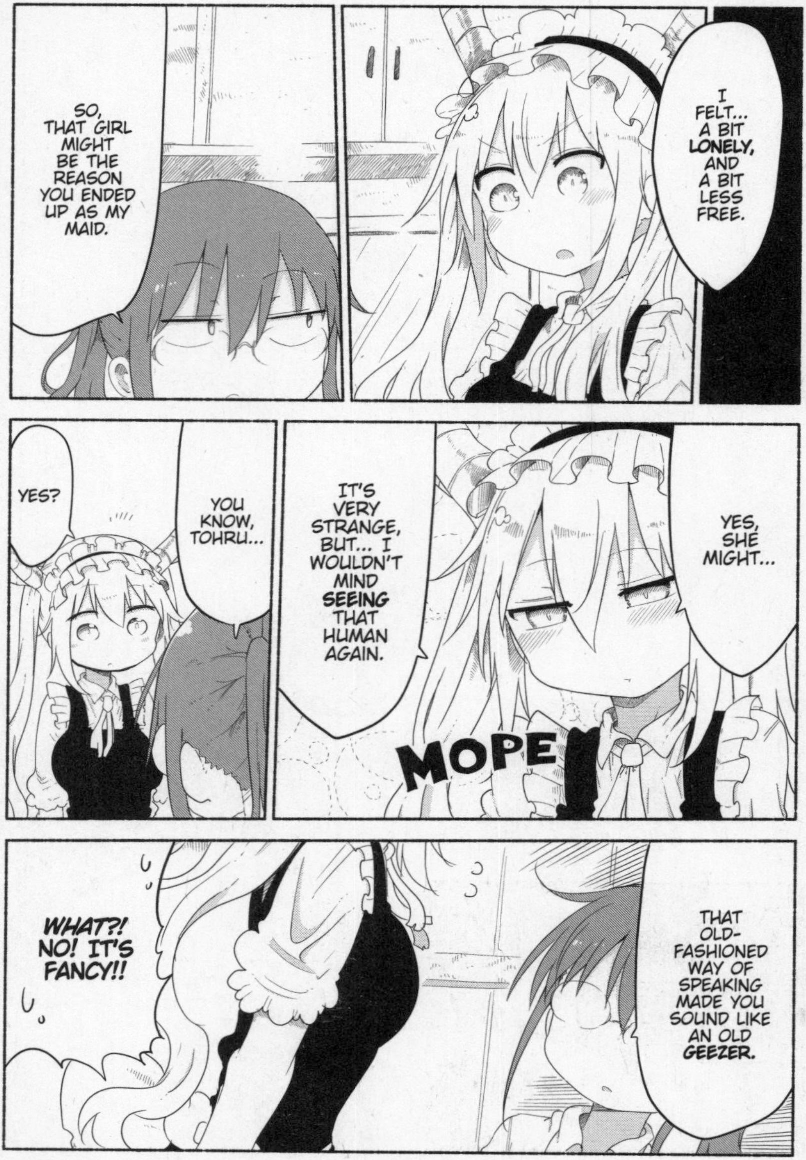
I FELT... A BIT LONELY, AND A BIT LESS FREE.
SO, THAT GIRL MIGHT BE THE REASON YOU ENDED UP AS MY MAID.
YES, SHE MIGHT...
IT'S VERY STRANGE, BUT... I WOULDN'T MIND SEEING THAT HUMAN AGAIN.
MOPE
YOU KNOW, TOHRU...
YES?
THAT OLD-FASHIONED WAY OF SPEAKING MADE YOU SOUND LIKE AN OLD GEEZER.
WHAT?! NO! IT'S FANCY!!

CHAPTER 28/END

Miss Kobayashi's Dragon Maid

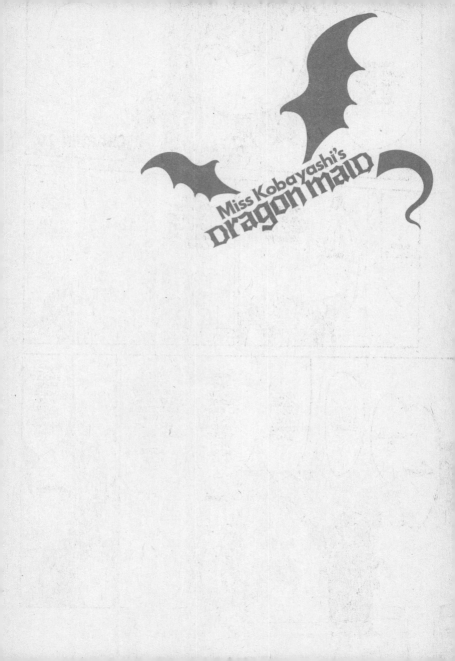

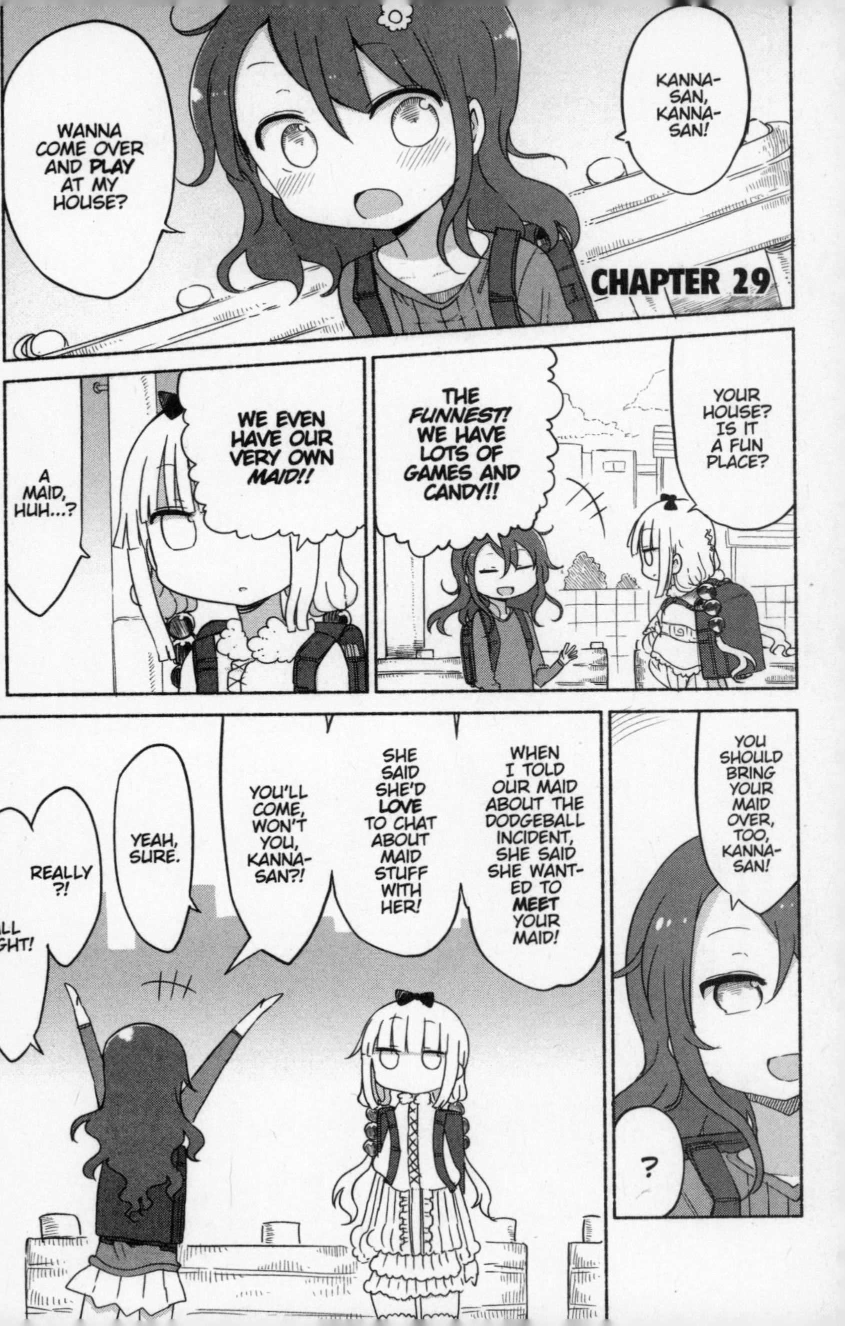
KANNA-SAN, KANNA-SAN!
WANNA COME OVER AND PLAY AT MY HOUSE?
CHAPTER 29
YOUR HOUSE? IS IT A FUN PLACE?
THE FUNNEST! WE HAVE LOTS OF GAMES AND CANDY!!
WE EVEN HAVE OUR VERY OWN MAID!!
A MAID, HUH...?
YOU SHOULD BRING YOUR MAID OVER, TOO, KANNA-SAN!
?
WHEN I TOLD OUR MAID ABOUT THE DODGEBALL INCIDENT, SHE SAID SHE WANTED TO MEET YOUR MAID!
SHE SAID SHE'D LOVE TO CHAT ABOUT MAID STUFF WITH HER!
YOU'LL COME, WON'T YOU, KANNA-SAN?!
YEAH, SURE.
REALLY?!
ALL RIGHT!

CHAPTER 29 : TOHRU & SAIKAWA-SAN

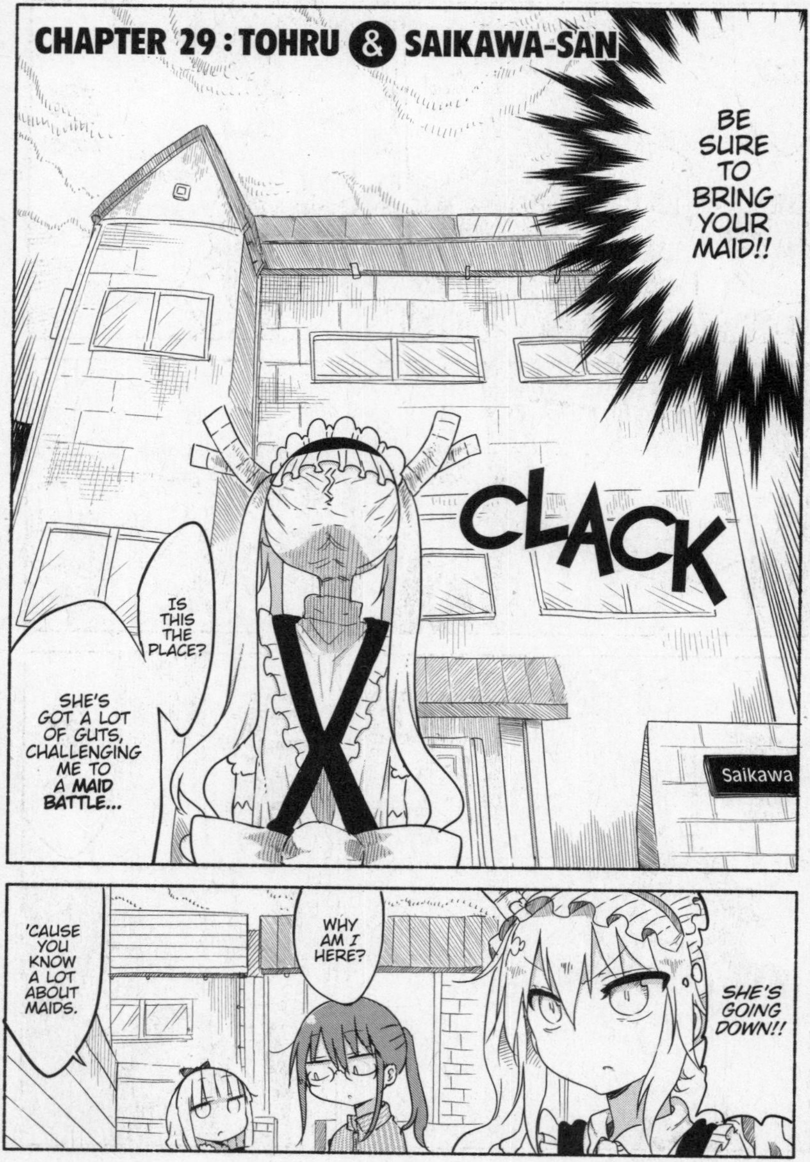
BE SURE TO BRING YOUR MAID!!
CLACK
Saikawa
IS THIS THE PLACE?
SHE'S GOT A LOT OF GUTS, CHALLENGING ME TO A MAID BATTLE...
SHE'S GOING DOWN!!
WHY AM I HERE?
'CAUSE YOU KNOW A LOT ABOUT MAIDS.

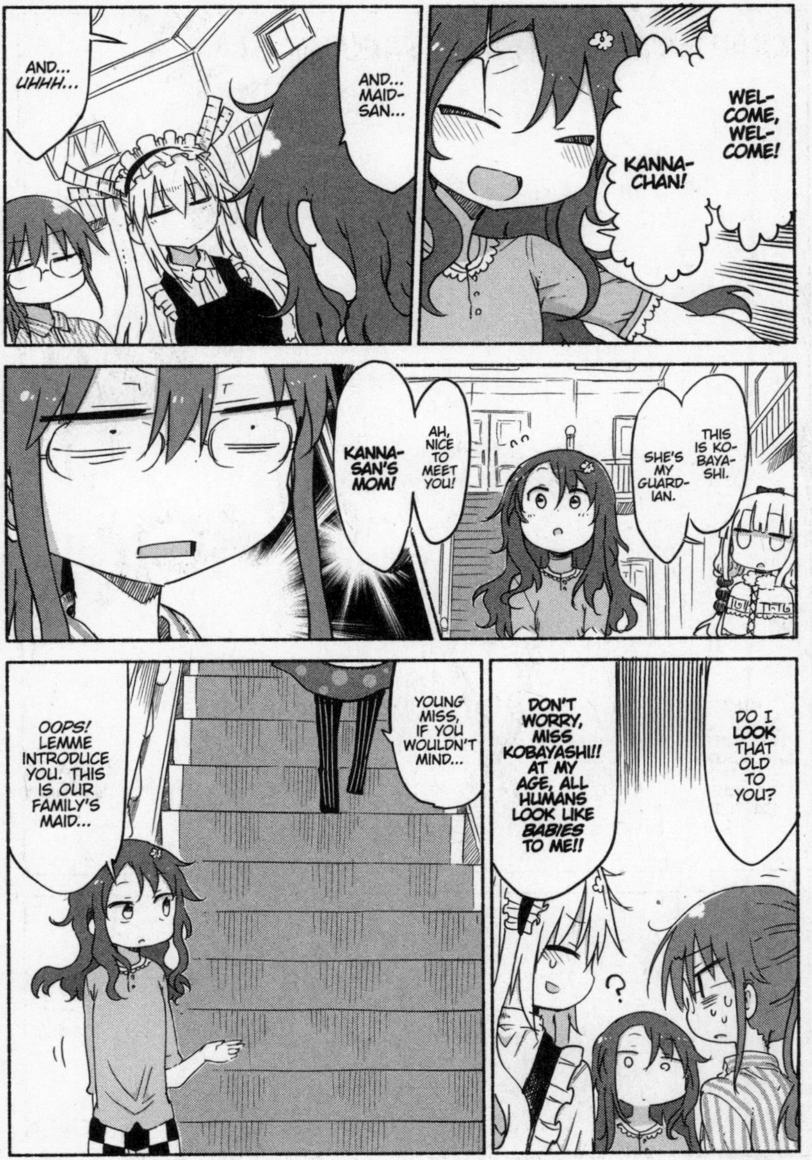
WEL-COME, WEL-COME!
KANNA-CHAN!
AND... MAID-SAN...
AND... UHHH...
THIS IS KO-BAYA-SHI.
SHE'S MY GUARD-IAN.
AH, NICE TO MEET YOU!
KANNA-SAN'S MOM!
DO I LOOK THAT OLD TO YOU?
DON'T WORRY, MISS KOBAYASHI!! AT MY AGE, ALL HUMANS LOOK LIKE BABIES TO ME!!
YOUNG MISS, IF YOU WOULDN'T MIND...
OOPS! LEMME INTRODUCE YOU. THIS IS OUR FAMILY'S MAID...

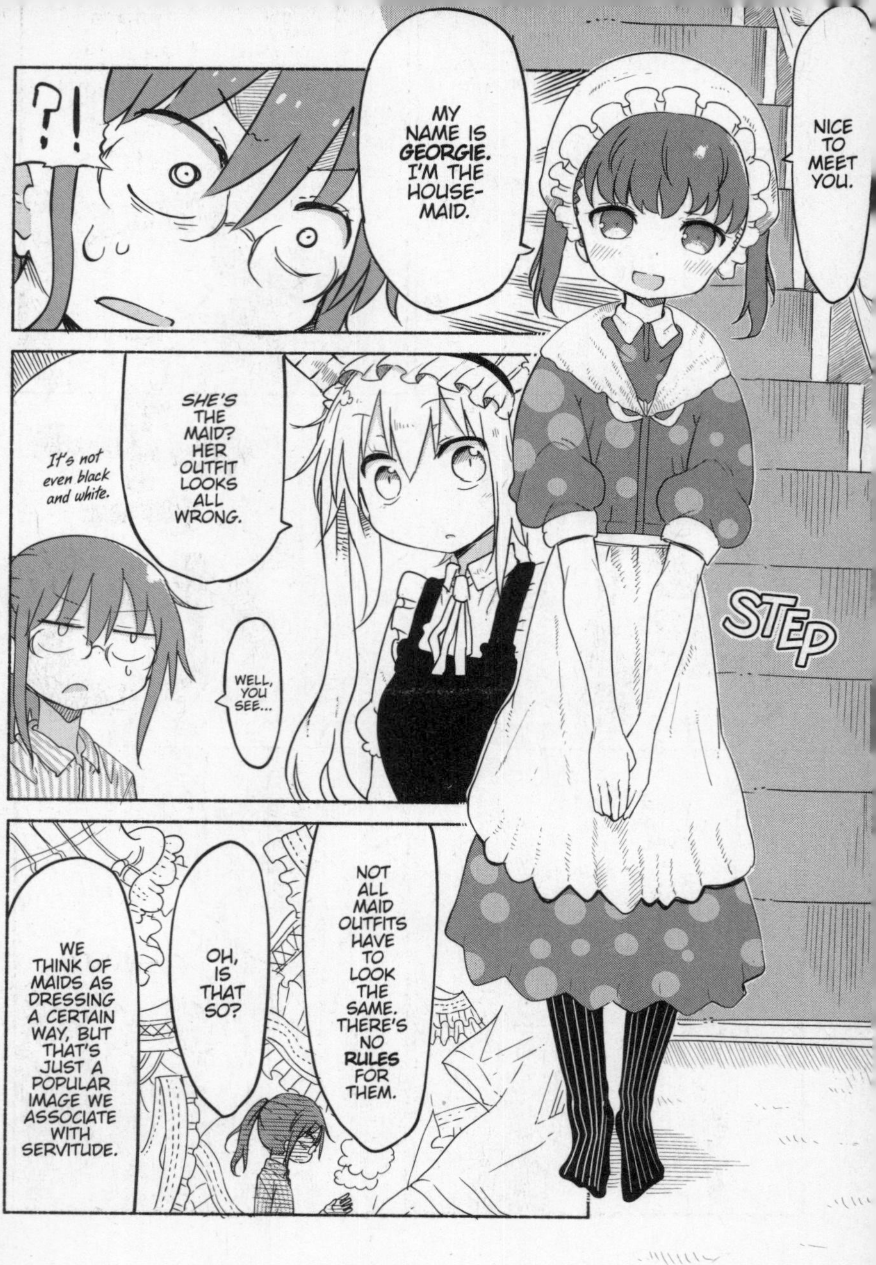
NICE TO MEET YOU.
MY NAME IS GEORGIE. I'M THE HOUSE-MAID.
STEP
?!
SHE'S THE MAID? HER OUTFIT LOOKS ALL WRONG.
It's not even black and white.
WELL, YOU SEE...
NOT ALL MAID OUTFITS HAVE TO LOOK THE SAME. THERE'S NO RULES FOR THEM.
OH, IS THAT SO?
WE THINK OF MAIDS AS DRESSING A CERTAIN WAY, BUT THAT'S JUST A POPULAR IMAGE WE ASSOCIATE WITH SERVITUDE.

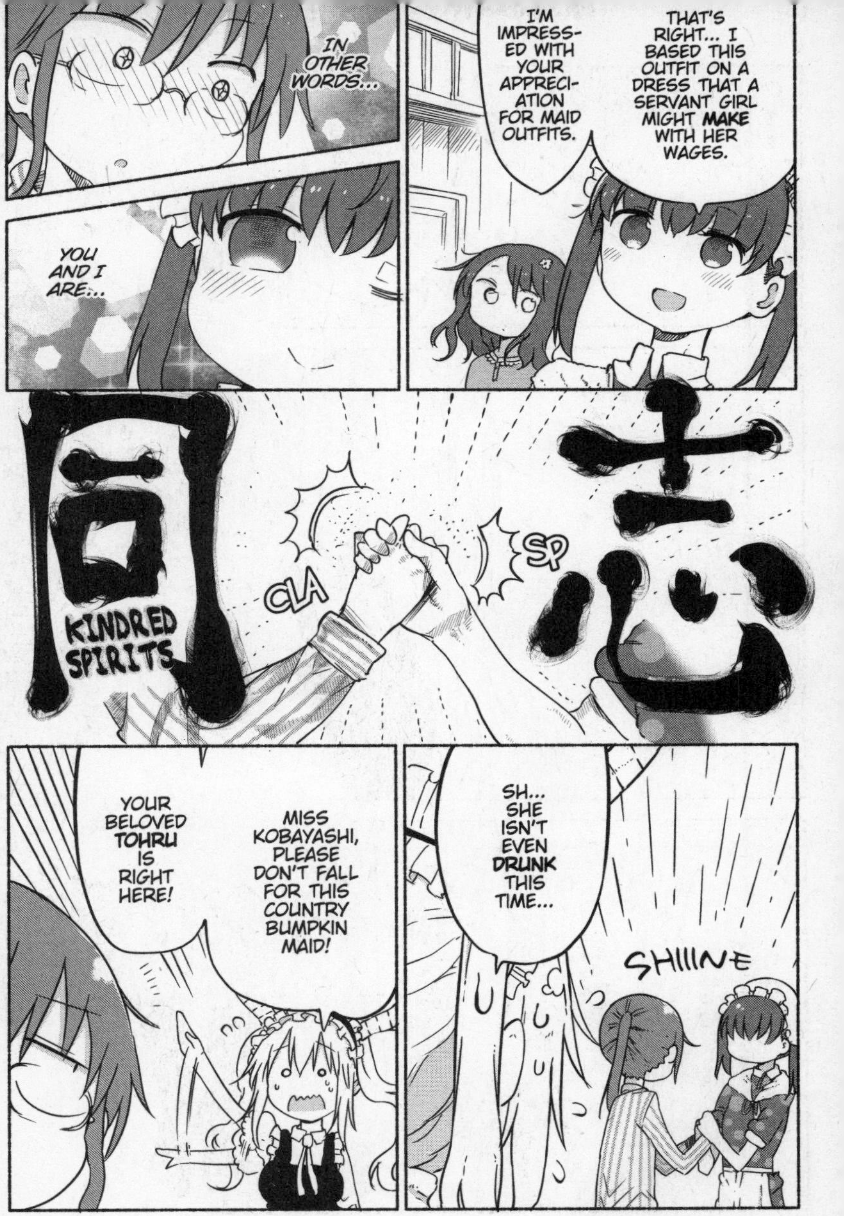
THAT'S RIGHT... I BASED THIS OUTFIT ON A DRESS THAT A SERVANT GIRL MIGHT **MAKE** WITH HER WAGES.
I'M IMPRESSED WITH YOUR APPRECIATION FOR MAID OUTFITS.
IN OTHER WORDS...
YOU AND I ARE...
同志
KINDRED SPIRITS
SP
CLA
SH... SHE ISN'T EVEN **DRUNK** THIS TIME...
SHIIIINE
MISS KOBAYASHI, PLEASE DON'T FALL FOR THIS COUNTRY BUMPKIN MAID!
YOUR BELOVED **TOHRU** IS RIGHT HERE!

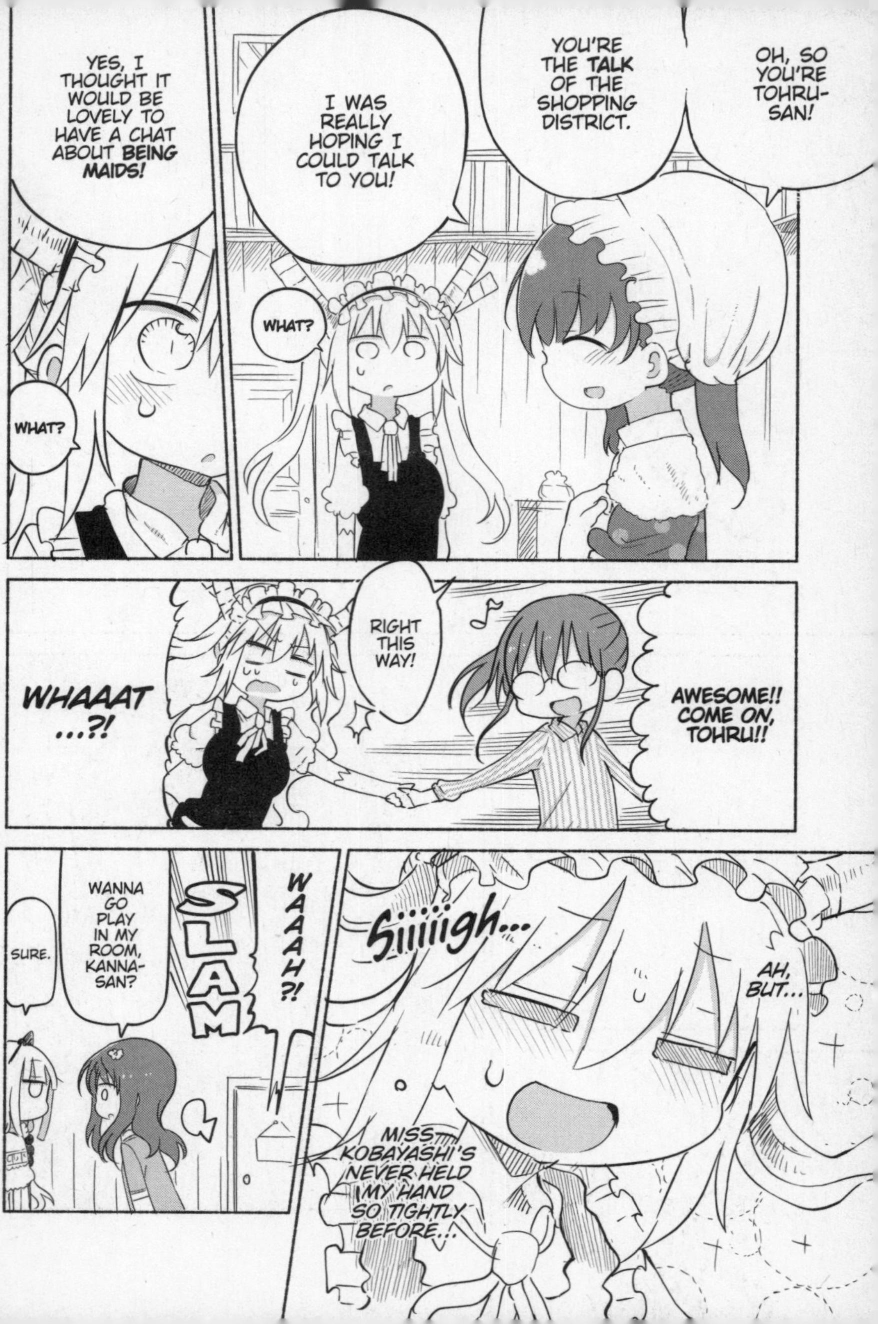
OH, SO YOU'RE TOHRU-SAN!
YOU'RE THE TALK OF THE SHOPPING DISTRICT.
I WAS REALLY HOPING I COULD TALK TO YOU!
WHAT?
YES, I THOUGHT IT WOULD BE LOVELY TO HAVE A CHAT ABOUT BEING MAIDS!
WHAT?
AWESOME!! COME ON, TOHRU!!
RIGHT THIS WAY!
WHAAAT ...?!
AH, BUT...
Siiiiigh...
MISS KOBAYASHI'S NEVER HELD MY HAND SO TIGHTLY BEFORE..!
WAAAAH?!
SLAM
WANNA GO PLAY IN MY ROOM, KANNA-SAN?
SURE.

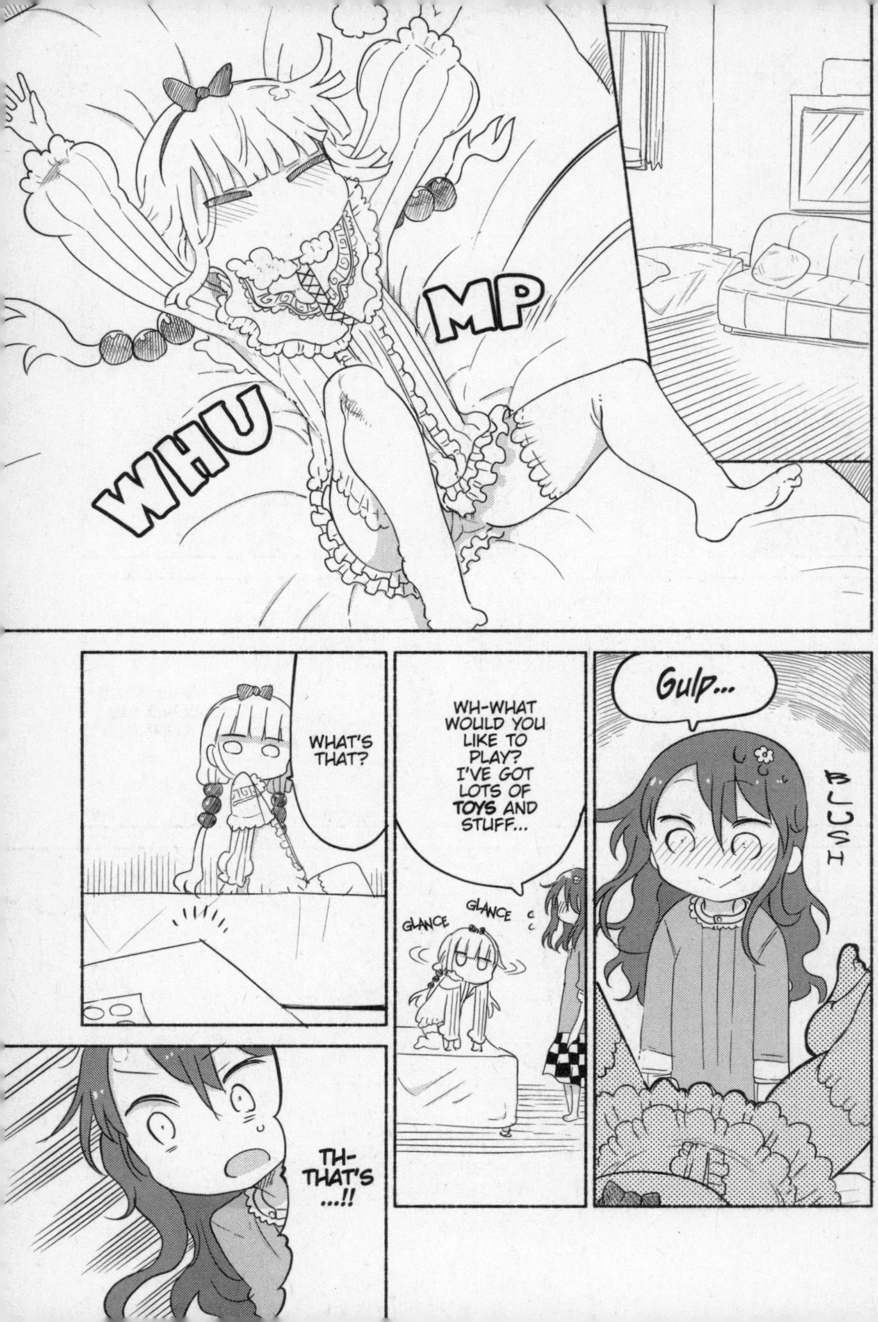
WHU
MP
Gulp...
BLUSH
WH-WHAT WOULD YOU LIKE TO PLAY? I'VE GOT LOTS OF TOYS AND STUFF...
GLANCE
GLANCE
WHAT'S THAT?
TH-THAT'S ...!!

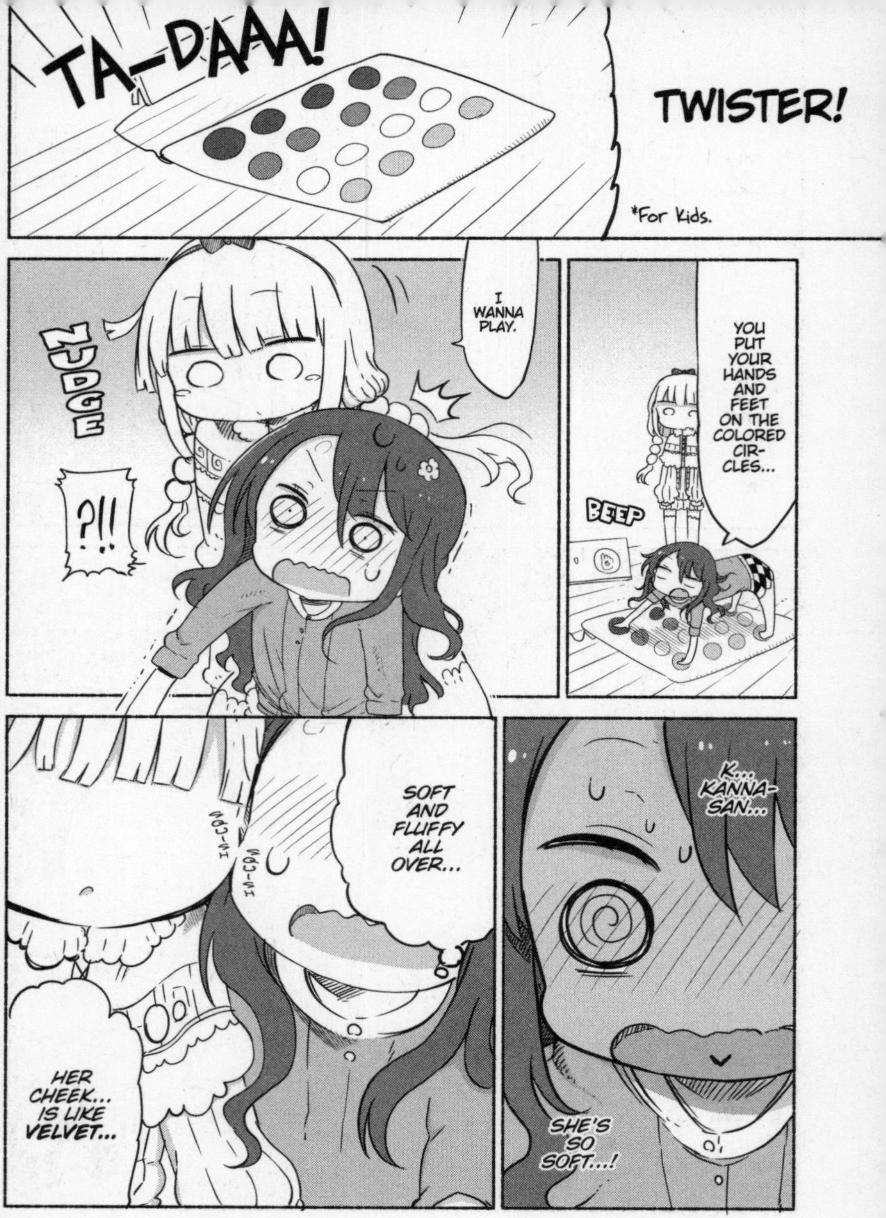
TA-DAAA!
TWISTER!
*For Kids.
YOU PUT YOUR HANDS AND FEET ON THE COLORED CIR-CLES...
BEEP
I WANNA PLAY.
NUDGE
?!!
K... KANNA-SAN...
SHE'S SO SOFT...!
SOFT AND FLUFFY ALL OVER...
SQUISH
SQUISH
HER CHEEK... IS LIKE VELVET...

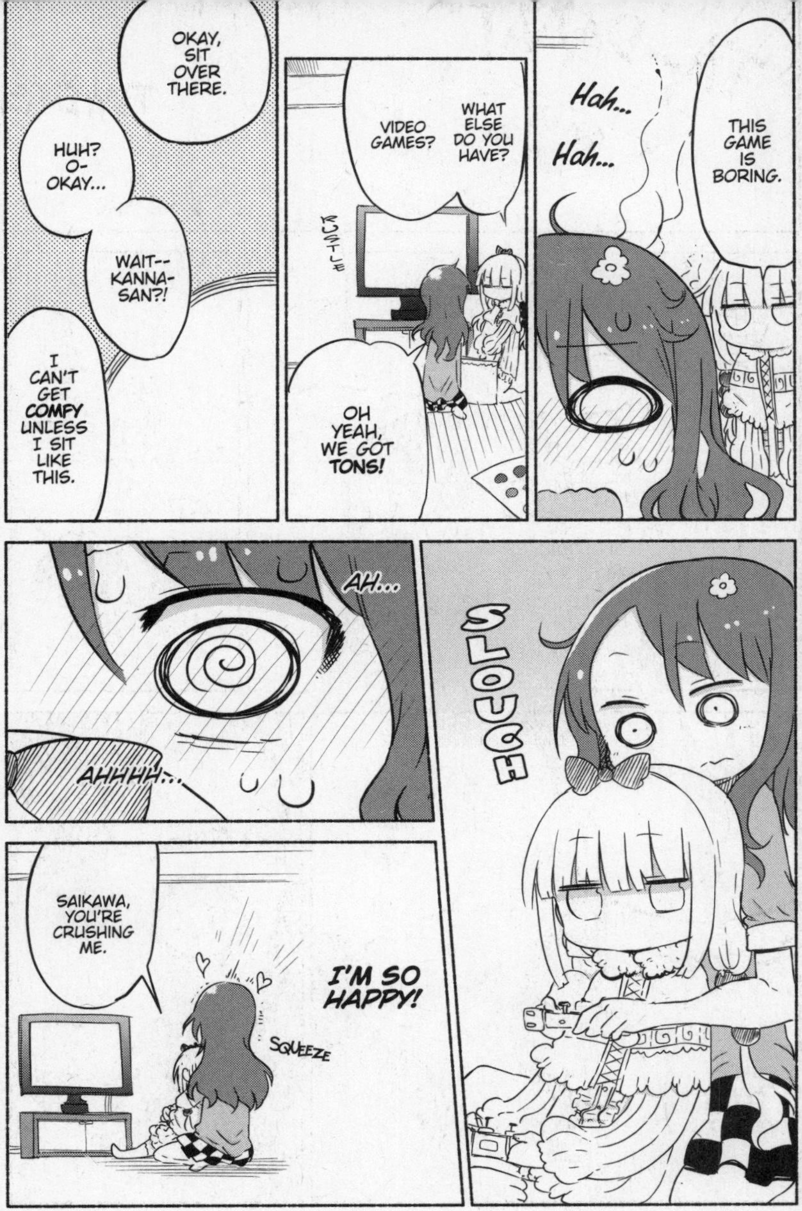
THIS GAME IS BORING.
Hah... Hah...
WHAT ELSE DO YOU HAVE?
VIDEO GAMES?
RUSTLE
OH YEAH, WE GOT TONS!
OKAY, SIT OVER THERE.
HUH? O-OKAY...
WAIT-- KANNA-SAN?!
I CAN'T GET COMFY UNLESS I SIT LIKE THIS.
SLOUCH
AH...
AHHHH...
I'M SO HAPPY!
SAIKAWA, YOU'RE CRUSHING ME.
SQUEEZE

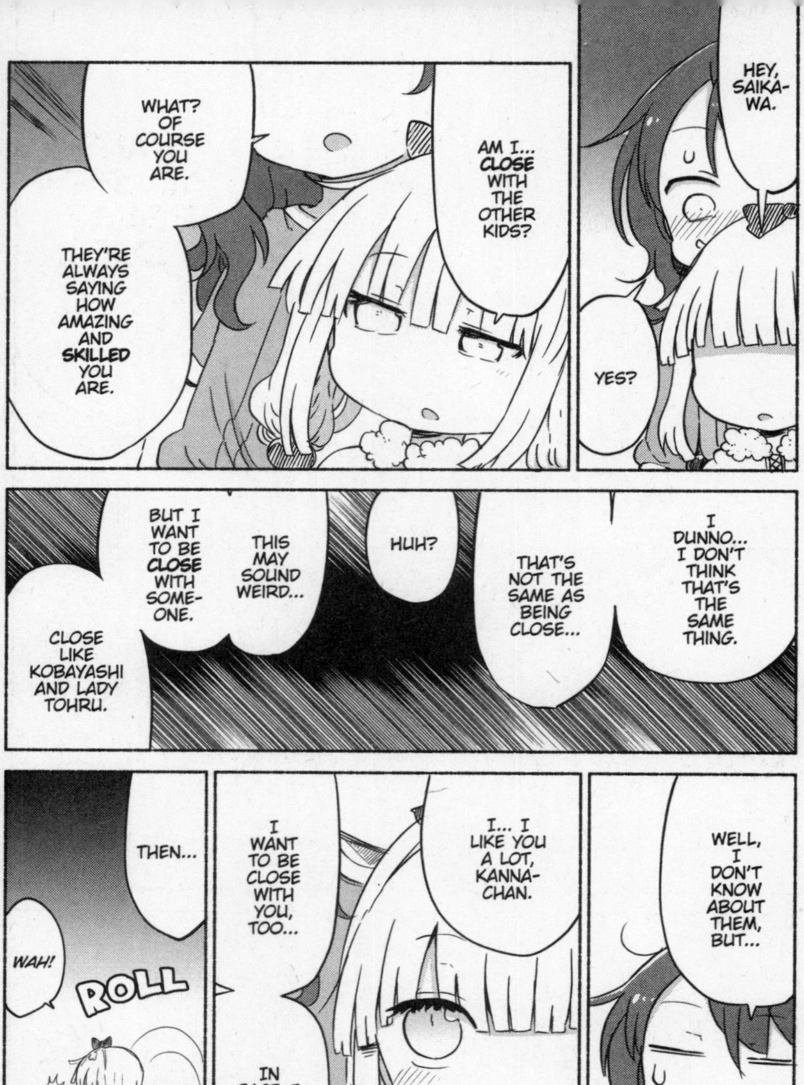
HEY, SAIKA-WA.
YES?
AM I... CLOSE WITH THE OTHER KIDS?
WHAT? OF COURSE YOU ARE.
THEY'RE ALWAYS SAYING HOW AMAZING AND SKILLED YOU ARE.
I DUNNO... I DON'T THINK THAT'S THE SAME THING.
THAT'S NOT THE SAME AS BEING CLOSE...
HUH?
THIS MAY SOUND WEIRD...
BUT I WANT TO BE CLOSE WITH SOME-ONE.
CLOSE LIKE KOBAYASHI AND LADY TOHRU.
WELL, I DON'T KNOW ABOUT THEM, BUT...
I... I LIKE YOU A LOT, KANNA-CHAN.
I WANT TO BE CLOSE WITH YOU, TOO...
IN FACT, I WANNA MARRY YOU!
THEN...
ROLL
WAH!

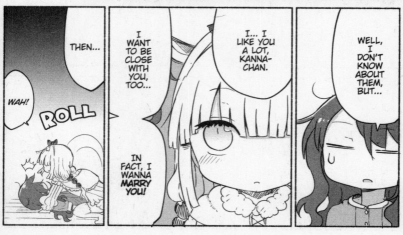

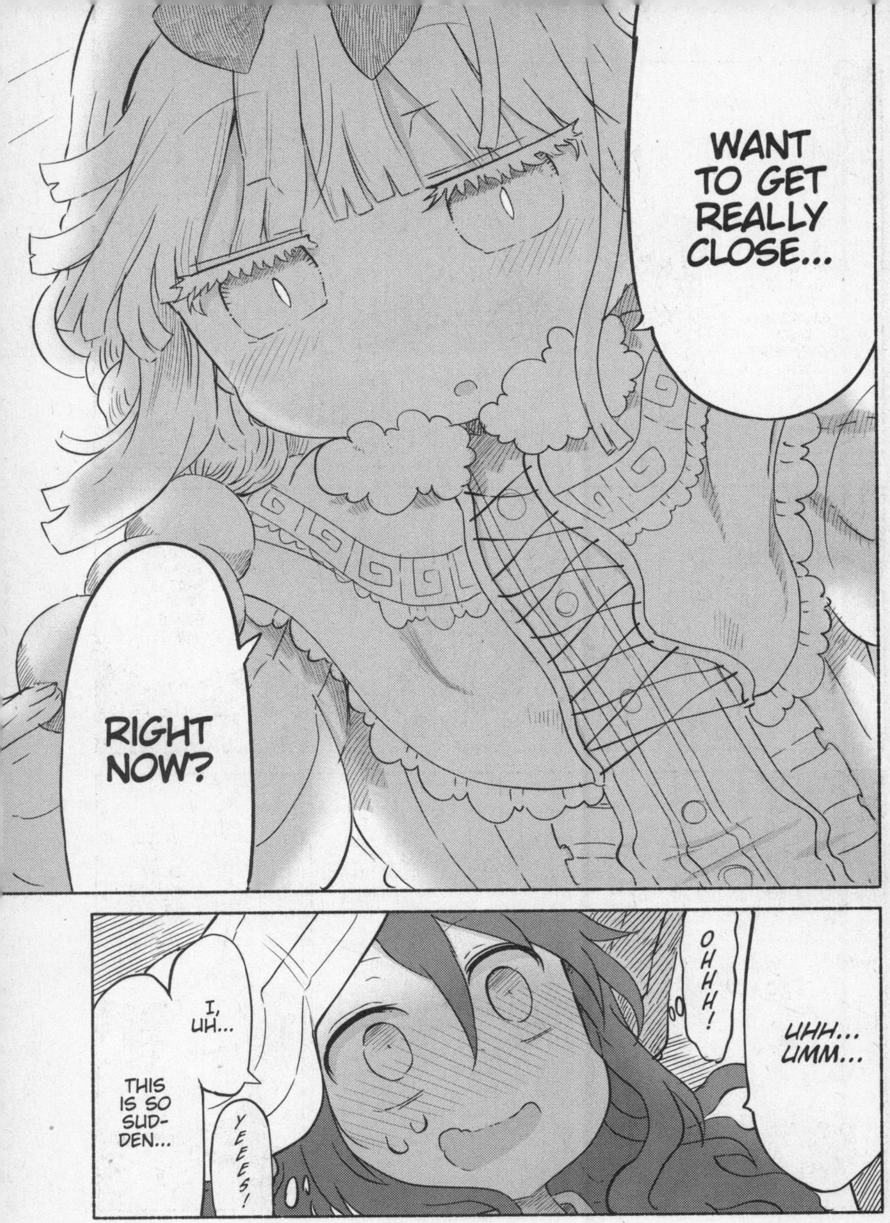
WANT TO GET REALLY CLOSE...
RIGHT NOW?
UHH... UMM...
OHHH!
I, UH...
THIS IS SO SUDDEN...
YEEES!

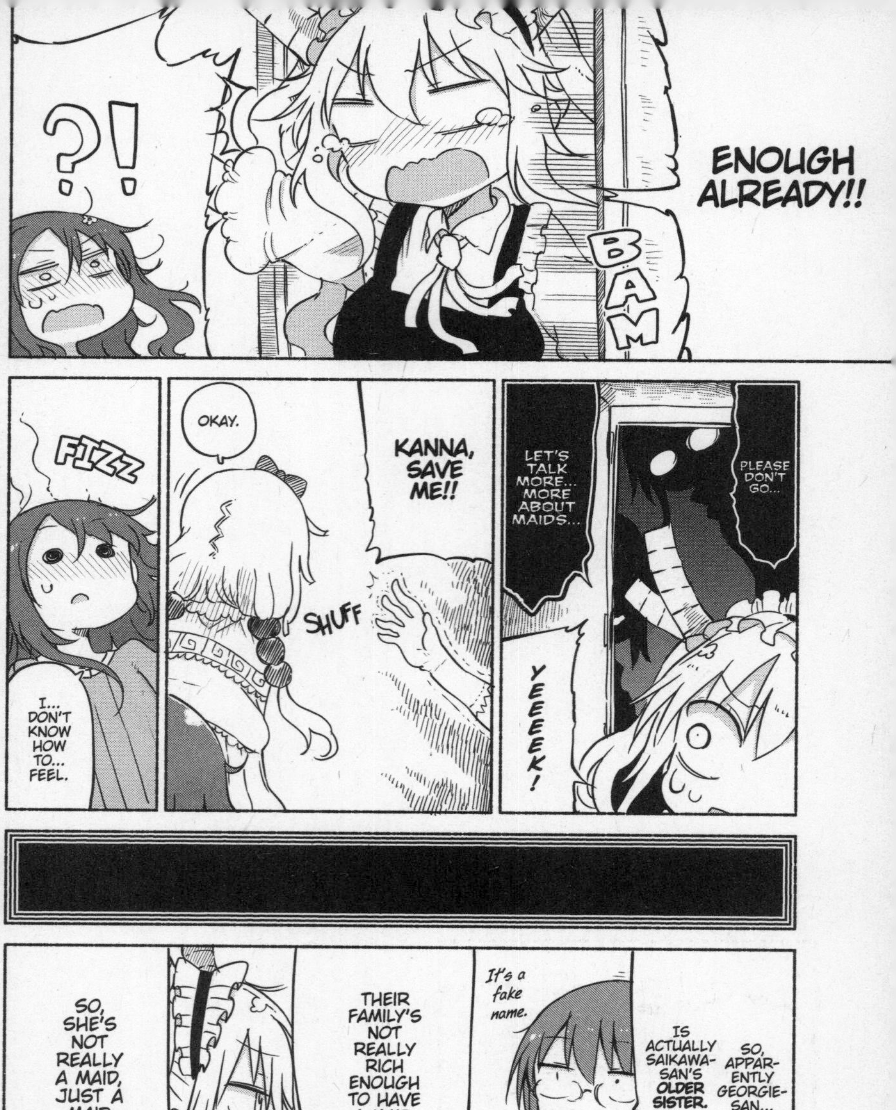
ENOUGH ALREADY!!
BAM
?!
PLEASE DON'T GO...
LET'S TALK MORE... MORE ABOUT MAIDS...
YEEEEK!
KANNA, SAVE ME!!
OKAY.
SHUFF
FIZZ
I... DON'T KNOW HOW TO... FEEL.
SO, APPARENTLY GEORGIE-SAN...
IS ACTUALLY SAIKAWA-SAN'S OLDER SISTER.
It's a fake name.
THEIR FAMILY'S NOT REALLY RICH ENOUGH TO HAVE A MAID.
SO, SHE'S NOT REALLY A MAID, JUST A MAID FANATIC.
Just like you.

CHAPTER 29/END

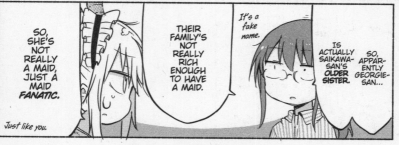

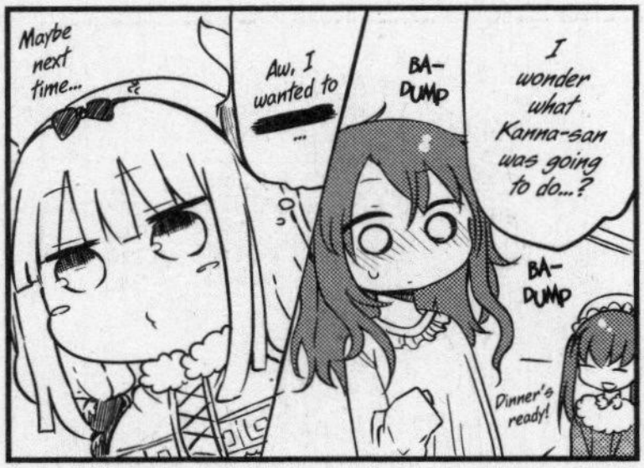
I wonder what Kanna-san was going to do...?
BA-DUMP
Aw, I wanted to [redacted]...
Maybe next time...
BA-DUMP
Dinner's ready!

Miss Kobayashi's
DRAGON MAID

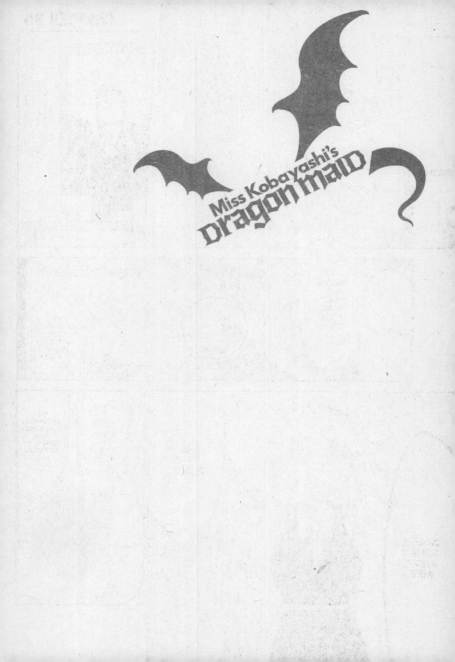

CHAPTER 30

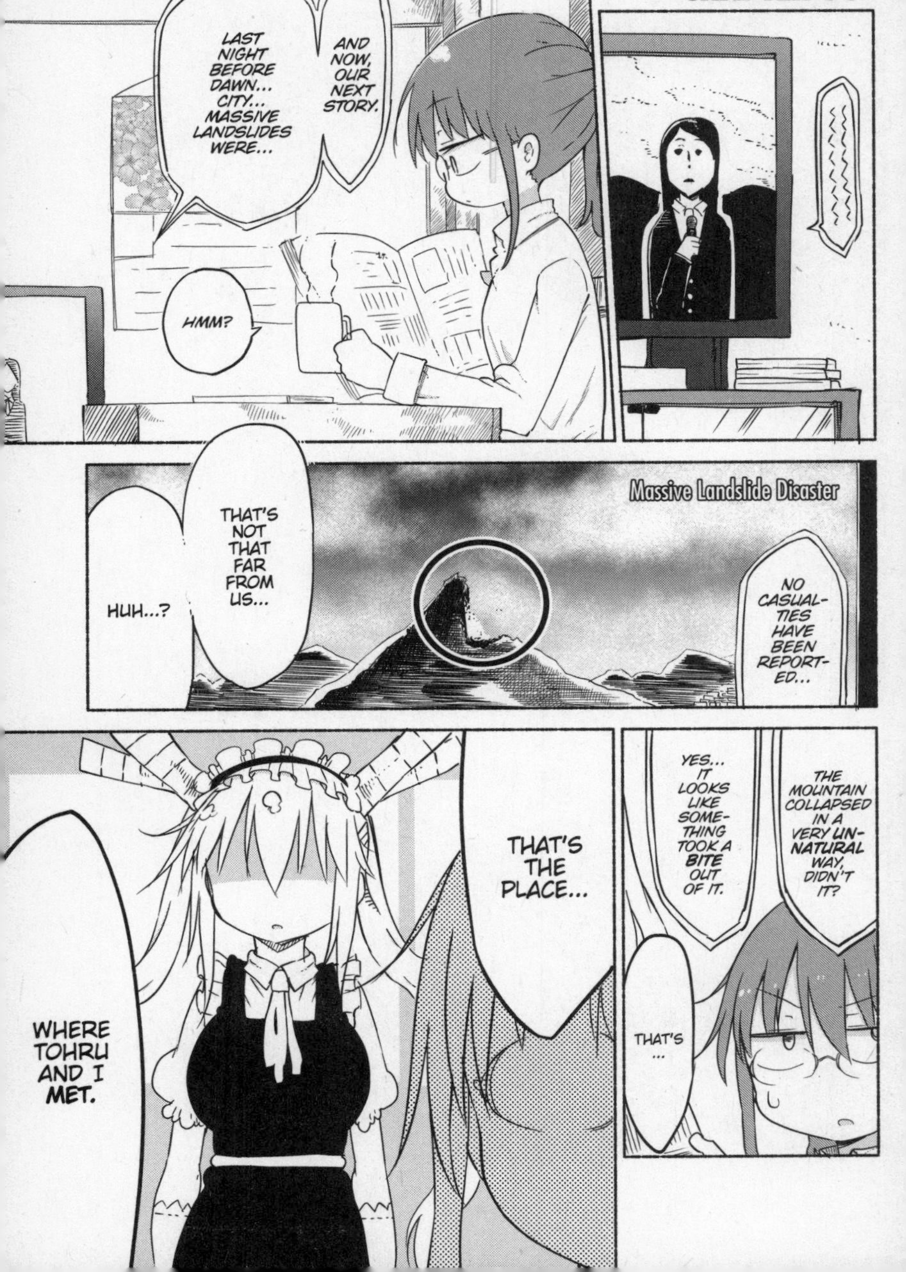
AND NOW, OUR NEXT STORY.
LAST NIGHT BEFORE DAWN... CITY... MASSIVE LANDSLIDES WERE...
HMM?
Massive Landslide Disaster
NO CASUALTIES HAVE BEEN REPORTED...
THAT'S NOT THAT FAR FROM US...
HUH...?
THE MOUNTAIN COLLAPSED IN A VERY UNNATURAL WAY, DIDN'T IT?
YES... IT LOOKS LIKE SOMETHING TOOK A BITE OUT OF IT.
THAT'S...
THAT'S THE PLACE...
WHERE TOHRU AND I MET.

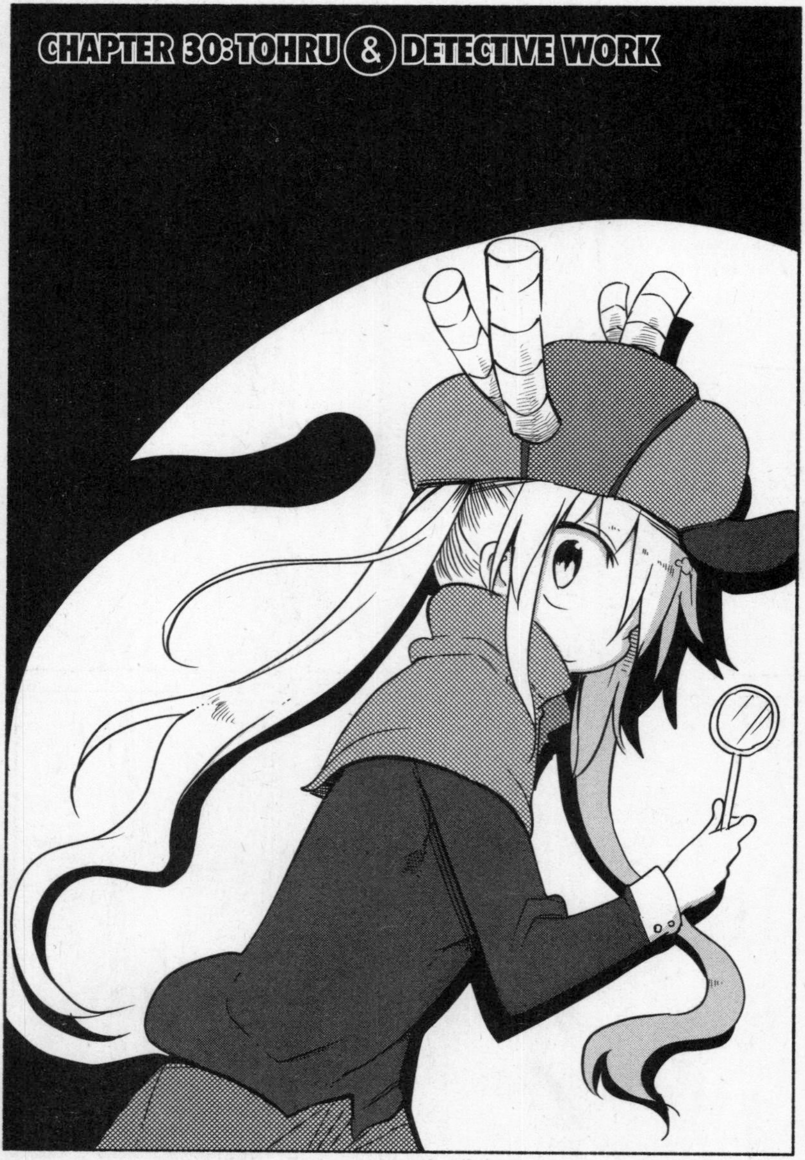
CHAPTER 30: TOHRU & DETECTIVE WORK

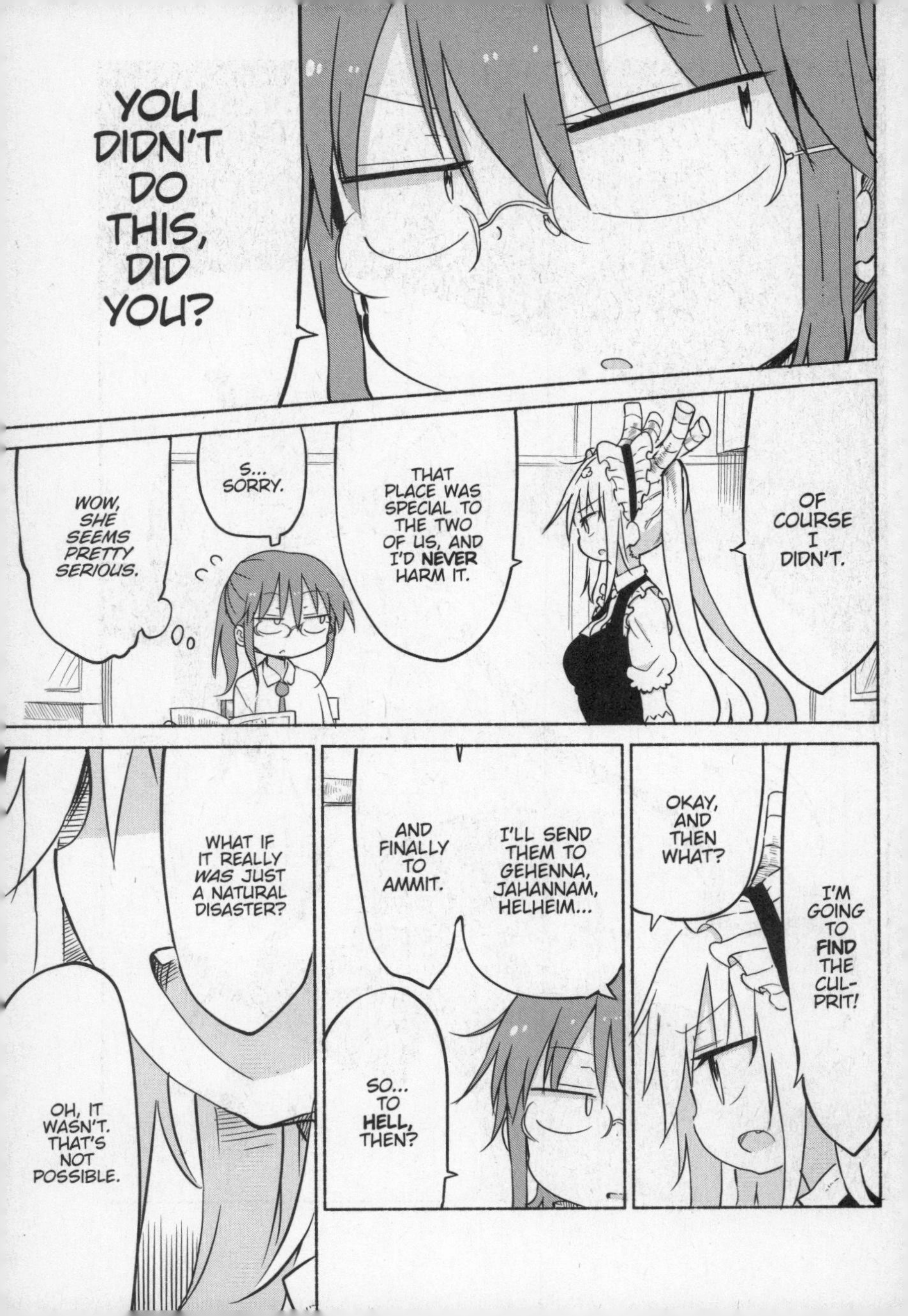
YOU DIDN'T DO THIS, DID YOU?
OF COURSE I DIDN'T.
THAT PLACE WAS SPECIAL TO THE TWO OF US, AND I'D **NEVER** HARM IT.
S... SORRY.
WOW, SHE SEEMS PRETTY SERIOUS.
I'M GOING TO **FIND** THE CUL-PRIT!
OKAY, AND THEN WHAT?
I'LL SEND THEM TO GEHENNA, JAHANNAM, HELHEIM...
AND FINALLY TO AMMIT.
SO... TO **HELL**, THEN?
WHAT IF IT REALLY *WAS* JUST A NATURAL DISASTER?
OH, IT WASN'T. THAT'S NOT POSSIBLE.

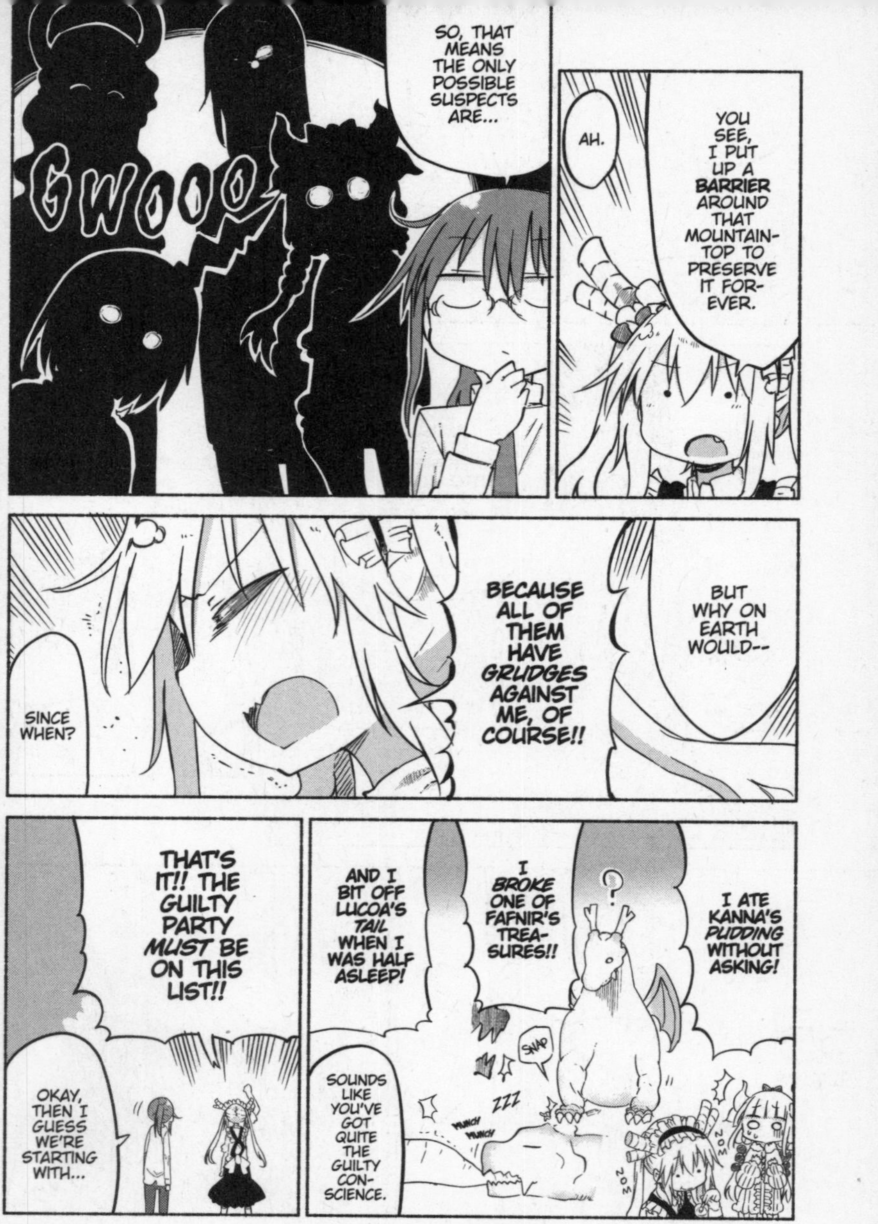
YOU SEE, I PUT UP A BARRIER AROUND THAT MOUNTAIN-TOP TO PRESERVE IT FOR-EVER.
AH.
SO, THAT MEANS THE ONLY POSSIBLE SUSPECTS ARE...
GWOOO
BUT WHY ON EARTH WOULD--
BECAUSE ALL OF THEM HAVE GRUDGES AGAINST ME, OF COURSE!!
SINCE WHEN?
I ATE KANNA'S PUDDING WITHOUT ASKING!
I BROKE ONE OF FAFNIR'S TREA-SURES!!
AND I BIT OFF LUCOA'S TAIL WHEN I WAS HALF ASLEEP!
?
SNAP
ZZZ
MUNCH MUNCH
NOM NOM
SOUNDS LIKE YOU'VE GOT QUITE THE GUILTY CON-SCIENCE.
THAT'S IT!! THE GUILTY PARTY MUST BE ON THIS LIST!!
OKAY, THEN I GUESS WE'RE STARTING WITH...

(Elma's grudge needs no explanation.)

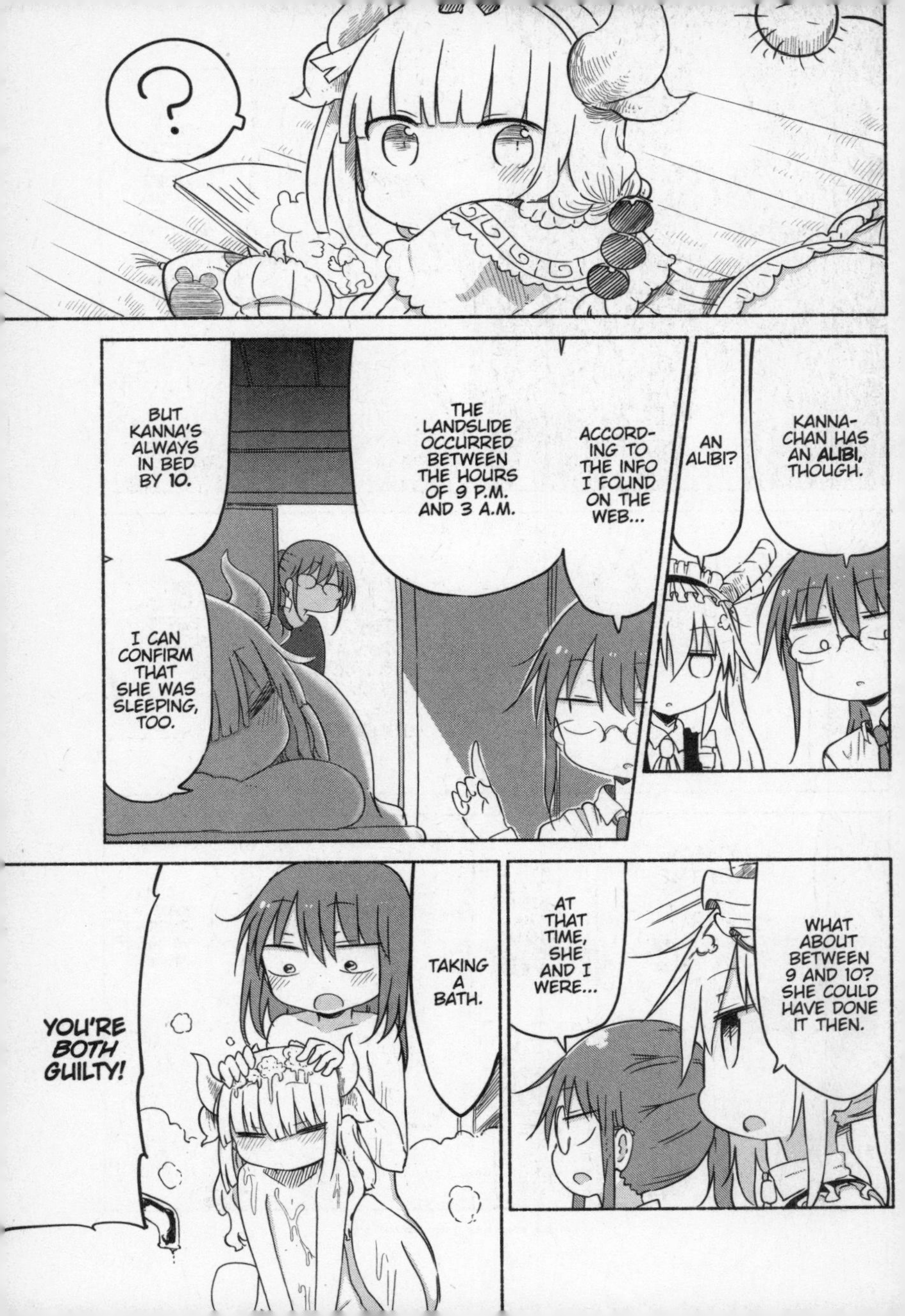
?
KANNA-CHAN HAS AN ALIBI, THOUGH.
AN ALIBI?
ACCORDING TO THE INFO I FOUND ON THE WEB...
THE LANDSLIDE OCCURRED BETWEEN THE HOURS OF 9 P.M. AND 3 A.M.
BUT KANNA'S ALWAYS IN BED BY 10.
I CAN CONFIRM THAT SHE WAS SLEEPING, TOO.
WHAT ABOUT BETWEEN 9 AND 10? SHE COULD HAVE DONE IT THEN.
AT THAT TIME, SHE AND I WERE...
TAKING A BATH.
YOU'RE BOTH GUILTY!

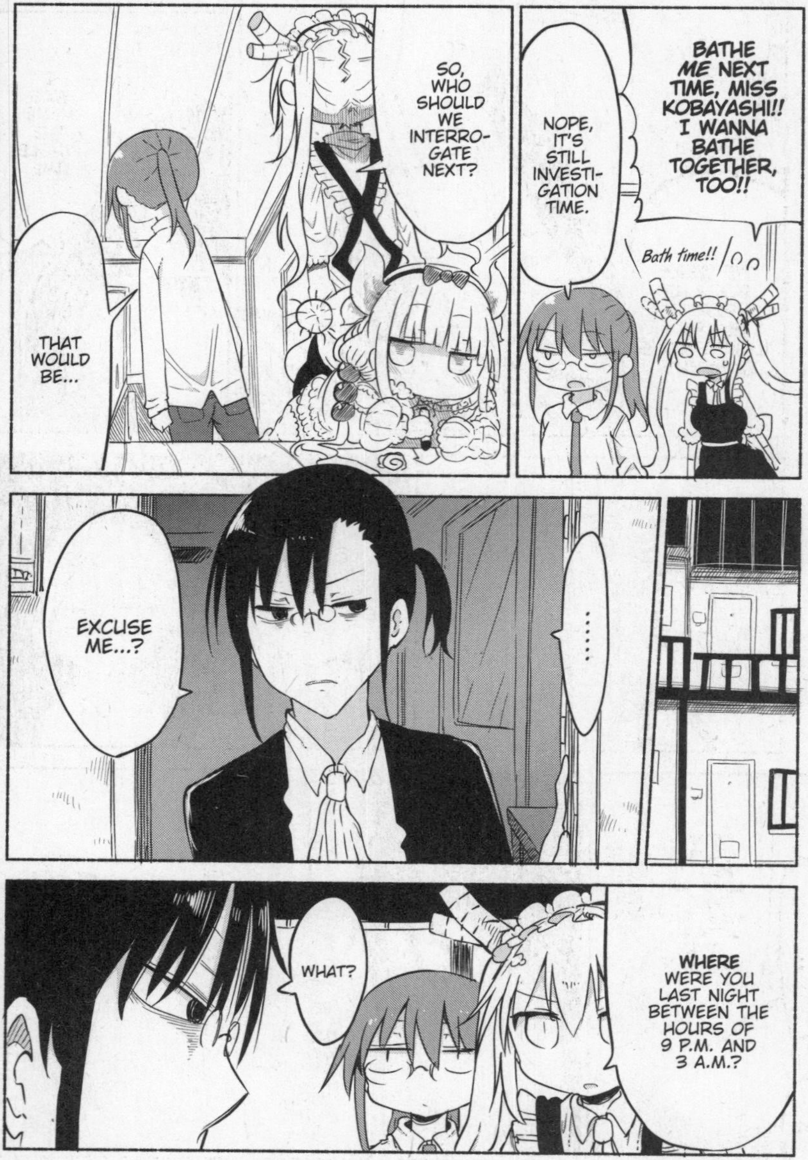

BATHE *ME* NEXT TIME, MISS KOBAYASHI!! I WANNA BATHE TOGETHER, TOO!!
Bath time!!
NOPE, IT'S STILL INVESTIGATION TIME.
SO, WHO SHOULD WE INTERROGATE NEXT?
THAT WOULD BE...
......
EXCUSE ME...?
WHERE WERE YOU LAST NIGHT BETWEEN THE HOURS OF 9 P.M. AND 3 A.M.?
WHAT?

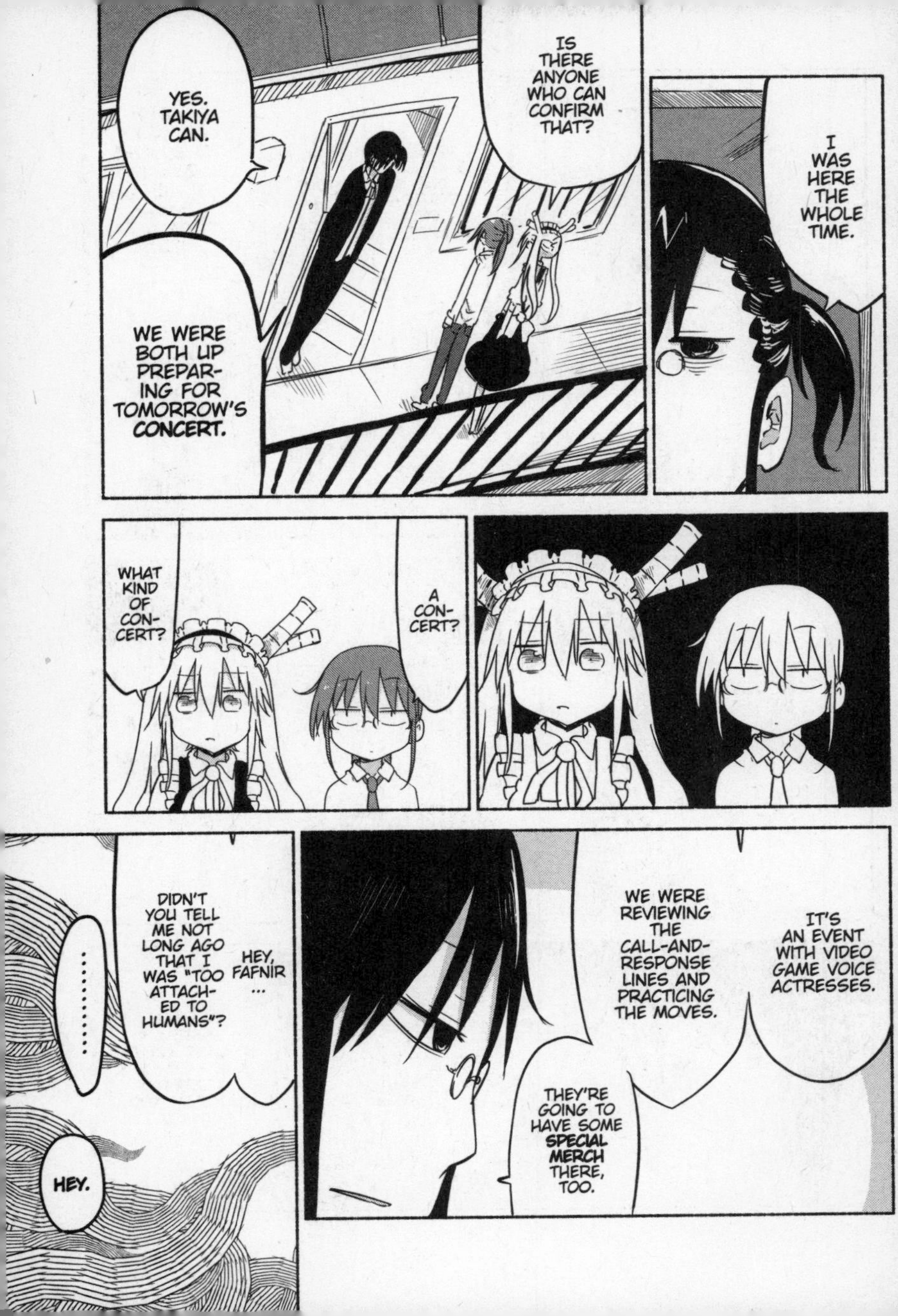
I WAS HERE THE WHOLE TIME.
IS THERE ANYONE WHO CAN CONFIRM THAT?
YES. TAKIYA CAN.
WE WERE BOTH UP PREPARING FOR TOMORROW'S CONCERT.
A CONCERT?
WHAT KIND OF CONCERT?
IT'S AN EVENT WITH VIDEO GAME VOICE ACTRESSES.
WE WERE REVIEWING THE CALL-AND-RESPONSE LINES AND PRACTICING THE MOVES.
THEY'RE GOING TO HAVE SOME SPECIAL MERCH THERE, TOO.
HEY, FAFNIR ...
DIDN'T YOU TELL ME NOT LONG AGO THAT I WAS "TOO ATTACHED TO HUMANS"?
......
HEY.

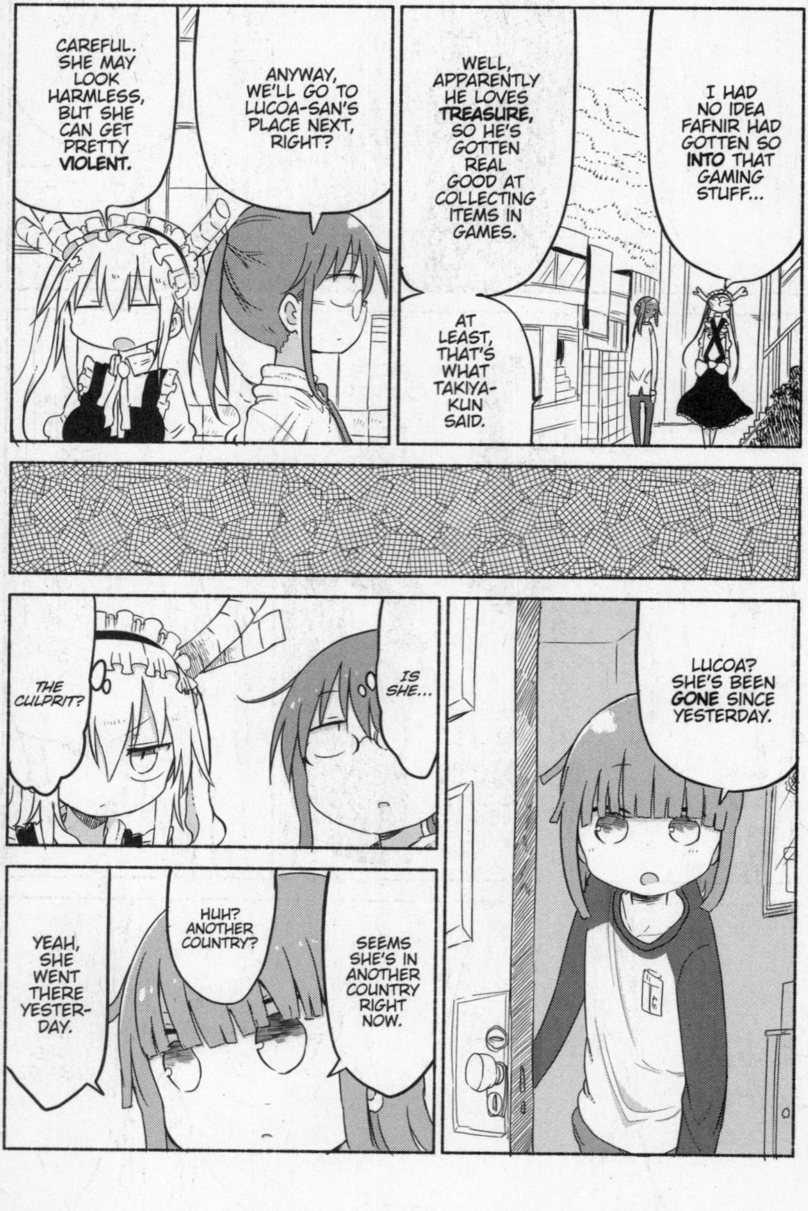
I HAD NO IDEA FAFNIR HAD GOTTEN SO INTO THAT GAMING STUFF...
WELL, APPARENTLY HE LOVES TREASURE, SO HE'S GOTTEN REAL GOOD AT COLLECTING ITEMS IN GAMES.
AT LEAST, THAT'S WHAT TAKIYA-KUN SAID.
ANYWAY, WE'LL GO TO LUCOA-SAN'S PLACE NEXT, RIGHT?
CAREFUL. SHE MAY LOOK HARMLESS, BUT SHE CAN GET PRETTY VIOLENT.
LUCOA? SHE'S BEEN GONE SINCE YESTERDAY.
IS SHE...
THE CULPRIT?
SEEMS SHE'S IN ANOTHER COUNTRY RIGHT NOW.
HUH? ANOTHER COUNTRY?
YEAH, SHE WENT THERE YESTER-DAY.

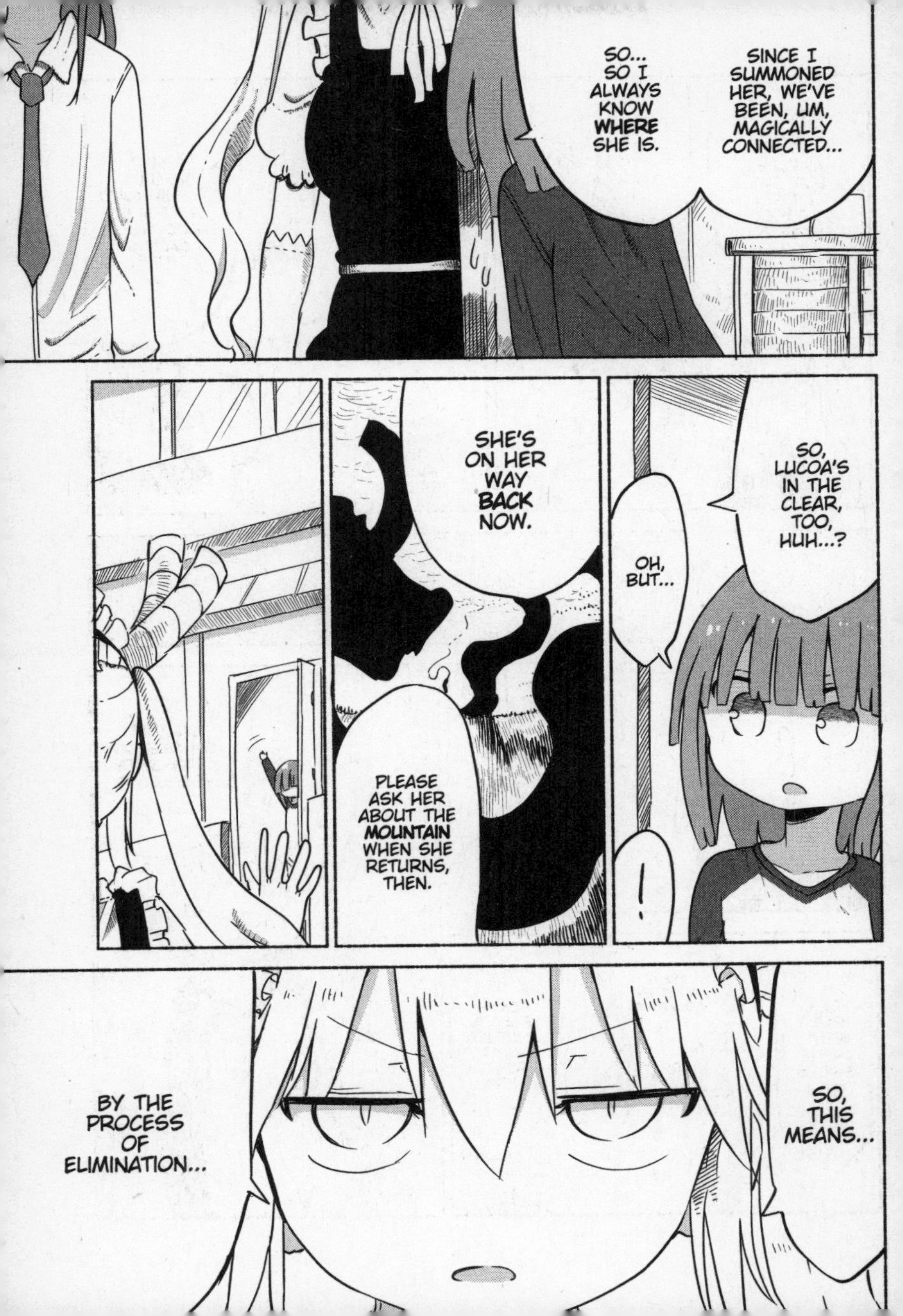
SINCE I SUMMONED HER, WE'VE BEEN, UM, MAGICALLY CONNECTED...
SO... SO I ALWAYS KNOW WHERE SHE IS.
SO, LUCOA'S IN THE CLEAR, TOO, HUH...?
OH, BUT...
!
SHE'S ON HER WAY BACK NOW.
PLEASE ASK HER ABOUT THE MOUNTAIN WHEN SHE RETURNS, THEN.
SO, THIS MEANS...
BY THE PROCESS OF ELIMINATION...

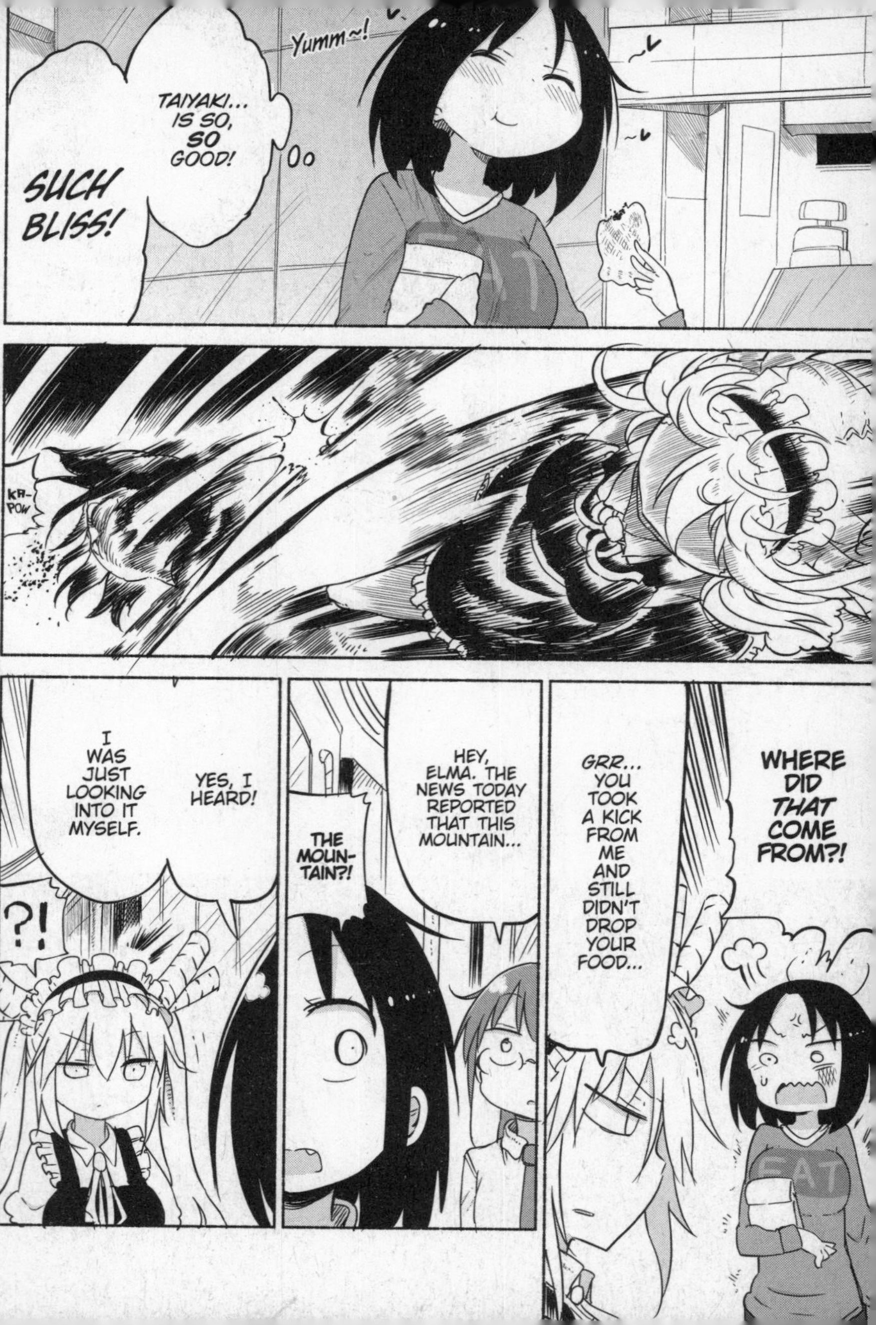
Yumm~!
TAIYAKI... IS SO, SO GOOD!
SUCH BLISS!
KA-POW
WHERE DID THAT COME FROM?!
GRR... YOU TOOK A KICK FROM ME AND STILL DIDN'T DROP YOUR FOOD...
HEY, ELMA. THE NEWS TODAY REPORTED THAT THIS MOUNTAIN...
THE MOUN-TAIN?!
YES, I HEARD!
I WAS JUST LOOKING INTO IT MYSELF.
?!

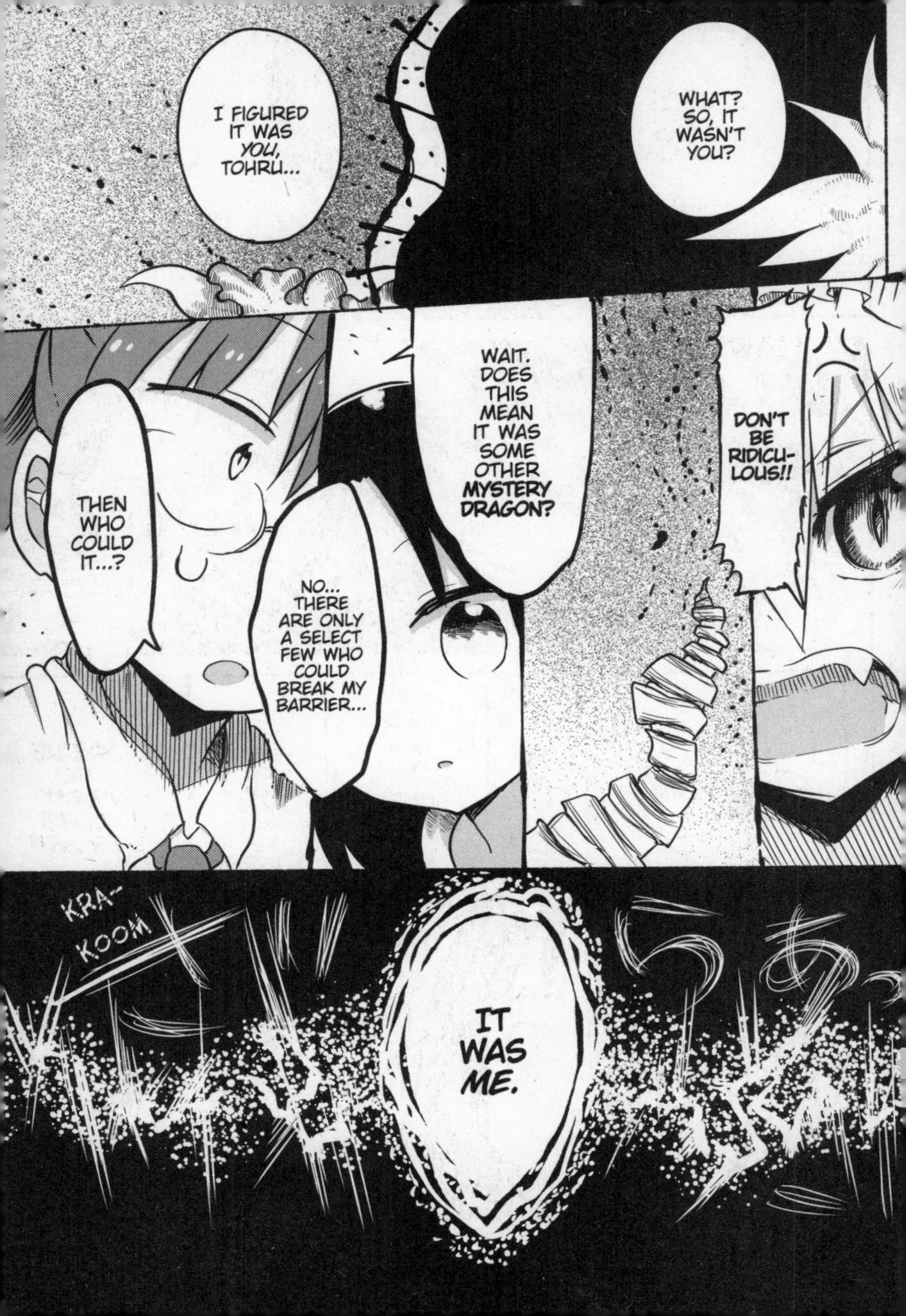
WHAT? SO, IT WASN'T YOU?
I FIGURED IT WAS *YOU*, TOHRU...
DON'T BE RIDICULOUS!!
WAIT. DOES THIS MEAN IT WAS SOME OTHER MYSTERY DRAGON?
NO... THERE ARE ONLY A SELECT FEW WHO COULD BREAK MY BARRIER...
THEN WHO COULD IT...?
IT WAS *ME.*
KRA-KOOM

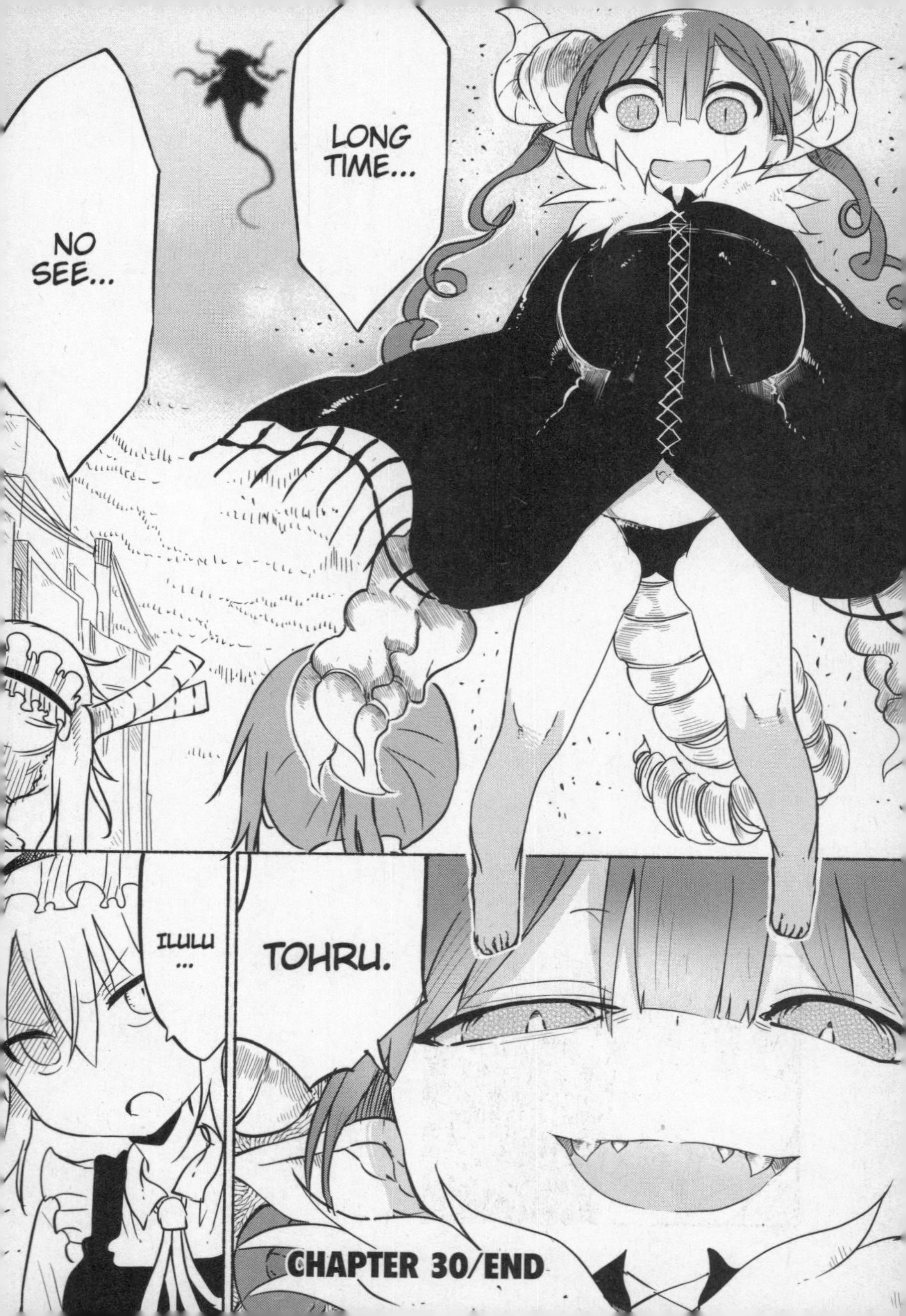
LONG TIME...
NO SEE...
TOHRU.
ILULU ...
CHAPTER 30/END

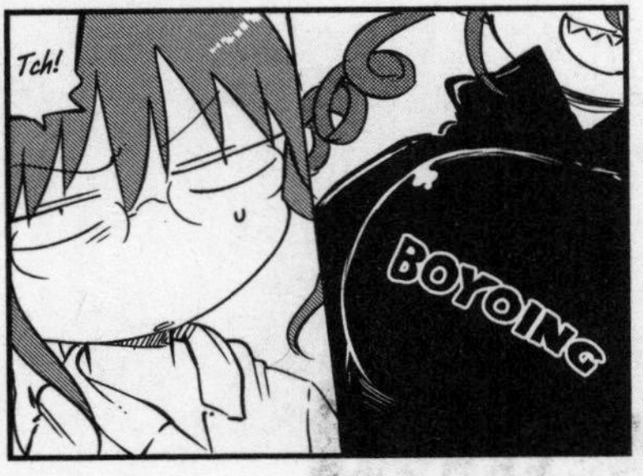
Tch!
BOYOING

AFTERWORD

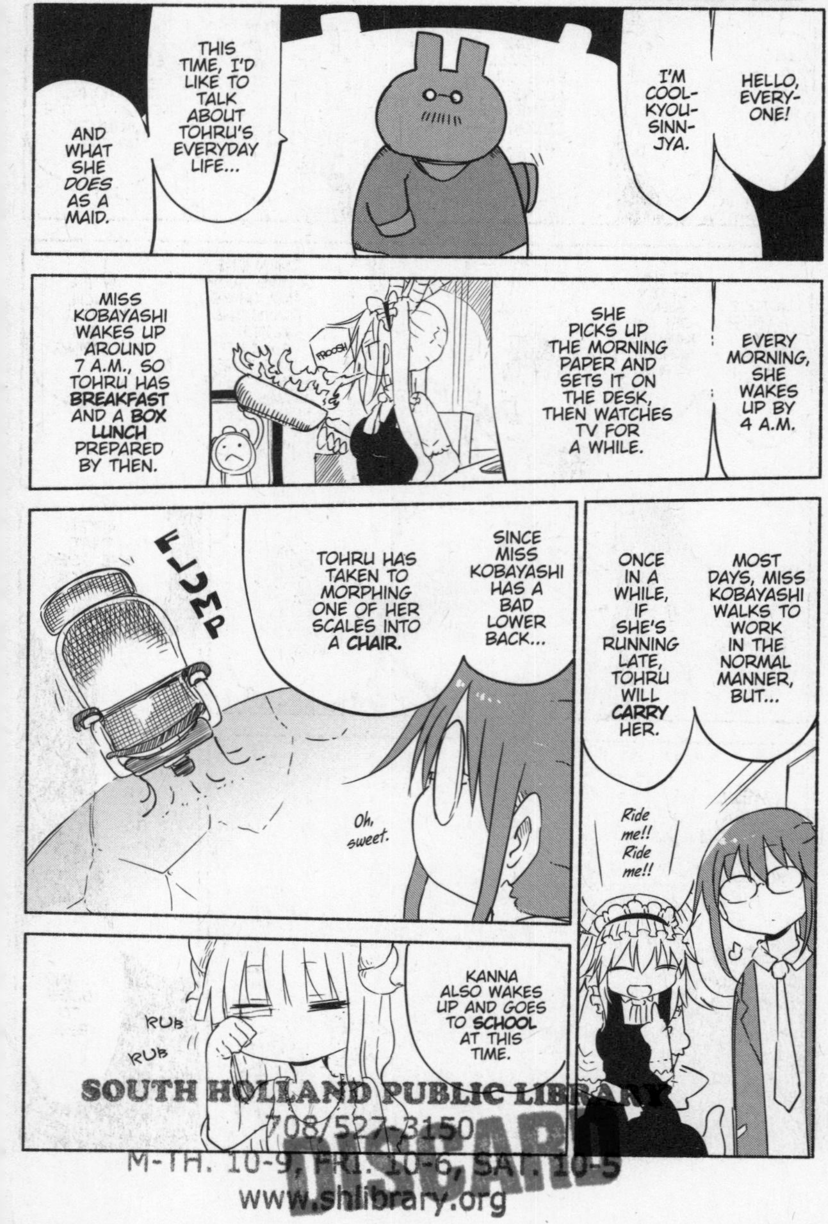
HELLO, EVERY-ONE!
I'M COOL-KYOU-SINNJYA.
THIS TIME, I'D LIKE TO TALK ABOUT TOHRU'S EVERYDAY LIFE...
AND WHAT SHE DOES AS A MAID.
EVERY MORNING, SHE WAKES UP BY 4 A.M.
SHE PICKS UP THE MORNING PAPER AND SETS IT ON THE DESK, THEN WATCHES TV FOR A WHILE.
FROOSH
MISS KOBAYASHI WAKES UP AROUND 7 A.M., SO TOHRU HAS **BREAKFAST** AND A **BOX LUNCH** PREPARED BY THEN.
MOST DAYS, MISS KOBAYASHI WALKS TO WORK IN THE NORMAL MANNER, BUT...
ONCE IN A WHILE, IF SHE'S RUNNING LATE, TOHRU WILL **CARRY** HER.
Ride me!! Ride me!!
SINCE MISS KOBAYASHI HAS A BAD LOWER BACK...
TOHRU HAS TAKEN TO MORPHING ONE OF HER SCALES INTO A **CHAIR**.
FLUMP
Oh, sweet.
KANNA ALSO WAKES UP AND GOES TO **SCHOOL** AT THIS TIME.
RUB
RUB

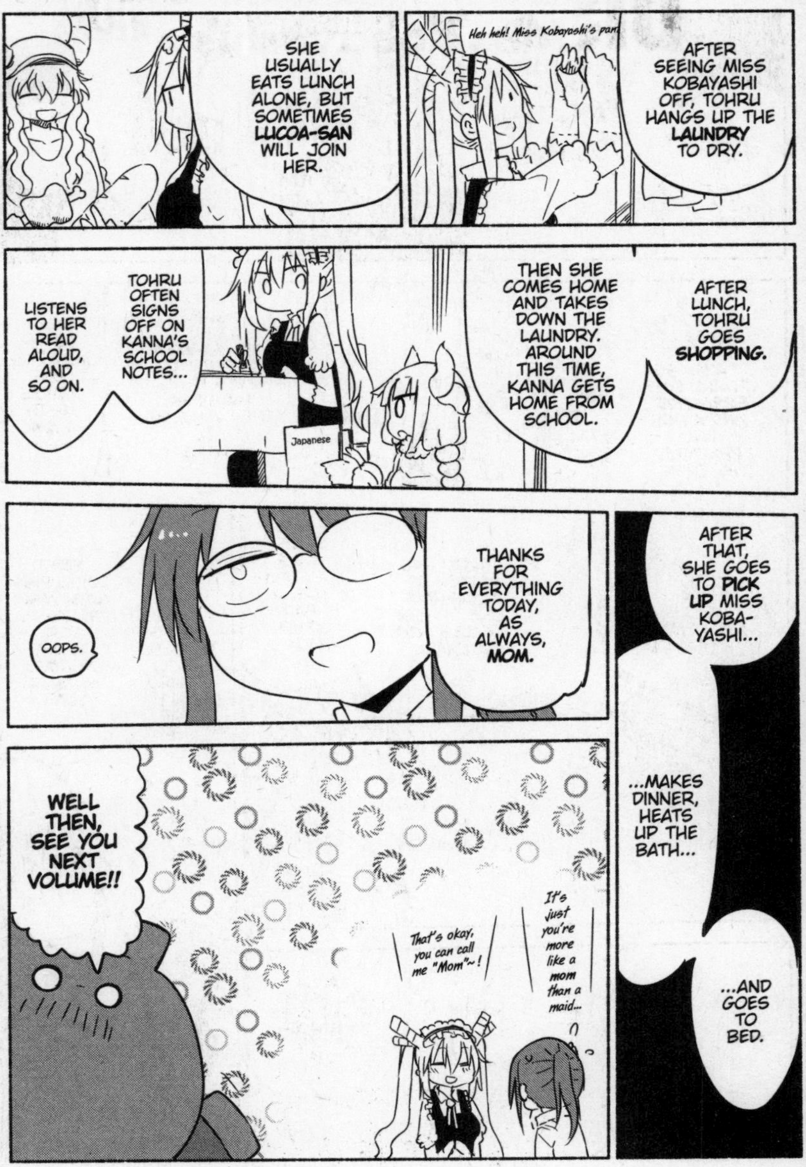
Heh heh! Miss Kobayashi's pan
AFTER SEEING MISS KOBAYASHI OFF, TOHRU HANGS UP THE **LAUNDRY** TO DRY.
SHE USUALLY EATS LUNCH ALONE, BUT SOMETIMES **LUCOA-SAN** WILL JOIN HER.
AFTER LUNCH, TOHRU GOES **SHOPPING.**
THEN SHE COMES HOME AND TAKES DOWN THE LAUNDRY. AROUND THIS TIME, KANNA GETS HOME FROM SCHOOL.
Japanese
TOHRU OFTEN SIGNS OFF ON KANNA'S SCHOOL NOTES...
LISTENS TO HER READ ALOUD, AND SO ON.
AFTER THAT, SHE GOES TO **PICK UP** MISS KOBAYASHI...
...MAKES DINNER, HEATS UP THE BATH...
...AND GOES TO BED.
THANKS FOR EVERYTHING TODAY, AS ALWAYS, **MOM.**
OOPS.
It's just you're more like a mom than a maid...
That's okay, you can call me "Mom"~!
WELL THEN, SEE YOU NEXT VOLUME!!

SEVEN SEAS ENTERTAINMENT PRESENTS

Dragon'maid
VOL.3

story and art by coolkyousinnjya

TRANSLATION
Jenny McKeon

ADAPTATION
Shanti Whitesides

LETTERING
Jennifer Skarupa

LOGO DESIGN
KC Fabellon

COVER DESIGN
Nicky Lim

ASSISTANT EDITOR
Jenn Grunigen

PRODUCTION ASSISTANT
CK Russell

PRODUCTION MANAGER
Lissa Pattillo

EDITOR-IN-CHIEF
Adam Arnold

PUBLISHER
Jason DeAngelis

MISS KOBAYASHI'S DRAGON MAID VOL. 3
© coolkyousinnjya 2013
All rights reserved.
First published in Japan in 2013 by Futabasha Publishers Ltd., Tokyo.
English version published by Seven Seas Entertainment, LLC.
Under license from Futabasha Publishers Ltd.

Seven Seas books may be purchased in bulk for promotional, educational, or
business use. Please contact your local bookseller or the Macmillan Corporate
and Premium Sales Department at 1-800-221-7945, extension 5442, or by
e-mail at MacmillanSpecialMarkets@macmillan.com.

Seven Seas and the Seven Seas logo are trademarks of
Seven Seas Entertainment, LLC. All rights reserved.

ISBN: 978-1-626924-85-7

Printed in Canada

First Printing: May 2017

10 9 8 7 6 5 4 3 2 1

FOLLOW US ONLINE: *www.gomanga.com*

READING DIRECTIONS

This book reads from *right to left*, Japanese style.
If this is your first time reading manga, you start
reading from the top right panel on each page and
take it from there. If you get lost, just follow the
numbered diagram here. It may seem backwards at
first, but you'll get the hang of it! Have fun!!

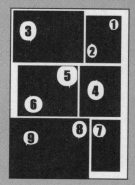